My Life Journey
from Darfur, Sudan to Boston, USA

My Life Journey

from Darfur, Sudan to Boston, USA

Victor Zaki

Library of Congress Control Number: 2020924174
ISBN: Hardcover 978-1-6641-4561-0
Softcover 978-1-6641-4562-7
eBook 978-1-6641-4563-4

Print information available on the last page.

Rev. date: 12/02/2020

To order additional copies of this book, contact:
Xlibris
844-714-8691
www.Xlibris.com
Orders@Xlibris.com
821811

CONTENTS

Acknowledgments

I give thanks first to my God. He protects me, guides me, and gives me peace and joy every day of my life.

Leila, my wife, is my companion. Her love and sacrifices make life full of happiness. Her support and encouragement helped me to write this book.

My children Tony, Jennie, and Diana gave me technical and computer support, and Sandra spent many hours reviewing the book and gave her valuable suggestions and grammar corrections.

Thanks to Fouad Lebbos and Shoukry Makar for reviewing the book and giving me advice.

Thanks to Ms. Maegan Arevalo, Iris Johannsen, and Xlibris team for their support in publishing this book.

Introduction

My name is Victor Zaki. I was born in Darfur, Sudan, and I live now in Boston, Massachusetts, USA. During my seventy-five years of life, I have lived in different cities and in different countries. I want to take you along with me on a delightful journey. I have enjoyed and was very happy in every city that I have lived in or even just visited.

I lived my childhood in the capital of Sudan, Khartoum. I finished my elementary and high school studies in Khartoum, then I moved to Assiut, Egypt, to study medicine.

I received my medical degree but even better than the degree, I found my beautiful wife.

As a medical doctor working in the Ministry of Health, we had to work in different cities of Sudan. I worked in Obeid in Western Sudan, Kassala, in Eastern Sudan, and Wau in Southern Sudan.

In 1972 we went to London, United Kingdom, to finish my specialization in ophthalmology. We returned to Khartoum for one year, then I was sent by the Ministry of Health to New Halfa in the Eastern part of Sudan.

In 1985, I came to Boston to get more knowledge and training in glaucoma. After four months in Boston, I returned to Khartoum.

In 1990, I returned to Boston with my family to work as a research ophthalmologist. In 1993 I joined the New England College of Optometry as a full-time student and I graduated and received my license to be an optometrist.

In April 2020, I retired from work, and now I am enjoying my life with my wife in Newton, Massachusetts, USA.

Come along with me as I take you to each city I have visited or lived in, and through the journey, I will describe snapshots of my life.

Chapter 01

My Ancestry

My grandparents from both sides came from a small town in southern Egypt. Akhmim is about five hundred kilometers south of Cairo, and it is near Sohag.

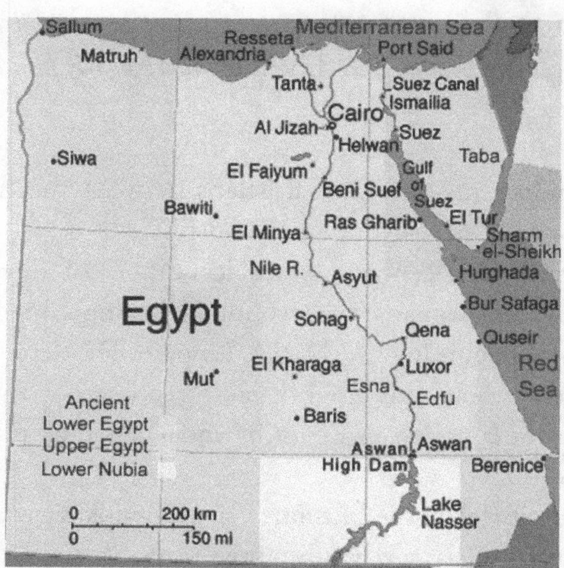

Map of Egypt

We are the grandchildren of the Pharaohs. We still use some words that the pharaohs used.

Egypt is identified in the Bible as the place of refuge that the Holy Family sought in their flight from Judea.

> [14] *When he arose, he took the young Child and His mother by night and departed for Egypt,* [15] *and was there until the death of Herod, that it might be fulfilled which was spoken by the Lord through the prophet, saying, "Out of Egypt I called My Son." (Matt. 2:14–15)*

Mark the evangelist is the traditionally ascribed author of the Gospel of Mark. He founded the church in Alexandria. Mark is the first bishop of the Orthodox church in Egypt.

The Egyptian church, which is now more than twenty centuries old, regards itself as the subject of many prophecies in the Old Testament. *Isaiah, the prophet, in chapter 19, verse 19 says, "In that day there will be an altar to the LORD in the midst of the land of Egypt, and a pillar to the LORD at its border."*

Isaiah 19:25 states, "25 Whom the Lord of hosts shall bless, saying, 'Blessed is Egypt My people, and Assyria the work of My hands, and Israel My inheritance.'"

Our grandparents became Christians between the first and the second century.

By the mid-third century, a sizable number of Egyptians were persecuted by the Romans on account of having adopted the new Christian faith. Beginning in AD 284, Emperor Diocletian persecuted and put to death thousands of Christian Egyptians.

The Muslim conquest of Egypt by the Arabs took place between 639 and 646 AD. [1]

When the city fell to the Muslims, Amr ibn-al-Aas gave them `three options: convert to Islam, pay substantial taxes, *the jizya*, or fight.

This heavy taxation forced many poor Christians to convert to Islam, and those who refused to convert continued to suffer and many were killed.

The payment of the Jizya tax also meant that Copts were required to wear special clothing to distinguish them from Muslims and that they could practice their personal status law apart from Shari'a law courts. This tax was abolished in 1855. So the Copts paid Jizya for about 1200 years.

Our grandparents insisted on their Christianity.

The Coptic language was spoken in Egypt from about the 2nd century CE. That represented the final stage of the ancient Egyptian language that was used by the Pharaohs. In contrast to earlier stages of the Egyptian language, which used hieroglyphic writing, hieratic script, or demotic script, the Coptic language was written in the Greek alphabet, supplemented by seven letters borrowed from demotic writing. Coptic also replaced the religious terms and expressions of earlier Egyptian with words borrowed from Greek.[2]

At that time of the Islamic conquest, the Coptic language was used in both religious and everyday life in Egypt.

After the Islamic invasion of Egypt, they forced the use of Arabic in all transactions and forbade the use of the Coptic language. By the twelfth century, however, Arabic became the common day use even among Christian Copts, who continued to use Coptic language only as a liturgical language in the Coptic Orthodox church.

I can understand and use a few Coptic words.

In Egypt now, the population is divided into the Copts the Christian Egyptians and the Muslim Egyptians.

In about the year 1900 AC, my grandparents from both sides moved from Akhmim, Egypt, to Sudan.

My father's parents settled in a small town in northern Sudan called El-Zeidab. My father was born there in 1910.

My mother's parents settled in Khartoum Bahri, where my mother was born.

My parents got married about 1930. They moved to different cities in central and western Sudan: Kosti, Obeid, and Al-Fashir.

So we are Sudanese of Coptic origin.

References:

1- Muslim conquest of Egypt
From Wikipedia, the free encyclopedia https://en.wikipedia.org/wiki/Muslim_conquest_of_Egypt

2- https://www.britannica.com/topic/Coptic-language

Chapter 02

Sudan

I am speaking about Sudan where I was born and lived.

The Sudan that I knew was a beautiful, peaceful, united country from the North to the South.

Wherever you went, every home invited you to come in and stay for a day or two. Nobody would ask about your race or religion

Map of Sudan

Sudan was 1 million square miles in the area, about 2.5 million square kilometers, more than 25 percent of the area of the USA.

It was the largest country in Africa and the Arab world by area before the 2011 South Sudan's secession.

I worked and lived in different parts of Sudan in its west, in El-Obeid, east in Kassala and Halfa El-Jadida, north in Khartoum, and its south in Wau.

In all those cities, I met simple loving people. They would invite me to their homes where I felt like it was my home.

The hate and ethnic cleansing led to the separation of the south of Sudan from the north in 2011.

The Sudanese Copts

The Sudanese Copts look different than most other Sudanese because of their skin color and because they are Christian.

They number up to 500,000, or slightly over 1 percent of the Sudanese population.

When Mohamad Ali, the ruler of Egypt 1804–1848, wanted to build the infrastructure in Sudan, he brought some of the Copts from Egypt to take top positions in every department in Sudan.

They worked in railway stations, the post office, tax department, judiciary, and others.

Sudanese Copts have a significant role in the country because of their high education. One of my relatives was the minister of health, and another was the head of the police force.

My brother was acting minister of transportation. My other brother was the head of the government chemical lab and consultant in World Health Organizations (WHO) specializing in water and food analysis.

Before coming to the USA, I was elected twice for secretary of the Sudanese Ophthalmological Society.

Most of the Sudanese Copts were leaders in medicine, law, pharmacy, and engineering. Because of their honesty, at a certain point, all the bank managers were Copts. After the rule of Omar Al-Bashir, in one day, he fired thirty-five bank managers, all of them were Copts.

Modern immigration of Copts to Sudan peaked in the early 19th century, and they generally received a tolerant welcome there. However, this was interrupted by a decade of persecution under Mahdist rule at the end of the 19th century.[1]

Anglo-Egyptian invasion in 1898 allowed Copts greater religious and economic freedom, and they extended their original roles as artisans and merchants into trading, banking, engineering, Medicine, and the civil service. Proficiency in business and administration made them a privileged minority. However, the return of militant Islam in the mid-1960s and subsequent demands by radicals for an Islamic constitution prompted Copts to join in public opposition to religious rule.

Gaafar Nimeiry's introduction of Islamic Sharia law in 1983 began a new phase of the harsh treatment of Copts, among other non-Muslims. After the overthrow of Nimeiry, Coptic leaders supported a secular candidate in the 1986 elections. However, when the National Islamic Front overthrew the elected Government of Sadiq al-Mahdi with the help of the military, discrimination against Copts returned in earnest. Hundreds of Copts were dismissed from the civil service and judiciary.

I know two Sudanese Copts among other Muslim colleagues who were imprisoned and tortured because of their positions in the trade union.

Christian schools were confiscated. They imposed an Arab-Islamic emphasis on language and history, teaching accompanied by harassment of Christian children and the introduction of *hijab* dress laws.

After the Sudanese Revolution of 2019, a Coptic Orthodox priest led the inauguration of the new Prime Minister of Sudan, Abdalla Hamdok.[2] A Coptic Christian woman was also appointed to serve in Sudan's new Transitional Council.

Refrerernce:

1- https://minorityrights.org/minorities/copts-2
2- https://en.wikipedia.org/wiki/Sudanese_Revolution

Chapter 03

Darfur, Sudan

I was born in Al-Fashir, Sudan, in September 1945.

Al-Fashir is the capital of Darfur, the western province of Sudan.

Darfur was a prosperous independent Sultanate from 1606–1906, interrupted by twelve years of *Mahdy rule*.

The monarchy was suspended after the Egyptian conquest of the region in 1874. But in 1898 it was restored after the defeat of the Mahdiyah. The Keira dynasty finally ended in 1916 when the British annexed Darfur to Sudan.

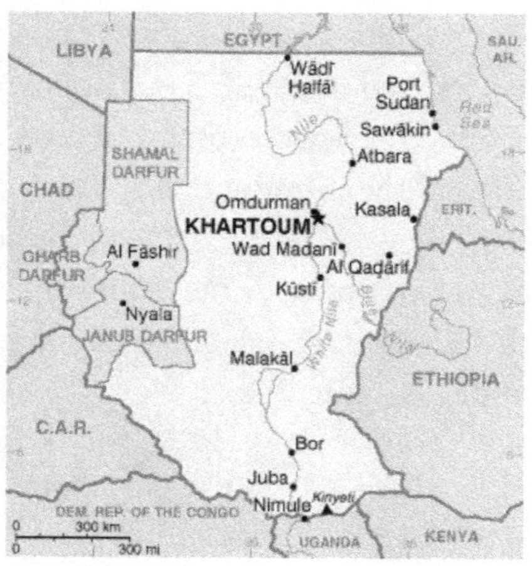

Map of Sudan showing Darfur province

Till now there is a two-story building, which was the palace of Sultan Ali Dinar palace 1898–1916 Fashir-Darfur, Sudan. He was the last sultan of Darfur.

The major tribes in Darfur are the **Zaghawa**, **Fur**, and **Masalit**. The predominantly nomadic **(Arab)** tribes occupied the more significant part of Northern Darfur, and the more sedentary groups (Non-Arab), mainly composed of peasant farmers occupied the western and southern regions of Darfur.[1]

The **War in Darfur** was a major armed conflict in the Darfur region of Sudan. It started to be dangerous in February 2003 when the Sudan Liberation Movement (SLM) and the Justice and Equality Movement (JEM) rebel groups began fighting the Government of Sudan, which they accused of oppressing Darfur's non-Arab population. The Government responded to attacks by carrying out a campaign of ethnic cleansing against Darfur's non-Arabs. The result was the death of three hundred thousand civilians and the displacement of 2.5 Million (According to United Nation's report), and also the indictment of Sudan's president, Omar al-Bashir, for genocide, war crimes, and crimes against humanity by the International Criminal Court.

In my opinion, the people of Darfur felt that the Government of Khartoum occupied them since 1916 when they lost their three-hundred-year-old Sultanate.

They will never be satisfied until they get back their independence. Or at least the same rights as other Sudanese citizens. Now there is a new government in Khartoum, and hopefully, the conflict and the displaced people can go back to their homes.

There is a beautiful place in Darfur called Gebel Marra.

It is a range of volcanic peaks in a massif that rises to 3,042 meters (9,980 ft). They are the highest mountains in Sudan.

I spent in Al-Fashir the first two years of my life.

These are some stories of my *Suboua*.

The tradition is to celebrate the arrival of the new baby on the seventh day of his birthday *Suboua* with a big party, inviting friends and family. Our friends gave us six lambs as presents. My father bought one. They cooked those to feed the attendants.

One of the lambs ran away. One of the servants wanted to go out to search for it. My mother told him we were too busy; there was no need to waste time searching for the lost lamb.

In El-Fashir, there were no churches. My father made some benches, bought Bibles, hymnbooks and invited all the Christian families to join for Sunday service.

So he started a church without a priest for all Christians from all denominations. This meeting continued every week until we left El-Fashir.

My father was a godly man, and he practiced what is written in the Bible:

> *37 Jesus said to him, "You shall love the Lord your God with all your heart, with all your soul, and with all your mind." 38 This is the first and great commandment. 39 And the second is like it: "You shall love your neighbor as yourself." (Matt. 22:37–39)*

I cannot remember anything from El-Fashir. I just noticed later in my life that I have a scar on my face. When I smile, the right cheek show more creases than the left side. The story was when I was about two years old, I managed to fall down fifteen steps of the stairs which connected our house building to the yard. I heard that the house was huge with a very big yard. My mother told me that when I went down, I injured my cheek. The wound was bleeding very heavily. My mother put some coffee powder on the wound and pressed hard on it. It worked well because the scar was minimum. In this accident, I lost the front upper two teeth as well. In El-Fashir there was no electricity or public water supply. We used to have a special person to bring water from the main reservoir. The water man used two large leather bags and loaded them on a donkey.

We moved from El-Fashir to Om-Durman in about 1948. I heard at that time they have to travel by a lorry from El-Fashir to El-Obeid which was a three days journey. From El-Obeid to Khartoum there was a train working. I think it was about a twenty-two-hour journey if the weather was good.

Reference:

1- http://exhibits.lib.usf.edu/exhibits/show/darfur-genocide/parties/tribes

Chapter 04

Omdurman and Al-Mahdi

My parents decided to move to Omdurman because my uncles from both sides of the family moved to Omdurman.

Omdurman is considered the national capital, and Khartoum is the official one where the government offices are.

Al-Imam Al-Mahdi's tomb

Muhammad Ahmad bin Abd Allah "Al-Imam Al-Mahdi" was born August 12, 1844—died June 22, 1885, Omdurman, Sudan.[1] He created a vast Islamic state extending from the Red Sea to Central Africa and founded a movement that remained influential in Sudan till now. He was born in Dongola in the North part of Sudan. Then he moved south to a small Island in central Sudan 912 kilometer from his hometown.

The island is called Aba island. It is a twelve kilometer long island in the middle of the White Nile.

There he combined orthodox theological study with a mystical interpretation of Islam. He started to preach; he proclaimed his divine mission to purify Islam and the governments that defiled it.

Some people followed him. On June 29, 1881, he was proclaimed by his disciples as the Mahdi, the messianic redeemer of the Islamic faith.

Within less than four years, Al-Mahdī, who set out from Abā Island with a few followers armed with sticks and spears, ended up making himself master of almost all the territory formerly occupied by the Egyptian Government, and capturing an enormous booty of money.

His extensive campaign culminated in the crowning victory of the capture of Khartoum, on January 26, 1885, after a vigorous defense by its commander, Major General Charles George Gordon, who, against Al-Mahdī's express order, was killed in the final assault. After many of the citizens of Khartoum had been massacred, Al-Mahdī made a triumphal entry into the stricken city and led the prayers in the principal mosque.

The withdrawal of the British expedition, which had failed to relieve Khartoum, left al-Mahdī free to consolidate his religious empire. He abandoned Khartoum, still heavy with the stench of the dead, and set up his administrative center at Omdurman. He managed to attract the people around him because he was attacking foreign invaders against Sudan and many believed his religious message.

Al-Mahdī's rule was brief. He was taken ill, possibly of typhus, and died in June 1885, only 41 years old. At his wish, his temporal functions were assumed by one of his followers, the caliph ʿAbd Allāh A-Taishi.

Over his grave, the caliph built a domed tomb similar in architecture to those customarily built over the remains of the more revered holy men. Partially destroyed by gunfire during the Battle of Omdurman in 1898 but later rebuilt by al-Mahdī's son ʿAbd al-Raḥmān and the Mahdist community.

In 1898 the British and Egyptian troops came in powerful force under the leadership of General Kitchener and occupied Sudan.

They named Sudan the Anglo-Egyptian Sudan.

The occupation continued for fifty-eight years until the independence of Sudan in 1956.

It was a democratically elected government sworn in Khartoum for the first time in Sudan.

Sudan's flag was raised at the independence ceremony by the prime minister Isma'il Alazhari and opposition leader Mohamed Ahmed Almahjoub on January 1, 1956

The family of Al-Mahdi had been trying to be the spiritual and if possible, the political leaders of Sudan, one generation after another.

Al-Mahdi's grandson, Al-Sadig Al-Mahdi, studied at Oxford University, United Kingdom, became prime minister of Sudan twice, and still is one the leading political figures in Sudan.

Our house was five minutes walk from Al-Imam Al-Mahdi's tomb. During *the Moulid* which is the annual celebration of the birth of Prophet Muhammad, there are usually many shops selling Halawat El-Moulid. Our father used to take us there to buy some. They are very delicious sugar cookies. They were red in color in the shape of dolls or a horse.

In addition to sweets, there are many people chanting hymns and dancing. Those are the Suffiya, who are a sect of Islam that usually praise God and Prophet Muhammed in hymns and dance. They typically wear green long, wide costumes. They dance in big groups in a circle, and the people surround them.

Our house was on a narrow, unpaved road. Our neighbors were of different ethnic origins—some Armenians, Syrians, and Jews.

We were one group playing every evening on the road.

Our house was very near to the city council.

In Om-Durman, we lived in a small house in a residential area called Hay El-Isbitalya which means the hospital neighborhood. Near our house, there was a hospital called Isbitalya El-Irsalya because it was a missionary hospital. I think an English missionary managed it. In this community, most of the people were Jews, Syrians, Armenians and a few Copts, and one Muslim family. I think this Muslim was even of Jewish origin because his name was Jewish. All the families were friends. The ladies visited each other in the mornings while the men were at work. All the children played together in the narrow, unpaved street. Our car was the only car that passed in that street. Only the main streets in the town were paved.

Our next-door neighbor was an old man called Amin, living quietly with his wife; they had no children. I remember once they had some visitors with a small kid. They asked me to play with the kid. I came and played with the kid, and suddenly he started to cry. The lady accused me of hitting the kid. I was upset and angry because I was innocent. From that day on, I recognized that sometimes there were wrong accusations.

In our house in Om-Durman, I remember one of our regular visitors was the person who sold dates. He used to come carrying two big goffa which was palm tree leaves basket with two handles. I remember every visit he would bring a different type of date. He insisted on giving each child a large number of dates to try them. Those were the best dates I ever ate. In every season of the year, he used to sell a different type of fruit like oranges or grapefruits. He used to only sell fruits.

Another visitor was a tall man called Khalid. He used to come with a big bike (for me it was huge). I am not sure if he was a classmate of one of my older brothers or a messenger from one of our relatives. He used to give us a ride on his big bike.

In the evenings, especially when there was a full moon, all the children of the street would meet and play together Al-Shilael. This was the top-rated game. The older children, the leaders, would divide the group into two. They drew a line on the ground, and everybody had to be in front of the line at the beginning and not look backward. Then the leader of one group would say, "Al-Shilael wey noo," which means where is the Shilael; all the children would respond, "Akallo Al-Doddo," which meant the lion ate it. Then the leader would ask, "Al-Shilael wain rah," which means where has the Shilael gone? The reply from the group would be, "Akallo El-Tomsaah," which means the crocodile ate it. Then the leader had to throw a small piece of a bull's bone backward so nobody could see it. After that, all the children from the two groups had to go and search for this piece of bone. If anyone found this precious bone, he would give it to another member of his group secretly till they bring it back to the beginning line, and they had to shout, "Shalalet." That was how that group won, and their leader would throw the bone in the next round. Usually, the selection of the bone was critical. It had to be of a specific size so that it would be just visible. Also, it had to be clean and without sharp edges. I remember one of the neighbor's children called Shalom made a small hole in our brick wall, mainly to keep this bone for the next day of play. I remember the players' number was usually about twenty children or more, and everybody of any age could join.

One of our neighbors at the end of the street was an Armenian. They had three daughters of our age or a bit older. I used to visit them with my sister. They had a revolving three-seat swing. It was red. I liked to take a turn when I visited them.

Once, we went to a party for the children in the next block. It was funny because a boy of about seven and a girl of the same age were dressed as a bride and groom, and they gave us *shaaryea*, which was skinny pasta made as a sweet. I think it was their first baptism.

The neighborhood activities were completely different from one family to another, according to their ethnicity. Once a week on Tuesdays, all our relatives would come and visit us, at least twenty adults and about thirty children. Sometimes the number was less, but usually more than twenty. In our age group, we typically played soccer with a homemade ball. We called it *kora sharab,* which meant ball of socks. We made it by putting a few old socks inside one sock. Then we squeezed the contents to the end of the hose and twisted it several times and turned it back and repeated this several times. You could add several socks and repeat the twisting until you reach the desired size. These balls were very friendly, and they bounced on the floor as if they were made of rubber.

Sometimes we played cards, especially when it was late at night. On other occasions, we created short plays and jokes and repeated them over and over. Sometimes we remembered the old joke, either we enjoyed it, or we forced ourselves to laugh.

We used to sleep over at our cousin's house, and they did the same at our house, especially on school vacations, sometimes for two or three consecutive days.

At our home, I used to play most of the time with my brother, who was two years older than me. Most of the time, we played *billey* (marbles). Our usual game was the one where we pushed the marble with our thumb only. The game aimed to hit your enemy's marble and push it away from the hole and at the same time reach the hole and aim your marble to enter the hole. We dug the hole in our yard where we used to play. It was a very small hole that barely fit the marble. My brother was very good at this game. I hardly remember any time that I managed to beat him in this game.

Every Sunday we used to go to the Coptic Orthodox church in Masalma. This area was known as being the most Christian-populated area in Sudan. Its name means *gave peace*. It was, as usual, the residency of most of the Christians in about 1885. When El-Mahady, the Islamic ruler came and took Om-Durman over from the English-Egyptian government, he asked the people from Al-Masalma either to become Muslims, to pay a yearly ransom of money *jizyia* to him or be killed. Most of the people were rich, so they paid the money. Very few people were poor, and they converted to Islam. Till now, some families have some Muslim relatives, and the rest of the family are Christians. So nobody fought the invading Mahady's army.

In the church, there was a bishop called Anba Bakhomious. He was a man with strong faith. Once while building a new church, one of the workers fell from the top of the church dome (about three floors height). Anba Bakhomious was watching, so he prayed for the man; the man then stood up and was completely intact. I remember every Sunday at the end of the church service while giving Lugmat El-Baraka, which means the blessed bread, Anba Bakhomious used to ask specifically for me, my uncle, or my father or one of my cousins. He used to call me "the blessed little kid." When I reached him among the crowd, he usually asked me to put my hands together and fill them with Lugmat Baraka. He regularly gave each person only one small piece, but for me, he would give me many pieces that I could hardly hold. My father had to put his hands under mine to collect what would drop from my hands. Till now, I feel that God is blessing me abundantly. If he gives everybody one thing, He usually gives me double. I felt this when I found myself growing in a loving and caring family. I felt the love of my parents and all my brothers and sister. When I went to school, God helped me in every step from elementary school through high school, college, and post-graduate studies in England and Sudan, and lastly, in my studies in Boston thirty years ago. When I thought of marriage, God chose the perfect wife for me. Sometimes when I think if I put specific criteria for the best wife that I could imagine, she would be far less than Leila, the one that God gave me. Then God blessed me with four children and eight grandchildren, and they are great to have. Then God gave me the greatest gift that anybody can get, that is His *peace.* For all my seventy-five years of life, I haven't felt worried at any time because I know that He will help me in every step.

I remember when I went to school for the first time. I was five years old. My mother took me to the principal of the school and convinced him that I was bright, and I would do well despite my young age. He asked me to read the letter *F* in Arabic, and I did. So he accepted me one year ahead of my classmates. Two years later, they found me getting good grades in my tests, so they let me skip one year.

We used to walk to school, which was about three miles from our house. On our way to school, we had to pass the central marketplace of Om-Durman.

Walking to school, Victor is the youngest

When I was in the fourth grade, and during the middle of the school year, we moved to Khartoum. In the beginning of the year, we started in our school in Om-Durman, then we moved to a school in Al-Shagarra while we were still living in Om-Durman. I remember my father used to drive us in the morning from our house in Om-Durman to Al-Shagarra, which was about thirty miles away. At the end of the school day, my older brother and I had to use the public buses, which were lorries modified to be buses, so they were open on the sides. In the winter it was terrible. We used to take those buses from Al-Shagarra to Khartoum then walk to my father's office in downtown Khartoum. We had to wait for my father to finish his work at about 2:30 PM and sometimes later. Then go with him in our car to Om-Durman. The school in Al-Shagarra was beautiful and small. They had a small pyramid built in the middle of the school's yard. The new strange thing for me was their habit of checking all the students each morning, for lice. I felt this was humiliating. I think we spent only about three months in this transitional period, after which we moved to a new school in Khartoum.

Reference:

1- https://military.wikia.org/wiki/Muhammad_Ahmad

Chapter 05

Khartoum and My Elementary and High School

Khartoum is located at the junction of the Blue Nile and the White Nile.

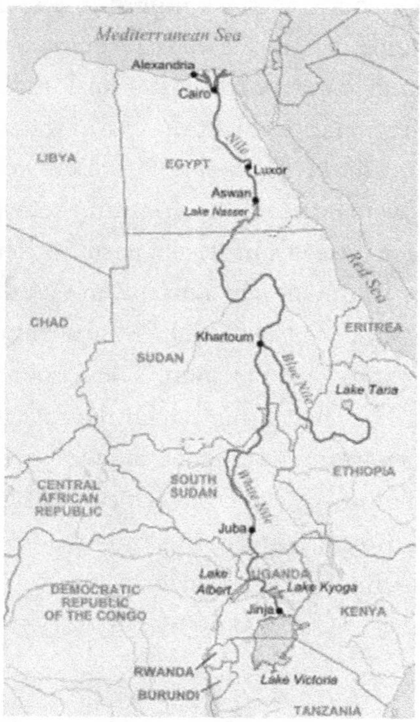

The River Nile

The River Nile is about 6,650 km long. It is the longest river in the world.

Khartoum is located at the junction of the Blue Nile and the White Nile.

Part of Khartoum are three cities: Khartoum 1, Khartoum 2, and Khartoum 3.

Khartoum 1 has high-quality houses, and Khartoum 3 has more simple dwellings.

We chose Khartoum 2 City.

Map of the capital of Sudan

In Sudan at that time, the system of getting loans and mortgages for houses was not available.

So my father bought a piece of land. He hired a contractor to build it. Before finishing the house, we moved in.

The builder was not accurate in his timing. So I was able to watch and learn how the builders used the bricks to build walls. I learned about the tools they used and their names. That is helping me now in doing some repairs in my house.

Picture with my brother in New home

Our new home, like all other houses in Sudan, had walls.

The weather in Khartoum was dry and hot. The average temperature fluctuated from 65°F to 110 ^{O}F. In the winter, the coldest was 65 ^{O}F for only one or two hours then would go up to 80 ^{O}F or above.

Everyone slept in the yard to enjoy the cooler weather.

And for privacy, we built walls.

The bike and me

I had some difficulty at the beginning of riding a bike.

Once at the beginning of my training, I was riding my bike on a side road.

Nobody was there except an older man crossing slowly. I saw him from far away. I started to use my bike bell to alarm him. He did not change his direction, and I was unable to stop the bike or change the course of the bike. Then I hit him. The kind man, in a low voice, told me, “My son, there is enough space, why didn’t you turn your bike to the right or left.” My answer was “If I knew, I might do it, this is the reason I rang my bike bell.”

Schools

The Coptic Orthodox church in Sudan built the first Coptic school in 1919. Those were for public education for everyone, Muslims or Christians. In those schools, most of the leaders of Sudan, like Ismael Azhari—the first prime minister of Sudan, he got their education.

I went to the Coptic school in Omdurman, then I continued my elementary and middle school in the Coptic school in Khartoum.

I remember it was effortless for me to pass the final exam, which was considered a significant step between primary school and middle school. I remember our music teacher used to teach my mother when she was in school. Her favorite song was called "El-Ghamh," which meant the wheat, in which the famous singer Mohamed Abd-al Wahhab sang about celebrating the wheat harvest. Till now, I like to hear this lovely song. We had a period for artwork. The teacher's name was Olga; she taught us how to make artificial flowers from a particular type of paper called *warag kureisha*.

During lunch period, I used to play with my friends *safragat* which is similar to checkers but with only six pieces. I was excellent at it. I would eat my lunch and play at the same time. Many students played *sakk*, which I was not interested in because it was very violent. They used to run very fast and push anybody in their way.

The next school year, I moved to middle school. We started for the first time to study English. Our English teacher was Fayez Fedeil. He was one of the best teachers that I ever had. The next year I had another English teacher called Shams. He was terrible; he used to hit us with a stick if we could not memorize the words. I had a difficult time learning my English during this period.

My favorite subject was mathematics. I also used to get good grades in science, geography, and to some extent, history. Arabic was another problematic subject, and it was challenging for me to memorize poems and grammar. I used to get high marks in Arabic composition. It usually compensated for my total marks in Arabic, so I reached at least the passing score. The regulations in our school were if you failed Arabic, you couldn't pass to the next year. I was able to get a pass in all my school years.

We used to have drawing classes. I never had a good grade. I typically drew everything in straight lines and angles. I used to get just the passing grade, which was 4 out of the total mark of 20.

Our new neighborhood was completely different from the old one. Most of the houses around were still under construction. On our school vacations, my brother and I, under the supervision of our older brother, used to have a lemonade stand. We used to sell lemonade and candies to the construction laborers around our house. I don't think that there was enough profit, but it was a good experience.

Victor and family 1959

My family

I spent all my life in a family living in peace and joy. My father was a godly man. He did what was right. My mother was a dedicated wife and mother. She tried to do everything to save money from making clothes for all the family, different types of cheese, and other delicious food.

I have four brothers and one sister.

My family

The ministry of education in Egypt joined the Coptic church in the management of the Coptic schools after 1952. Egypt was the ruler of Sudan.

Egypt had its schools as well.

All Egyptian schools followed the school curriculum in Egypt.

The Sudanese government had a different curriculum with more emphasis on English.

The Catholic church built Catholic schools. They taught all subjects in English.

The only university in Sudan was Khartoum University.

The competition was very high, and they required excellent English.

My parents decided when I was in middle school to transfer me to Catholic school. That would increase my chances of getting into Khartoum University.

I found a big difference from my old school.

They started school by reciting the Lord's Prayer.

Most of the teachers were Italian monks wearing long white robes. After three months, I discovered that my English was not good enough to continue.

So I returned to my old school.

I later found God's plan was for me to continue with Egyptian schools and to college in Egypt.

The first few years after we moved to Khartoum 2, my father used to take us to school in his car and pick us up at the end of the day. Later in around 1954, he opened a new branch of the company in El-Gedaref in the eastern part of Sudan. Baheeg and Nabeel used to ride their bikes to school. I was young so Baheeg used to take me on his bike. Later on, I managed to go to school on my bike.

I continued using the bike in all my college years.

The Arabic club and my difficulty in swimming

After we settled in our new house in Khartoum 2, we joined the Arabic club, owned by the Egyptian embassy. Most of the members were Armenians, Greeks, a mixture of other races, and a few Copts. The annual fees were very high, and to encourage families, the costs for a family were the same as for a single person. In this club, there was a swimming pool, which was the best in Sudan at that time. There were also tennis, basketball, volleyball courts, ping-pong, and roller skating rink, and even a billiard table. I tried hard to learn swimming, but I was unable to coordinate breathing and swimming. I had no problem swimming underwater for a reasonable distance, but I have to come to the surface to

We used to go swimming every day during our school vacations and about twice a week during school days for many years, but I was unable to improve my swimming skills.

Graduation from high school

The families usually sat in the big garden each around a table. The young adults and children went to play or swim and would come to join the family to eat and go back to play again. We usually went to the club in the afternoon to start swimming, and the rest of the family would join us later. Most of the people stayed until about midnight. The swimming pool was usually open from the morning till midnight except on Mondays because they drained the water for cleaning. They used to serve high-quality food at reasonable prices.

Chapter 06

Gedaref without Electricity or Water Supply

Gedaref is a middle-sized city in the southeastern part of Sudan. It lies on the road that connects Khartoum with the Ethiopian border about 410 kilometers (250 mi) from the capital. Three mountains surround the city.

The climate of Gedaref is hot and rainy in the summer. The rainy season extends four months with an average annual rainfall of 30–35 inches.

The majority of Gedaref people in the 1950s lived in huts.

Each house consisted of two, three, or more huts. In addition to the bedrooms, there was a hut designed as a kitchen called *tukkull* and the house had a wall called *sareef.*

They usually raised the floor a level higher than the rest of the house to keep the rainwater away. One hut was called *ghottia* and several huts called *ghuttatti*. Some people lived in brick houses but still added a ghottia in the yard. The huts were cooler than the brick buildings.

Huts were used in Gedaref in Western Sudan.

Huts in Gedaref

The materials, lumber and straws, were available and cheap. The design of the guttyia kept the rain away, but the air could still pass through. I never lived in a guttyia but went in many times. It felt very cool compared to a brick building.

The only problem with these huts is the risk of fire. In the period just before the rainy season, fires easily started because of the dry weather and wind, and it would jump from one hut to the next. In a few hours, the fire could consume hundreds of huts. Lack of water was another added factor. Some gangs intentionally started fires because as soon as the fire started in an area, everybody would start to move their valuables outside their huts and if possible away from the whole area. The thieves then would pretend that they were helping by carrying the valuables away and then disappear.

The fertile soil and heavy rainy season encouraged the development of a mechanized farming scheme introduced in Gedaref in 1954. The government decided to start a large agricultural project. They distributed the land around Gedaref into four acres each to anybody who owned a tractor and harvesting machine. Each new owner was obligated to plant one acre each year with sorghum, which is similar to wheat, another acre with cotton, the third with either sesame or peanut. The fourth acre was left without any plant for one year. They found that rotating through the different crops each year would keep the land in good condition.

This entire operation depended on natural rain. During June, July, August, and part of September, heavy rains would fall. They usually waited for the first few showers of rain, and some weeds would grow. Then they used tractors and discs to mix the ground and plant the new crops. The next few months, they just waited for the heavy rains to do the job. In January, the crops would be ready for collection. Everything was automated.

A huge grain silo built by Russia in the 1950s.

My father worked in a company importing and selling tractors and grain-harvesting machines. My father was the manager of this company in Gedaref in 1954.

There was a repair shop as well.

I worked as a clerk in that repair shop. I remember my father was rigorous at work. The company fired any employee if he came late twice without a good reason. At the same time, my father was very kind. I remember he got a new watch. He had a free lottery for all the employees for his old, good working watch. The winner was a laborer whose salary was five cents an hour.

My salary was 10 cents an hour. I remember at the end of my vacation, I earned $13.50, so I bought a watch for myself.

I learned how to organize the billing of the repair shop. I also learned how to respect my work and how to be punctual.

During the time my father was in El-Gedaref, there was no electricity or water supply. We lived in an apartment on the second floor. We had a refrigerator that worked on kerosene. It was just like any ordinary electric refrigerator, but we have to fill it with kerosene every two days.

We had a water tank on the top of the roof so we could take a shower and use the tap water. The toilet was the standard toilet. The water itself came from deep wells outside El-Gedaref.

We had a particular filter system for the drinking water. For safety. We used to boil the water then put it in the filter then fill the fridge bottles with it. Despite all of this, the water tasted salty, compared to the River Nile water of Khartoum.

For light, there were two sources—the *retina*, which was a strong source of light that worked with kerosene.

There was a unique table for the retina or a lampstand. It was a small table, one foot by one foot, and about six feet tall, so the light from the retina would shine all over the room.

Matthew 5:15 states, "Nor do they light a lamp and put it under a basket, but on a lampstand, and it gives light to all who are in the house."

Most of the houses had one retina and three or more *fanouses*.

The fanouse was simply a kerosene lantern. At night most of the people carried a larger version of penlights, which used two or three type C batteries.

For the streets, there were specially designed retinas. Each evening a city employee would come to each light pole on the street and bring the retina down by rotating a small handle. He would turn the retina in the same way as at home and then bring it back up. Only a few of the main streets had light.

We had a butane gas cooker and used butane canisters. We usually needed to fill it every month. In Khartoum, we used the same system. But in Khartoum there was electricity.

There were handheld personal fans mostly used by old ladies; my aunt used them all year long. We called them *marawih* and *marwaha* for a single one. It had a small stick as a handle connected by colored threads to about ten tiny rods (the moving particles). These very beautifully designed color threads entirely covered all the wooden sticks, and a colored cloth covered the handle.

In El-Gedaref, there were two cinemas, of course. As in all other parts of Sudan, they were in an uncovered space.

Many times, when there was heavy rain, the show would simply continue, and the viewers covered themselves. They rarely stopped the show because of the rain.

The weather in Gedaref in the rainy season was excellent, cloudy, and slightly cold. We felt this, especially when we came from Khartoum, where the weather was hot and dry, and the sun was scorching all day.

The best time was tea time. At dusk, all the family used to sit down to drink tea (usually with milk). My father loved the tea to be served in high-quality china tea sets. My mother usually prepared a homemade cake. Maybe the beauty was the slightly cooler weather, no school or homework, and all the family relaxing together. It was a lovely family time.

In Gedaref, there were two churches. A Coptic Orthodox church and Presbyterian Arabic church. Sunday mornings, we would go to the Coptic church. My father insisted that we would be there exactly at opening time.

Sunday afternoon we would go to the Presbyterian Sunday school. On Monday evening, both priests came together to our home and spent a few hours visiting us. My father believed that Christians were one body in Christ.

We used to have many friends visiting our home and we visited theirs as well. One of them was Indian. Once we were in their house, and he showed us a glass cup. He said, "This cup does not break." Then suddenly, he threw the cup to the floor and nothing happened to the cup. After thirty years, this same man came to my clinic in Khartoum for an eye exam.

Another friend from Gedaref was the manager of a bank in Gedaref. At that time he had two daughters and one-year-old son. The son came for an eye exam with his wife and children.

It was a small world!

My father used to drive a four-wheel-drive Land Rover.

I remember once we were traveling from Khartoum to Gedaref, and then the rain started, we lost our way because all the roads were unpaved and you just have to keep track of other cars. It was about an eight-hour drive. We noticed a light far away. We drove toward the light and at last, we found a gubba which is a dome-like building characteristic of Muslim religious leaders.

We stopped and the driver came down from the car, and we saw a tall man; his hands were locked in chains. The driver was trying to greet him, but the man gave no response and continued to come toward us. It was scary. At last, somebody else came from inside and gave us directions. I learned that those religious leaders called fakki worked as doctors and kept mad people with them for treatment, sometimes for several months. The relatives usually paid the bills.

I visited El-Gedaref when I was working in Halfa Al-Jadeeda after 1975. I found that they managed to bring the water supply to the town, in addition to electricity. Also, there was a paved road to the capital Khartoum and the seaport, Port Sudan.

Chapter 07

Cairo, First Time to See Egypt

In Sudan, there was only one university, which was Khartoum University. My two oldest brothers finished their studies there. There was only a limited number of students that could go to Khartoum University and only one or two students each year from the Egyptian schools in Sudan. They required them to pass an English language test. I took that test but didn't pass it. I applied to the Egyptian universities.

The application form gave the student ten choices. I applied to the colleges of engineering and science in all the four Egyptian universities available at that time Cairo, Alexandria, Ein Shams, and Assiut, in addition to the college of accounting in Khartoum branch of Cairo University. My brother Joseph reviewed my application and told me that I had to fill the last space; otherwise, they may not look at the form. He suggested that I write Medicine Assiut. I told him I didn't want to study medicine. He said to fill it just to complete the application.

The committee accepted me in Medicine Assiut and accounting in Khartoum branch. When I received the results, I already tried the college of accounting in Khartoum and found that I would not be able to continue in that college because the subjects were difficult to understand. I had many discussions with my brothers. I also called my father and mother, who were at that time on vacation in Europe. We decided that I would go to Assiut and from there, I would try to transfer to the college of science.

I was 100 percent convinced that I didn't like to study medicine. In Assiut, the authorities refused the transfer me to science.

When I finished the third year in medical school, I applied to Khartoum University, college of engineering. They accepted me this time but as a first-year student, and I had to pass an English exam. I was unable to pass the exam.

After a few years, I discovered that this was God's plan for me to study medicine to see His greatness in creation and to believe more strongly in Him. The other part of God's plan for me to study in Assiut was so that I could meet Leila, my future wife.

The preparation to go to Assiut, Egypt, was quick because classes had already started a month before we received the acceptance results. When I traveled to Egypt in November 1961, I was sixteen years old, and this was my first visit to Egypt.

I was going to study in Assiut, but I had to first go to Cairo, the capital because there were no direct flights to Assiut and because I had to register in the Sudanese Embassy in Cairo and the secret police in Cairo.

Before I left Khartoum, I studied the Cairo map, from where I had to land first by airplane to the place of the Sudanese Embassy in Cairo and the Egyptian immigration department in Cairo. My brothers advised me that in Cairo, I had to act as if I were Egyptian.

Some swindlers in Cairo try to take advantage of foreigners. Now I remember this and laugh. Because as soon as we speak, any person in Egypt can easily recognize our Sudanese accent.

The plane took four hours to reach Cairo. All the airplanes at that time called Vi Count had four big fans. About three years later, a new jet airplane called Comet was introduced, and the time between Khartoum and Cairo was reduced to two hours and twenty minutes.

I was completely surprised by the significant tall buildings in Cairo when I saw them from the airplane. In Khartoum, at that time, the highest building was a three-story building. When I arrived at Cairo Airport, I saw the airport was about six stories high and of high-quality facilities, such as automatic doors and clean toilets for passengers. From the airport, I took a bus to downtown Cairo with other passengers. I carried my suitcase and walked according to the map to a hotel which I had the name and address of from Khartoum.

After I settled in the hotel, I walked outside to the streets to see Cairo for the first time. I felt that I was now in a new world.

The first thing I bought was one kilogram of grapes. We didn't have grapes in Sudan.

The next morning I planned to go to the Sudanese Embassy in Cairo. I had the address from my cousin, who was one year ahead of me and was studying at Cairo University. I knew that I could reach the embassy by taking the trolley bus number 15, and it would be the second stop in Garden City. I took the trolley bus and after two stops, I started to think maybe I took it in the wrong direction. I asked the bus driver, and he told me that I had to go in the opposite direction to reach Garden City. He said I could reach it in this direction, but it would take me about one hour longer. I also went to the main Egyptian immigration office in Cairo.

I had to register as a foreigner. They called the building El-Mogamma, which means the place that contains everything. It was a big old building about fourteen floors high. There were no elevators or at least not working ones. The first two floors had 215 offices for passports and immigration.

There was no information office or directions, not even any signs to indicate that this office was for this business. There was a crowd in front of each office, no lines or any organization. The last problem was if you ask any person about the place for registration of foreigners, for example, he would simply say it was on the sixth floor and when you go there and ask another person, he would tell you, no it was on the second floor, where I was. When I finally reached the right place, the officer said to me that I need to add to my application a *damgga*. It was a specific type of stamp which value ranges from five cents to one dollar. When I asked about where I could get it, they told me from the post office. The nearest post office was about five blocks away. I went and bought it, but when I came back, I found that the office was closed.

They closed at noon. Later I discovered that I could buy damgga from some people inside the building. Those persons were not related to the office, but they helped anybody to fill the forms. They told me they could fill the form for me.

I thought that this form is simple, and I could fill it. I thought that this was for illiterate people only. I discovered later that they charged a little amount of money to fill the forms, and at the same time, they sold the damgga. In my future visits to El-Mogamma, I became a regular customer to those valuable people.

In all my movements in Cairo, I tried to walk, using my map. It was beneficial to me to know the different places and directions. I used to walk each day for at least ten hours.

I remember one day I visited my cousin in the El-Giza area. I walked from Cairo's central railway station to his place. It took me about two hours to walk one way. Now I know the directions to many places in Cairo.

I found that the streets of Cairo were very crowded compared to Khartoum streets. Almost all the sidewalks were full of people. There were well-built sidewalks in every street, not like Khartoum, with none.

In Cairo, there were hundreds of fancy stores. They beautifully presented their merchandise. Later I discovered that I could only trust the big stores like Omer Affandi, Chicorel, Seddnawy because small stores cheated, and you had to bargain with them over the prices.

The food was very cheap. There were fancy restaurants that were very expensive. Still, many others were cheap like the foul (fava) beans and taamyeh places where the price of a sandwich of foul or taamyeh mixed with fresh vegetable salad and tahini salad, cost at that time one and a half cent. In addition to all this, they usually gave a small plate of mikhallal, which is pickles for free and a bottle of red pepper mixed with water for clients who like it hot. Those foul and taamyeh restaurants usually specialized in those two items only, and they didn't sell anything else. Other restaurants specialized in *kushari*, which was a mixture of cooked rice, lentils, spaghetti, fried onions, and spicy tomato sauce. They sold a big bowl for two cents. I was hardly able to finish it. In the same place, you could order rice pudding in a medium-sized bowl for one cent. Those dishes were very delicious. All such restaurants were crowded. In Cairo, they stayed open almost twenty-four hours a day, and you could go out and eat at 2:00 AM or even 4:00 or 5:00 AM. It was nearly impossible to pass any street in Cairo without seeing these restaurants.

Cairo and all Egyptian cities, even small towns, were characterized by their *gahawee,* which means coffee shops. In the main streets and especially in the shopping areas, you could see those gahawee. Each gahwa was an empty shop filled with small metal tables. Around each table, there were usually two to four wooden chairs. Most of the gahawee had additional tables outside facing the street.

There were regular customers for each gahwa. Usually friends came daily in the evenings after they finished their work. They would spend hours chatting. Some customers were old or retirees, so they would come in the mornings instead. Others were visitors from other cities who would come to drink coffee or tea and relax for a few minutes before they continued on their mission to the capital. The regular customers usually came to play *tawla,* which is backgammon or domino. Some of them came just to watch TV, which, at that time was not affordable for most families. Others enjoyed looking at ladies and girls walking by.

In Cairo, I used to sit in a particular gahwa near the central railway station in the area of Midan Ramses. This gahwa was near the middle-class hotel I used to stay in Cairo. I used to drink my tea there because it was of better quality and cheaper than the hotel tea. They called it *shay kushary.* They put the tea leaves and sugar in the glass cup and the boiling water on top. There were no tea bags at that time. Most of the other places boiled the tea leaves in the teapot for a long time before serving it. In the winter, they also served a special milky hot drink called *sahlab.* I liked it in the winter and especially early in the mornings. I think it is a mixture of rice powder, milk, some sesame seeds, and cinnamon.

In Khartoum, I think there were only two gahawee in the center of the market area, in contrast to Cairo, where each small street had at least two or three.

In Cairo, the price of the room in the middle-class hotel differed. I usually chose the rooms not facing the streets, and they were much cheaper. For a much lower price, you could share the room with one or more people that you didn't know. I never did that because you couldn't guarantee such people. Also, you could get a lower price for higher floors, for example, the sixth floor. Most of those hotels had no elevators, and even if they did, they usually didn't work. During all my university days, I stayed in Cairo at hotels even though my aunt Tafeeda lived in Masr-Elgadeeda. I think the reason for that is because I never saw her before I went to Cairo. Also, Masr-Elgadeeda was about forty-five minutes from downtown Cairo by public transportation, which was very crowded at that time.

After a few days in Cairo, I managed to finish all my paperwork in Cairo and took the train to Assiut. Assiut is about 387 kilometers south of Cairo.

Chapter 08

The Social, Economic, and Political Situation of Egypt during 1961–1968

Mohammed Ali was a military commander in an Albanian Ottoman force sent to recover Egypt from a French occupation under Napoleon. Following Napoleon's withdrawal, Muhammad Ali rose to power through a series of political maneuvers, and in 1805 he was named Wāli (ruler) of Egypt and gained the rank of Pasha.[1] The tenth ruler of Egypt from Muhammad Ali's dynasty is King Farouk. He was the King of Egypt until 1952.

King Farouk and his relatives owned 65 percent of Egypt's land. The British troops were in Egypt, and a British-French company owned the Suez Canal.

A military coup took over the government on July 23, 1952. The actual leader was the thirty-five years old Gamal Abdel-Nasser.

The new military regimen of Egypt started a socialist system. After a few months, they took over all the private businesses, companies, banks, big stores, factories, even private schools and put everything under the government's power.[2]

The previous owners of those facilities were appointed as employees in the government with a minimal salary or dismissed. Most of the rich people at that time left Egypt. They took the land and distributed it to the farmers.

They also nationalized the Suez Canal from the British-French company.

They tried to take a loan from the World Bank to build Aswan High Dam. When the bank refused, Nasser asked the Soviet Union to help, and they did. President Nikita Khrushchev came to Aswan to attend the ceremony at the beginning of the building. I was pleased with this great achievement. A new song came out to celebrate this. I went to see this site and felt very proud as if I were the one who achieved it.

The Aswan High Dam captured floodwater during rainy seasons and released the water during times of drought. The dam also generated enormous amounts of electric power—more than 10 billion kilowatt-hours every year. Power generation began in 1967. When the high dam first reached its peak output, it produced around half of Egypt's production of electric power, and it gave most Egyptian villages electricity for the first time.

Jamal wanted to bring industry to Egypt, he started to use the military in manufacturing projects. Those factories were built and operated by military personnel. They called them the military factories. They built refrigerators, washing machines, cabinets, and many more essential things that people needed.

They declared that every student had the right to continue their university studies for free. For us, there were no tuition fees. The Sudanese Embassy used to give some students financial aid. I think about five dollars a month if they proved that they did not have enough financial support from their parents. I received no money.

The Egyptian government revolved around and copied the communist system but declared that it was a democratic-socialist system. There were general elections but just to select the local committees of the only party in the country Al Ittihad Al Ishttiraki. The top government leaders were about six military officers headed by Jamal Abd El-Nasser.

They appointed some civilian ministers as heads of the government departments. In most cases, they tried to select the best, most educated people for such jobs.

Freedom of speech was not allowed at that time. The military regime took over all the newspapers and selected their writers.

The secret police were powerful. Anyone who spoke against the government and the military leaders went to secret jails. I heard about many who were tortured at that time. Most of them didn't appear again. I remember one of them was my chemistry professor, Eissa. He was the head of the chemistry department at Assiut University. We heard that he was part of the Islamic group, who opposed the government. He suddenly disappeared, and we never saw him again.

The secret police were responsible for observing foreigners. We, as Sudanese, had to report to the secret police in Cairo and Assiut within three days of our arrival to Egypt. Once I was busy until the fourth day when I found secret police knocking at my room door and telling me that I was one day late for my registration with them. The secret police usually wore *galabia* and a black coat. By their clothes, we could guess that a person was an undercover police. I think for important tasks, they should select more hidden secret police.

Jamal Abd El-Nasser was very proud of Egypt as a nation, and he wanted it to progress rapidly in all directions. He built a powerful military force. He started to buy his weapons from the Soviet Union and France and even from China when America refused to help him. He used to send weapons and money to different opposition groups in various Arab and African countries to get rid of their rulers. I remember he used to attack the king of Saudi Arabia and King Hussein of Jordan in his public speeches. He used to talk about King Hussein as the little king. His public speeches usually lasted more than two hours, and everyone listened and enjoyed them.

I remember that he used to attack the USA, and once he said we were going to do whatever we wanted and if the United States did not like that, let them drink from the Mediterranean Sea, and if that was not enough for them, they could drink from the Red Sea as well. He was trying to be good and lead Egypt to be a prosperous country. Because he was the only ruler, all his assistants were unable to say their opinions, especially if it was against his.

Nasser was from a middle-class family. His father was working in a post office. He saw the big difference in the income of the elite class, who were mostly of Albanian origin and the ordinary Egyptian poor. So he adopted the socialist system, so all the poor people could get cheap food, accommodation, and free education. Nasser was the president of Egypt in all the period that I spent in Assiut from 1961 till 1968. All this period there were almost no increases in the prices of the main food items. He decreased the rent in that period by 15 percent. He put new rules that prevented landlords from increasing apartment rents or to ask their tenants to evacuate them. Nobody at that time thought about building new apartments. If any of the tenants wanted to leave the apartment, they asked for ransom money from the landlord, *khulow rigel*, usually about several thousand dollars, especially if the rent of the apartment was low. Most of the monthly rents at that time ranged between five and twenty dollars. Later on, most of the owners asked for khulow rigel from the new tenants, still about several thousand. It was an illegal transaction, but everybody did it.

At the end of my time in Assiut, my Egyptian colleagues told me that I could get several thousands of pounds as khulow rigel when I left my apartment. I refused to do that because it was not right.

The government built many public housing units, *masakin shabia*, to fill the gap in apartment shortages.

They also make all the university education free.

They promised to secure a job for every university graduate. The government usually made a list of all the students who graduated from all four universities at that time, and I think from all two-year colleges and appointed them as government employees. Very few were able to join the private sector and usually those who worked with their relatives. In some cases, government jobs are not related to studies in college.

Nasser's ideas were good about appointing all the graduates, but economically, it was wrong because there were no incentives for employees to work. Everybody was guaranteed to get their salary at the end of the month and knew that by law he would get their salary increase every year, and nobody could fire him. Most of the private factories that were getting good profits under their private ownership started to lose profits under government ownership. There was a lot of corruption among the senior officials and managers of those newly public companies. Most of those were relatives of the top of the new ruling leaders of the country, so nobody could dare to ask them.

Gamal Abdel-Nasser was an honest man.

He did a lot of good things for his people. But the economy was not good for the following reasons:

1. Nasser was dreaming of creating a United Arab country for all Arab nations in the Middle East.

   He spent a lot of money to change the Arab monarchies to republics that later on would join them in his imaginary Arab nation.

   He managed to do this with Syria and Iraq. The three countries agreed to unite in one country with one flag and one leader—United Arabic Republic. Iraq did not continue at the agreement after the final preparation.

   The Syrians went off the union after three and a half years, and Iraq kept only the flag with the three stars, which was the flag of the united country for twenty-eight years. Egypt kept the name and the flag with two stars for fourteen years.

2. Nasser sent troops to fight in Yemen to change the regime there but failed.

   He tried to help the Palestinians to get their land back from Israel. So Egypt had to go into wars with Israel.

3. His social agenda had significant benefits for the poor, but he was unable to finance it.

4. The financial institutions that he got from the rich became a financial burden on the government. The managers were

corrupt, and the employees didn't care because they had a secure job.

5. To keep the price of all commodities low, below the actual price, he started to sell everything cheaply and pay the difference from the budget.

Most of the essential food items were sold only in specific government stores, Gameia Taawonia. The government paid the difference in the prices of these subsidized items to keep them cheap. Those items were sugar, flour, meat, chicken, food oil, soap, tea, a specific type of fabric for winter clothes, blankets, and many other things. Most of the rationed items were of low quality. For example, the soap was dark brown because of the impurities. The rice was a mixture of rice and dirt.

Every family had a card with all its members recorded on it. With this card, only they could buy the ration items from a specific Gameia Taawonia. Only a few of those items were available outside the system but were usually very expensive.

The first time I tried to cook by myself in Assiut, I bought all the ingredients except oil. I went to almost every store in Assiut asking about oil; all their answers were no. Nobody told me that this was only available in Gameia Taawonia. As a foreigner, I had no right to buy from there. So I decided not to cook anything except eggs and rice pudding.

No imported items were available in Egypt. And because of the general deterioration of the Egyptian factories, everything you bought was of terrible quality, and you couldn't complain because this was the only available in the market. I used to get many things from Sudan except for food. I usually bought Lipton tea from Khartoum for me and some of my close Egyptian friends. My dentist in Assiut asked me to buy for him from Sudan a piece of fabric to make a suit.

The government used to tell the people that they should sacrifice the luxurious items that the imperialist countries (USA, England, and France) were trying to sell them and only use their Egyptian-made items. But the fact was because the economic system was wrong and due to the corruption, the quality of the Egyptian products was deficient and could not compete with foreign-made products.

In Boston, I buy fancy shirts from the stores and discover that they are Egyptian made. When the next president came, Anwar Al-Saddat, he opened up the economy.

This was the political, social, and economic situation of Egypt when I lived in Assiut. Now I go back to my train journey from Cairo to Assiut.

Rreference:

1- https://www.britannica.com/biography/Muhammad-Ali-pasha-and-viceroy-of-Egypt
2- https://www.britannica.com/biography/Gamal-Abdel-Nasser

Chapter 09

Fun on the Train from Cairo to Assiut

I went to Ramsis Railway Station. It was the central railway station in Cairo. All the trains coming and going to Cairo from all around Egypt started here. To my surprise, the station was very crowded. Everyone was running to reach their train. The trains were crowded. When a train stopped, a considerable number of passengers squeezed themselves at the door, of course, with their bags, no lines.

Some *shayaleen* could bring your bag inside the train and find a seat for you. They forced themselves and pushed other passengers away. They received money for doing that. They usually asked for a lot, and you had to bargain. The other alternative was to push yourself among the crowds through the train door.

It was a familiar thing to see some people coming from deprived areas, and the man pushed his wife and children inside the train through the train windows. It was a dramatic scene and a complete shock to me.

I discovered the reason for the crowd. Not all the people crowded were travelers. Three or four friends accompanied every passenger. All of them were trying to go inside the train to secure a place for their friend.

The train stopped for a short period, and you had to get in as soon as possible. When the train started to move, you saw many people getting down; those were the friends of the traveler. I managed to go in and find a place to sit.

I noticed that part of the train trip was to chat with the people around you. Most of the people read the newspaper or weekly magazines on the trains for some time, but the rest of the time, they had conversations with other passengers. I chatted with the person next to me. He was, I think, a government employee.

I had no idea how many hours the train would take until I reached Assiut. God was ready with the person who was sitting next to me.

I was surprised when I noticed that most of the train passengers at the beginning of the trip were putting on their full suits. As soon as the train started to move from Cairo, they exchanged their jackets with pajama tops.

In Egyptian trains, there was a lot of entertainment. First, the people who sold the newspapers would come inside the train during the train stop and pass in between the passengers and shout, "*Gomhoria, Akhbar, Ahram*", "*Rosa, Mosawar, Kawakib, Sabah* El-Kheir." Those were the popular newspapers and weekly magazines. They also called out, "Igraa El-Hadsa," which meant "Read about the accident." In every paper, there was at least one accident every day. I noticed those newspaper sellers rode the train for one stop only. Then they rode another train going in the other direction. They were clever by this, to avoid paying for train tickets.

Secondly, some people passed and shouted, "Sameet we gibna," this was a popular type of bread covered with sesame. They sold it with boiled eggs and Feta cheese. We usually ate this sameet more often when we are traveling.

Then the third person was the tea person. He often came with a tray full of glass cups full of fresh hot tea. He used the spoon to click it on the cup and said, "Is-haa ma-aya shay sukhn," which meant, "Wake up, I have hot tea." I usually drank tea on the train, especially in the winter.

The fourth person who sold cold drinks would come and click the bottle opener on the glass bottles and say, "Ma-aya Kakola sagaa," which meant, "I have cold Coke."

A fifth was a person who sold *turmos,* which was boiled lupine. Those were just a few of many who passed and shouted and tried to sell their items. It was impossible to try to sleep on any Egyptian train.

During the train stop, there was usually a crowd of people outside the train trying to get on (no lines in Egypt). Nobody waited for the exiting passengers to get out first. Most of the passengers carried heavy bags and *sabat akel*, which was a characteristic big basket made of bamboo with a big handle at the top. In this sabat they usually put what they wanted to eat during the trip and sometimes took food for the relatives they were visiting. The travelers inside the train tried to keep the windows closed, and the people from outside tried to open them. In most cases, a person would enter the train and open the window, and then his friends would throw the bags and sometimes his wife from the outside.

In my last few years in Assiut, they introduced modern trains with permanently closed windows, air conditioning, and you couldn't use it without booking. They called this train El-Magari because it was from Hungary (Magar in Arabic). I used those trains on all my trips afterward.

My train partner asked me if this was the first time for me to go to Assiut, and I answered yes. He then mentioned that he was on a business trip to Assiut. He asked me if anybody would be waiting for me. I told him no. He said that he was staying in a hotel near the train station and if I wanted, he could show me the hotel.

The trip to Assiut took seven hours. The scenery was outstanding compared to train trips in Sudan, where the land was bare with nothing growing except a few dry bushes. In Egypt, there was a big strip of land around the River Nile with green vegetation. The farmers were working on their farms. Their wives were taking their buffaloes to the Nile or the central canal to drink water and were taking a bath while they washed the family clothes. It gave the impression of life. The train traveled along the Nile the whole trip, and on the other side, you could see the paved road.

The train passed many small and big towns with beautiful, modern large buildings or just mud-built homes.

Chapter 10

My First Week in Assiut 1961

When the train approached Assiut, my train companion started to change out of his pajamas and into his suit. He then pointed to a few new buildings. Each had five stories and surrounded by large spaces of green grass.

Victor in Assiut

There were well-paved streets with newly planted trees on each side. He told me, "This is Assiut University."

Assiut University buildings were white with all the windows lighted. It gave the feeling of something new and elegant. I was happy and looking forward to joining such a beautiful university.

The train, at last, stopped at Assiut station. The station had a new modern building. It was not big, but tiles covered all the sidewalks. Khartoum Railway Station, there were no pavements, and you had to take a big step from the train to reach the floor. Assiut station was an improvement.

Assiut Railway Station

When we went outside the station, I saw for the first time a *hantoor* which was a black carriage that could accommodate two passengers and two small children. A horse pulled each hantour. Most of the horses were dark brown. The driver usually sat on top of the car just behind the horse and carried a very long whip. He typically used the whip to make a noise to encourage the horse to move quickly, and many times he used the strap to hit the children who liked to get a free ride by sitting on the back of the carriage.

I noticed that the hantour was the primary means of transportation in Assiut at that time.

There were few 1924 Ford cars in use in certain lanes from one point of the city to another.

Leila waiting the old Ford car to be fixed, Assiut 1977

Old Ford Taxi

You couldn't hire the whole car as a taxi. You could pay for one seat. The driver usually filled the car with many passengers. Before the car reached the police checkpoint, the driver would ask some of the passengers to sit in the luggage space in the back of the car and close the hood over them until he passed the police, then he would release them to join the other passengers in the front. They called those Ford cars *labo labo*. I think this name came from the noise of its horn. The horn was not an electric one but consisted of a rubber ball connected to a long metal horn. When the driver wanted to use it, he would push his hand outside the car to reach the horn and press on the rubber ball. As in all other parts of Egypt, they used the horn all the time.

There were very few buses in Assiut for in-town transportation. The private cars were few, and only a few wealthy people, doctors, and some of the university professors had them. I think at that time the number of private cars in Assiut was less than twenty.

Most of the people used the hantour if the place they were going was far away or if they were going to the railway station and had luggage. The first time I used the hantour, I was terrified because I felt it was not stable. It had two big wheels in the back. When the horse moved, the whole carriage moved, and you had to get in quickly. I asked the driver how he could stop the car if there were an emergency or suddenly a child came in front of the carriage. There were no breaks.

Now I imagine that the driver thought of me as insane because who in Assiut would ask such a silly question.

Anyhow he answered and told me he could stop or reduce the speed by pulling the liggam which is the leather strap that he held the horse's head with.

The Hantour

I noticed that the hantour had bells that the driver could press by his foot. The hantour wheels were big and wooden, covered by a strap of thick rubber band. Most of the time, the rubber bands were not complete. When the hantour moved, you felt the wheels were moving up and down and to the right and left, especially if the hantour was old.

Till now, I do not like to use the hantour. I remember once the horse slipped, and we jumped down immediately. Some of the hantour drivers drove very fast. I remember my father-in-law Hyzkial Bestourous was with me, and he felt that I was not comfortable with the high speed the hantour was going, so he told the driver, "Why are you driving fast as if you are Ramses the First the pharaoh!"

In Khartoum, there was no hantour. Even in Cairo, there were a few, just for the tourists and the newly wedded couples.

I went with my train friend to Lokandet Al-Tahreer, which meant the freedom hotel. It was an old two stories hotel, ancient and everything looked dirty, even the outside of the building. I don't think that they painted it after they built it at least fifty years earlier. I asked for a separate room. This was the last time I saw my train companion. I settled in the room and slept.

After a few minutes, I felt a painful insect bite. I woke up, removed the covers and looked, and found nothing. A few minutes again, I felt another bite. I repeated the search, but there were no insects at all. The bites were going on all night. It was a terrible night. The next morning I found all my skin swollen, and the sites of the bites were there.

I asked about the university and how to reach it. I took the hantour for the first time. I found it funny to ride the hantour as if you were in an open space with no doors or windows, just a cover for the back and head. You could see the streets better with the hantour than the cars. I went to the Jamaa El-Gadeeda, which meant the new university. The medical school student affairs were in one of the two buildings in the modern university. The registration went OK. When I came out of the office, I saw my friend Adel with some other Sudanese students. I knew that Adel would join Assiut University, but it was a pleasant surprise for me. I asked him where he was staying? I decided to go and change my hotel to their hotel to be away from the insect bites. Adil was a friend from high school in Khartoum. I went with Adil and the other Sudanese friends to their hotel. It was a surprise for me to find that their hotel was the same Al-Tahreer.

Later I learned that my insect bites were actual insect bites, and the insects were called bed bugs. These were small crawling insects without wings, about half a centimeter in diameter. They lived in the old mattresses. They come out at night toward the heated areas of the mattress, which was where the person was sleeping in bed. The bed bugs were brilliant; they disappeared very quickly when you took off the covers. These bed bugs were not present in Sudan because they only lived in cold weather. Bed bugs usually lived in old second- and third-class hotels.

Assiut was the largest town in the southern part of Egypt. It is called the capital of the *saieed*, which means the south. As with all the cities south of Egypt, it is along the River Nile surrounded by a small strip of fertile land. Most of the people are slightly darker in color than the Cairo people. In Egypt, in every town, people have a distinctive accent. You could guess the origin of each person from their accent. All the people from the south of Egypt are called Saiedda. They differ from the people from the north by their accent; it is called Saieedy. The accent of the north is called Bahry. Bahr means sea, and they say people living near the Mediterranean Sea. Most of the people from the south, when they want to show that they are modern, they try to use the accent of the north. The people from the north feel that Saeidda are primitive and know nothing and to some extent not intelligent. There are many jokes about this. In reality, Saeidda were usually straightforward in their relationships with others, and they didn't cheat. The reverse is true of the northern Egyptians, Baharwa. I am happy because I studied in Assiut. I like the characters of the Saeidda. They are just like the Sudanese.

In Egypt, I found that there are three groups of people.

The first group was the farmers. These men wore galabyeh, which was just like the maxi dress. It was usually made of cotton material and almost always of striated colors. They liked green, blue, and brown colors. In the winter, it was usually thick in material, and they typically wore more than one galabyeh, one over the other and wore long thermal underwear underneath. Over their heads, they wore libda which was an especially made small light-brown cap that covered only the head and made of lint-like material.

Their wives wore very long black dresses that must touch the ground, *garar*. You could see the dust in the air following the lady. They covered their hair with *harda* which was a big black scarf that covered their heads and shoulders. Young ladies wear colorful galabieh.

At work, the men usually wore suits in the winter and trousers and shirts in the summer. The ladies wore modern clothes, just like any Western lady. They didn't cover their hair, and they wore makeup.

After I left Assiut and after President Saddat took over, the Islamists enforced their agenda by persuasion or many times by force. They asked all Muslim ladies to wear hijab.

The third group was the people who were educated but were originally from the farmers' group but got some education. The men wore galabyeh at home and modern clothes at work. The ladies wear stylish clothes, but their dresses were usually longer than the others, and they covered their heads with a small scarf when they went out.

Assiut was a beautiful town but not as clean as central Cairo. The sidewalks were mostly paved but not properly maintained. There were usually holes in the sidewalks, and many of them were covered with just dust. The city used to appoint specialized employees just to clean the streets. You could see them using their brooms to push the waste papers and other garbage from one spot to the other. Most of them were not serious, just like all government employees at that time. Generally, the people in Egypt and Sudan threw any waste papers or garbage in the street. There were no fines for littering.

After a few days, one of the employees in the student affairs office came to the lecture room and asked about me. When I went out, he told me that your parents came, and they were waiting for you in the office. I met them. They were on vacation in Europe, visiting my brother George and his wife, who were at that time in Belgium in a training course. My parents were staying in Windsor Hotel, which was a first-class hotel. I took my belongings from Lokandet Al-Tahreer and stayed with them. My father was an expert in the Egyptian way of life, and he asked the Sudanese porter of the building, called Basheer, for a room for me. He gave him a good amount of money, and he found a studio for me. We rented it for three Egyptian pounds and seventy-five cents, which were about eight dollars, which was considered quite expensive at that time. My colleagues rented a three-bedroom apartment for five pounds. My room was on the second floor. The building had seven floors and had functioning elevators. It was called Emarat Al-Masarani Emarat means the building, and Al-Masarani was the owner's name. I met the owner because he was the manager of Windsor Hotel on the top three floors. He was a wealthy man about sixty-five years old.

He advised me not to use the elevator because the consumption of electricity was high. He mentioned that he was climbing the stairs to save money.

Emarat Al-Massarani

The building was big. On the ground floor, there were some shops—a first-class restaurant, El-Hatti, a pastry shop Akhir Saa, two shops sold soft drinks and ice cream, candies, and chocolates. One of those two candy shops was very famous called Andrea. The owner was a Greek lady. The other shop Nefartiti was less popular and was owned by an old Egyptian man Hakeem and his daughter.

There were two book stores. One was very popular, and most of the university students bought their needs from there. The owner was an older man and he worked together with all of his four sons. They had a printing press in the bookstore. The other book store was a small one, and I think the owner hardly covered his expenses.

There was a shop that sold fresh fruits, Fakahani. And there was a shoe shop as well. The main business of the shop was to shine shoes and make shoes for some people. There were three seats, you sat on a high chair, and the shoe shiner sat down and polished the shoe while you wore them. They did an excellent job. They cleaned the shoe from dust first with a shoe brush, and then they put a fluid like a dye then the shoe polish. At last, they rubbed the shoe firmly with a cloth. They were always busy. The owner of the store was called Hilmi. He usually sat at the inner end of the store and made new custom-made shoes.

In all the coffee shops, Gahawi, shoe shiners passed and looked at your eyes, and if you bend your face down, they would shine your shoes. They carried a wooden box with the top designed so the client could put his foot over it. They usually did one shoe first then clicked with the wooden brush over the box as a sign for the client to switch his foot with the other one. They carried with them a small cardboard box for the clients who like to take off their shoes while the shoe shiner cleaned them. The cardboard box was for the client to put his bare foot on them. You may think that those shoe shiners would be children or young adults, but surprisingly most of them were very old.

The first and second floors of my building were offices for lawyers and a dentist. In the same flat where my room was, there were three lawyers.

There was an office for *Al Ahram* newspaper. This office received the ads for the newspaper's main office in Cairo. The habit in Egypt was to put an obituary for the deceased persons in the newspaper. The richer the family was the bigger the ad. Sometimes, they did it in the three main available papers. The friends and relatives put ads as well for the same person. All Egyptians started their day by looking at the obituary pages, usually two or three pages long. Also, families congratulated their sons and daughters on graduations or marriages. Even some employees congratulated their bosses on their new promotions in hopes of getting their own promotions in the future.

My room was a fairly big one, about fifteen feet by twenty feet. Attached to the room was a private bathroom. My father went with me and bought a metal bed, a wooden desk, and two chairs.

We went together to Gharb El-Balad which meant west of the city to buy a mattress and a comforter, *lihaf.* In Assiut, you had to purchase the cotton, the fabric, and ask someone to make the mattress. You have to watch them because they could cheat and put in lower-quality cloth or old cotton. I saw how they, *yonfuddo el-gutton*, used a big wooden stick about five feet long and attached a metal string to separate the cotton.

Yonfuddo el-gutton, they moved the string forward and backward in the cotton, so the string made the cotton more fluffy. This was new to me because in Sudan, they used a small bamboo stick to hit the cotton to make it more fluffy. With my new mattress and new room, I never had the bed bug bites.

Gharb El-Balad was one of the old parts of Assiut. The streets were narrow, unpaved, and muddy because everybody threw the water to keep the dust down. We also bought wabour jaz, which was a kerosene stove.

I used a small electric heater most of the time except for heating water for the bath.

The majority of Egyptian families were using wabour el-jaz at that time. The butane gas was, to some extent, new and only used by higher-class families. The beautiful thing about wabour el-jaz was that you could put it on any table or the floor. The bad thing was the bad odor of the burnt kerosene. I tried to avoid using wabour el-jaz because in the winter when the windows were closed, you felt that you couldn't breathe. There was no alternative to wabour el-jaz because there was no hot water and no heating system.

I found Assiut to be very cold in the winter compared to Sudan. In Assiut, in winter, the temperature went down to freezing levels, but in Sudan, the minimum it ever reached was 60 degrees Fahrenheit. I found the best heating system for me was the small electric heater. I used it to make my tea, hot chocolate, and fried eggs. On cold nights, I used the electric heater to warm my feet. This was the only way to continue sitting on the desk.

In bed, I used the lihaf, which was the comforter for the first time as a cover in addition to the blanket. In Sudan, we only used the lihaf as a portable mattress. On cold nights, Assiut was cold even with all those coverings. I remember that if I wanted to turn or move my leg while sleeping, I found the new parts of the bed very cold, so I would have to go back to my original warm position.

My father bought a bike for me. It turned out to be very useful to me because I had to travel at least three to four miles every day from my room back and forth to the different university buildings.

When my father felt that I was settled, they left. I think they stayed only one week in Assiut.

I noticed my father tried to give me everything I needed and in good quality. The apartment was the best in a high-standard place (first-class hotel). The furniture was of high quality at that time for students. They even gave me the convenience of a bike. He showed his love, which reminded me of my heavenly Father God because His love to us gives us all our needs, air to breathe, food to eat, and water to drink.

> *29 And do not seek what you should eat or what you should drink, nor have an anxious mind. 30 For all these things the nations of the world seek after, and your Father knows that you need these things. 31 But seek the kingdom of God, and all these things shall be added to you. (Luke 12:29–31)*

Chapter 11

Why Did God Push Me to Study Medicine?

In high school, we studied the theory of evolution. According to this theory, it claimed that life started on its own.

Some scientists like Oparin claimed that many millions of years ago, life started spontaneously. Inorganic matters were present on the earth. Superheated water vapor reacted with other inorganic matters to form organic matter. The organic matter condensed together to form primitive living creatures.

I was a bit confused between this theory and what was in the Bible. *Genesis 2:7 says, "And the Lord God formed man of the dust of the ground and breathed into his nostrils the breath of life, and man became a living being."*

At the beginning of medical school, we studied the amoeba.

Amoeba is a tiny single cell, living on its own. It ranges in size. The largest is about 2 mm. We learned that amoeba was a living creature. The living creature must show certain characteristics: breath, eat, have the ability to create another creature.

We learned in medical school that when the cell died, it would lose its life and decay. So chemicals were the same, but they were missing one important thing, which was life. Chemical reactions between two chemicals would end with another chemical product, and sometimes the byproduct was energy but not life.

Harvard University started a project called the "Origin of Life Initiative" in 2007 and allocated one million dollars every year to find out how life began. Till now, they found nothing. The project is still ongoing.

Life can only come from a living creature. Life comes from the breath of a living God.

Genesis 2:7 states, "And the Lord God formed man of the dust of the ground and breathed into his nostrils the breath of life, and man became a living being."

When I discovered this fact, I realized that God wanted to give me the correct scientific facts to show me that the theory of evolution is just a wrong theory and has nothing to do with science. And I know now why God pushed me to study medicine despite my resistance. I thank God for His love for me.

Chapter 12

Assiut University 1961–1968

Before the July 1952 Egyptian revolution that changed the government from a kingdom to a presidential system, there were three universities. The oldest was Cairo University, the second was Ain-Shams University in Cairo and in Alexandria. The criteria for admission were the grades at the end of the high school exams, Tawgeeheya. This was the reason that every student had to make his best effort to get high grades.

In my final exam grade for high school, I wrote that I wanted to study engineering.

The higher the grade, the better the chance of being accepted into the university. A committee looks into all the university applications and decides what the grades are needed to enter each college in each university in Egypt. For example, they may decide that to enter Cairo University college of engineering, you must get an 85 percent average in the Tawjihiyya. For the same college in Alexandria, you may only need 78 percent, and for agriculture, you may only need 62 percent. This is how you could guess a person's Tawjihiyya grades by the college they attended. The top schools were either medicine or engineering followed by pharmacy, then science then veterinary medicine then agricultural science. All the nonscience colleges like languages, history, and law were different because starting in high school, you had to choose either the science division or the arts division. In the Tawjihi exams there were two exams, one of them for science and the other one for the arts. You couldn't take both exams.

Around 1956, the Egyptian government decided to open a new university in Assiut. They agreed that at that stage, they needed more scientists for the country to progress. They decided that Assiut University must be just for science colleges. They started by the college of science and engineering followed by agricultural science. Then in 1960 they opened the medical school. We were the second batch in this new college. The blueprints for all the buildings of all the colleges were ready from the beginning. They started the actual construction of the college of science during my first year in Assiut. College of engineering was two years later then agriculture. I heard they finished the college of medicine building about ten years after I graduated.

All the new buildings were in a large vacant land to the north of Assiut City and between it and the Turaa Ibraheemeya, which was the largest built canal in Egypt that runs parallel to the River Nile.

The new buildings and the area around it were called El-Gamaa El-Jadeeda, which meant the new university. They converted a high school to be part of the university. We used to call it El-Gamaa El-Gadeema, which meant the old university. This was just like any other high school, old building, and mostly used for labs because the lecture rooms were small. Only the college pharmacy students had their lectures there because their number was relatively small. We had to go between the old and new universities on the same day sometimes twice. The distance between them was about one and half mile. The good thing was that the road that we had to take was along the Turaa Ibraheemeya, and there were big shady trees that covered the entire road. It had the best fresh air that you could possibly breathe and the best scenery. The only thing that I was not happy about the Gamaa El-Gadeema was the way they cleaned it every morning. Small dark-brown tiles covered all the corridors. They used to clean the tiles with a cloth wet with what I think was kerosene. The result was a very slippery surface. Everybody slipped many times a day even if you were very careful. The building was two stories high, one built of granite or similar material. In contrast, the

Gamaa El-Jadeeda' had all new buildings with five levels. They were painted white and decorated with a few brown bricks. In the beginning, there were only two buildings for the college of science. They were big with two small elevators, but nobody used them. The stairs were wide to accommodate the large number of students coming at once from the lecture rooms. At first, we were a bit lost because all the floors were very similar. Sometimes you would go to the lecture room on the second floor instead of the third. The only clue was seeing your colleagues. There was a two-way street between the two buildings. At the end of the street was the cafeteria. It had a small store where the workers stayed and sold sandwiches and drinks to the students. The store was connected to a large shaded platform, maybe 300 feet in length and 100 feet in width. All the shaded area was covered by a roof but open from all sides. There were at least a hundred small tables and chairs in all this shaded area. You had to go to buy what you needed from the store and come back to sit to eat and drink. In the winter, we used to take the chairs and sit outside the shaded area to enjoy the sun. Assiut was always sunny, even in the winter. During all my years in Assiut, I never saw rain. I used to eat sandwiches *jibna roumy*, which was just like American cheese. For drinks, there were cold drinks like Coke and hot drinks like tea. I used to drink tea. They sold cookies and candies. I used to buy Arabisco, which was a type of wafer cookie. I liked the vanilla flavor, not the chocolate. For the candies, my best friend Saleem used to buy Nadler, which was just plain candy, and he liked to give it to his friends. The shoe shiners came to the cafeteria. I guess the income from the cafeteria was high because all the students from all the colleges went to eat and drink there. The university leased the cafeteria to private contractors, the same ones who leased the cafeteria of Assiut Railway Station.

In the first year, we used to have our lectures in large lecture rooms. The medical students joined the pharmacy students for most of the lectures. I was the only Sudanese student in medical school. There were three Sudanese students in the college of pharmacy in the same year. One of them, Gamal, was living in the same building with me. For me, it was nice to have some friends from Sudan in the same class.

The first year was tough. When I spoke with any Egyptian colleague, they would ask about the meaning of many words that I said because of my Sudanese accent. Some of them would just laugh when I spoke. After a few months, I started to recognize what were the Sudanese words that the Egyptians didn't use then avoided using them. I was unable, and until now, I cannot change my accent to an Egyptian one. This was the reason that as soon as I started speaking to any Egyptian person, they could recognize my accent and would ask the typical question, "Where are you from?" This was very annoying to me at the beginning because I had to answer this question every time I went to buy fruits, vegetables, bread, or anything. Some of them would proceed to mention that "but you don't look Sudanese." They meant that I wasn't black. After a few months, the questions became less. Apparently it was because I tried to avoid using the Sudanese words and maybe because most of the people that I used to contact knew me and heard my life story.

Most of the students in Assiut medical school were Egyptians. In the first Eadady year I met one of the students and he was from Thailand. He was Muslim and could hardly communicate in Arabic. After a few months, he left for Cairo to continue his studies there.

For the first two years in medical school, we had an Iraqi student. His name was Korial. He was Christian and became a good friend because he was in my group in all the labs. He was very handsome and apparently also rich. After he finished the second year, he transferred to Cairo University. There were about five Palestinian students in our class, one of them was my friend Feraje. The Egyptian government used to give them monthly allowances. My Egyptian colleagues complained about how the Egyptian government gave the Palestinian students money to study, and when they graduated, they went to work in the rich Gulf countries while the Egyptian students got no money during their education and after graduation. They had to spend two or three years in the army and may end up going to war which was mainly to defend and regain the Palestinian land.

There were some dorms for the students. They called them Masakin El-Talaba which meant student houses or El-Madeena El-Jameaya which meant the university town. They started out as only four of them. They gave them the Arabic alphabets, so they were building A, building B, and so on. They were in the area of the Gamaa Jadeeda. Every building was huge and made up of five levels. They had the same design and white color as all the other university buildings. The students had to pay four Egyptian pounds. I remember that it was about five dollars each month to stay in and included three meals a day for the whole month. For the foreign students, the university designated a special building in Assiut but just facing the Gamaa El-Jadida. It was a three-level building; they called it Beit El-Mughtaribeen, which meant the foreigners' house. I heard that the decision of separating the foreign students from the Egyptians was dictated by the security authorities in Assiut. Only one or two Sudanese students stayed in this building and only for a few months.

Most of the students, Egyptians or foreigners, lived inside Assiut town. Three or four students usually used to hire an apartment and share the expenses. Most of them do their cooking. The university offered a lunch meal for students living outside the Medina El-Jameaya. You could buy lunch tickets each for four cents. I tried it for some time because usually we had lectures after lunch, and it was more convenient to eat in the university than to go back to Assiut town to have lunch and come back to the university to finish my lectures or labs. I found the food was extremely bad. They usually served tabeekh and ruz which was tomato sauce with meat and rice. The meat was always half-cooked and very difficult to cut or chew. Even the vegetables were half-cooked. The tomato sauce was just water with faint brown-colored fluid. Also most of the time they served gulgas (artichoke) which I never ate before in Sudan, and I didn't like to eat it. In many cases, I ended eating only the banana or the orange they gave. Also maybe the way they served the food was not a nice one. You take a metal tray with four separate compartments. Then you passed in a line so each cook filled one compartment with one item. They used a long metal spoon, *maghrafa,* to take the tabeekh from a dirty-looking huge pot. I still remember how the grease and dirt were over the outside of those pots. Sometimes you think maybe because of the number of the students in thousands in each serving area, but I think this was just part of the bad services because the workers were just government employees, and nobody could fire them. Most of the time I used to eat a sandwich as lunch from the cafeteria, and then when I finished my classes, I went to one of the restaurants in downtown Assiut to eat there. My favorite restaurant was a small one owned by a person called Zakhir, and his son was Redda. He used to serve well-cooked food, and his prices were very moderate. He used to cook the tabeekh in a clay pot called *tajin* and each tajin was for one person only. Also, I used to eat well-cooked rice, and the meat was well cooked. Some clients eat tabeekh without meat, especially at the end of the month. They called it *sketto.* I usually order mine with meat. I think he was charging seven to ten cents for the whole meal. Sometimes, maybe once a month I go and eat *kebab* and *kuftta* in El-Hatti who was in the same building where I lived. I think the cost was about twenty cents. This place just served roasted meat, kebab or roasted minced meat, kuftta. They serve tahini salad with food and bread. It was always delicious.

Our school day usually used to start at 8:00 AM. I usually wake up early and drink tea with some cookies. At about 10:00 AM, I usually had my breakfast in the cafeteria which was mostly a sandwich, jibna roumy. If I finished my classes at two or three, I just went immediately to Amm Zakhir to take my lunch then go home. If I had labs and I had to stay late, I usually took another sandwich from the cafeteria at about 2:00 PM and then go home and prepare a good dinner. I decided not to cook tabeekh in my room. I found that I am not patient enough to wait for the tabeekh to finish cooking. Another factor was the way the butlers treated their customers in Assiut. They tried to cheat and give you what you didn't like to take. I could not argue with the butler since he was holding a big knife! I used to prepare fried eggs. Some days I did it with tomatoes and Feta cheese. I usually eat three or even four eggs if I miss the good lunch in Zakhir's restaurant. If I had the restaurant's lunch menu, I usually restricted my dinner to a sandwich. I used to buy dinner sandwiches from Daoud. This was a grocery shop owned by an old man called Daoud. He prepares the sandwich, for example, mortadella or salami and added *mish,* which was a special, very old Feta cheese mixed with hot pepper. This was my favorite till one day I discovered that all the mish was full of small living worms. When I mentioned this to my Egyptian friends, they laughed and said, "Dude, el-mish mino feeh." This was a proverb in Egypt which meant that the mish was expected to have worms. They also told me that "we don't consider el-mish to be good if it has no worms." This was the end of those delicious sandwiches for me. Now I was thinking that maybe they were delicious because of those worms. After this incident, I shifted to another grocery store owned by a Greek called Paulo. He had a very delicious basterma sandwiches. I remember once I went to him with my bike. This was not my habit. I usually walk to his store. After I bought what I wanted, I walked to my house, as usual, leaving my bike in front of his store. Lucky enough when he closed his store, he discovered my bike. He put it inside his store till I came asking about it the next morning. He was a nice person.

I had the habit of buying *basbousa* (a special very sweet like a cake with coconut) at least three times a week. I bought the basbousa from a Halawanee called Akhir Saa. They served it warm and I usually ask for gishtta which was a whipped cream to be added on top. Some days when my friend Adel came to visit me during the afternoon time, we usually went and bought basbousa from a small shop owned by a person called Taha. His shop was about four feet by four feet. He opened it only at 4:00 PM and brought with him about four big trays of hot basbousa. Within half an hour he would sell all his basbousa and close his shop. His basbousa was the best in Assiut.

Chapter 13

Friends and Interests in Assiut 1961–1968

During this period, I was a very active reader. I used to read the *Al Ahram* newspaper every Friday. The Friday edition was a special thick one, thirty-six pages or more, compared to Sudanese newspapers, which were only eight pages long. The price was one cent for many years but increased during my last years in Assiut to one and a half cents. The famous Egyptian writer Mohammed Hassanein Heikal used to write a long political article in each Friday's edition, analyzing the political situation in Egypt during that time. He was a friend and adviser to President Jamal Abd El Nasser. This was the reason that, to a great extent, what he wrote almost presented what Nasser wanted to do. Sometimes, he wrote ideas that appeared to be opposed to the government stance. I feel this was just to give the impression that there was some form of freedom of speech. I never enjoyed his writings, but I read every article to be aware of the political situation in Egypt. My friend Adel was fond of him and thought that he was a good writer and thinker. We used to argue about his articles every week. I used to read the weekly magazine *Sabah Al Kheir*. It was an excellent magazine, and I liked the way their writers presented their ideas. I used to read other newspapers and weekly magazines whenever there was something of interest. In those years, the Egyptian government put a great effort to publish many books either written by Egyptian writers or translated by them. These books were printed on paper covers and were mostly inexpensive. For example, there was a series called *Igraa* which meant read. The price for the book was only one and a half cents. I read many political books such as the communist revolution in the Soviet Union, the *Manifesto of the Communist Party* in China, Stalin, and Lenin. Most of the political books printed in Egypt at that period were about the communist system. I read many religious books as well. I used to buy them from the library of the Coptic Orthodox church and from another bookstore related to the evangelical church. My Egyptian friend Saleem used to give me some.

I read some books about other religions like *Confessio* and *Buddha*. I had two books about yoga, and I found them useful in their relaxation methods, especially when I traveled. I also read books about science, for example about petroleum and how it was formed as well as engines, light, air, and the circle of water in the earth. I read a few fictional books. There were excellent writers like Taha Hussein who was blind since he was seven years old. He received his PhD from France and married a French woman. He eventually became the minister of education in Egypt. Another famous writer was Tawfeek El Hakeem who won the 1980 Nobel Prize. There were other good writers like El Aquad and Yousif El Sebai. Sebai was later assassinated in an international conference in Cyprus. In general, I didn't like fiction. I feel that the writer had to lie because he was telling me a fake story and had to persuade me to believe it. But still, I read many stories and saw many movies during that period, many of which I couldn't recall now. I think the Egyptian government was very wise to keep the prices of the books down. At least for me, it gave me a chance to read more books.

My two best friends were Adel and Saleem. Adel was from Sudan. I felt that he matched me in my thinking and behavior. He was in the college of science. We used to spend our spare time together and discuss everything from politics to religion, social life, and our futures. Adel lived with Sameer in the same apartment. Adel was very sensitive to cold weather and hot weather. In the winter he used to turn the kerosene stove wabour el-jaz on just to warm his room. He kept it on till it consumed all the kerosene.

Once I joined a team to build a social club in a small village near Assiut; it was a volunteer job and we spent the entire Friday carrying bags of sand. It was fun.

In sports, I used to play tennis with my friend Sameer. Assiut University had great tennis courts. I also actively walked many miles each day. I remember once I decided to walk to Mangabad, which was about ten miles from Assiut. I couldn't remember who walked with me. We went and came back right away without stopping. It was a long walk. My friend Sameer used to go bird hunting at night. I never joined him because I didn't like killing animals.

Assiut was hot in the summer and very cold in the winter. In summer, my friend Adel simply sprayed water on his bed to keep it cool. Most of the time we spent the time either in my room or his room. Adel was a very practical thinker and at the same time liberal. He believed in the equality of people and that every government had to work to reach this goal. He was a godly person. He attended church meetings and was a good believer. He was very fond of science and new inventions. In sports he was an active soccer player. I never liked soccer because I felt that the players fought for the ball and sometimes kicked each other with their feet, which I hated.

Adil and I used to eat our dinner together whenever we met. We sometimes went to a dairy shop that served *rugag*. Those were thin sheets of baked wheat dough. It was served with warm milk and sugar. It was the equivalent of corn flakes. Adel liked to eat yogurt mixed with honey and honey with bread or yogurt alone. He sometimes mixed honey with *halawa tahinia*. This was made from sesame and sugar. This tasted terrible to me.

When we didn't have to study, we would go together to gahwa, a coffee shop, to play tawla, which was backgammon. We drank tea and had our shoes shined. When Adil went alone to the gahwa, he usually watched TV. I was and till now never fond of TV. In Assiut, there was one coffee shop that sold Cream Caramel; we used to go there every now and then to eat it.

Adel was a regular customer of the movie theater. Sometimes I joined him. There were some great films in that period, most of them were American films. In Assiut, there were three movie theaters. One was Cinema Shitwee, which meant the winter movie theater. It was a very modern place, and as expected it was covered and warm in the winter and was open all year long. It presented one film for about five days then switched it to another one. It had about six shows each day, starting at 10:00 AM. The seats were cushioned and bendable. When the film was about to start, the light dimed gradually, and the curtains opened smoothly. I remember once we went there with my friend Gamal, the film was about a chase and the bad guys were silently following the good guy and about to kill him. All the audience were in suspense watching, and suddenly Gamal in a loud voice shouted, "Wah." All the audience laughed. Gamal liked to make jokes; this was a nice one. There were two other movie theaters in Assiut, both of them were open without a roof. They closed in the winter. One of them was called Cinema Assiut El Seify the other was Cinema Masr El Seify. Both of them had bad-quality, uncomfortable wooden chairs. Whenever winter approached, they tried to keep open as long as possible. In their last days before closing, the audience sometimes burned some chairs to keep warm. Those two summertime movie theaters used to present two films each night. The first Arabic film was followed by the American then they repeated the first one again. You can see the three shows with one ticket. After three days they changed to the other two films, but they started this time with the American one first. I went to those two movie theaters only a few times, and I was never able to finish the two films.

The Egyptian government had and I believe still has a very strong censorship system for films. They don't allow some films and simply cut other parts of the film that they think don't match with their government policies or are not decent or appropriate. Almost 95 percent of Arabic films were Egyptian. There were a few Lebanese films at that time. I remember I saw a Lebanese film and I was astonished when I found that the Egyptians made Arabic translations just like American films. The Lebanese accent or dialect was different from the Egyptian, and it was difficult for the average Egyptian person to easily understand the film.

I had a transistor radio. There were no cassette recorders at that time. All the recorders were big and used big tapes. Usually, there were two rolls, one empty and one had the tape. At the beginning each roll was about five inches in diameter. Later in the 1970s they reduced it to about three inches only. All the tape recorders needed a direct electrical supply. The battery-operated ones were introduced around the late 1970s. This was the reason that only a few people had tape recorders at that time. We had one in our home in Khartoum. I used my radio to hear the news and the *Sawt El Injeel* which meant the voice of the Bible. This was an Arabic Christian program. They usually presented some hymns and comments and readings from the Bible. This radio broadcast was transmitted from Cyprus.

I didn't like to hear songs on the radio. At that time, in Assiut, most of the foul and tameeya or aseer gassab food places had loud music on. They exaggerated this to the extent that when you walked into the market area in Assiut, you could hear the songs continuously. Most of the songs were Umm Kulthum songs. She was a famous singer who was about seventy years old then. She used to have a musical show on the first Thursday of every month which started at 10:00 PM and continued for at least three hours. The Egyptian radio broadcast it live. Almost all Egyptians heard it and enjoyed it very much. I remember my Egyptian friend Mahir asked me where I was going to hear Umm Kulthum. I told him simply that I didn't like to hear her. He became very angry and told me that I had no taste for good music, and he left me immediately.

Assuit like all other Egyptian cities created a lot of business during Ramadan, the fasting month of Muslims. During the whole month, all the markets opened at late hours. In all the main streets you could see the people selling gattaief and kunafa. They made them in a large metal plate. The plate was about two and a half feet in diameter, and they put under this plate a butane gas cooker.

The kunafa and gattaief were the same dough. For the kunafa they put the fluid dough in a metal pot that had about ten tiny holes underneath. The owner of this practical small factory started to rotate the pot with the liquid dough over the hot metal plate. This resulted in very fine strings of cooked dough. Some people ate it simply with milk and sugar. Others baked it in a tray after putting layers of a mixture of sugar, peanuts, coconuts, and butter. In the end they pour sugar syrup over the whole tray. Gattaief was rounded about three inches diameter discs of cooked dough like mini pancakes. I never ate it. You could buy kunafa and gattaief at night till 3:00 AM. In the month of Ramadan. Muslims fast from dawn to sunset. They usually got up or continued to stay awake till about 3:00 AM when they eat their last meal, which was called *suhoor*, then they fast. There were special people who walked at this time and used a drum and shouted with special songs to wake people up to eat their suhoor. They were called *musaharateya*. They usually collected money from the people they served for the whole month.

The Egyptian radio and TV put special programs for Ramadan. Some were religious but most were nice entertaining programs. All the restaurants change their serving hours. They serve dinner at sunset instead of the usual time which was 2:00 PM–3:00 PM. I had no changes because the owner of the restaurant I usually went to was Christian Zakhir.

My Egyptian friend Saleem from El Menya which was about 120 miles to the north of Assiut. He was in my class in medical school.

Victor and Leila in Eglish class 1962

He was a good Christian. He usually attended the evangelical church. He lived with other friends from El Menya. He had bronchial asthma, which was initiated if there was any change in the temperature. I noticed that one day when he just moved from a sunny area to a shaded area. He was nice and at some time his mother, who was about seventy years old, stayed with him for a few days. I studied with him a few times, but most of the time we just discussed and spoke about college and our colleagues and teachers.

Chapter 14

First Time to See My Aunt in Sohag

When I landed for the first time in Cairo in 1961, I was really amazed to see a completely different country with different people and cultures. I found that the best way to not get lost was to walk. When I walked for the first few days, I discovered that I could see many new and interesting places. I decided after this experience to visit more places and more cities. After I settled in Assiut for a few weeks, I thought of visiting my aunt in Sohag. I heard about my aunt who was my mother's sister. She was born in Sudan and on one of the family's vacations to the relatives in Egypt, she got married to one of her distant relatives. I contacted them and arranged a time and found a bus that I could use. The distance between Assiut and Sohag was seventy-nine miles, the bus usually took two hours. The bus was very dirty and the people were mostly *falaheen* which meant farmers. When the bus stopped in Sohag, I found somebody shouting in a loud voice, "Victor, Victor!" I was next to him. This was the best way to recognize me. The person was my older cousin. He was about fifty years old, a short, slim man with gray hair. He was wearing gray pants and a white shirt and a black jacket with white stripes. He had a tie that was shifted to one side. He was very friendly and introduced himself as "your cousin Fawzy." This was the first time for me to see him or any other member of this family. He told me that their house was a few blocks from this place and asked me if it was OK for me to walk. I told him yes. I liked to walk at least so I could get to see more of the place. When I reached their street, I found it unpaved and muddy from the water that every house was pouring out. It was a habit there that every flat poured out the dirty water onto the street. Some people poured it from the ground floor, others from the second or third floor. It was very common that while walking, you find a lady was pouring the water from the third floor just in front of you. This may be the water after washing the clothes, or if you were unlucky, it may be after washing the greasy dishes. At last, we reached the house. They owned the house. On the ground floor, there was a sitting room, kitchen, and dining room. My aunt and two of her unmarried daughters were living on one floor. Fawzy and his wife and two children were living on the top floor. On the top of the house, they had a homemade mud oven called *forn balady* which was characteristic of all the old Egyptian houses. It was made of mud and varied in size but in most cases, about four feet in diameter and built as a dome. There was a bottom compartment for the firewood separated by a metal thick sheet from the top compartment which was for the bread and food to be baked. Every family used to bake their own bread, and it was considered a great shame if a family bought bread from the market. Most of the families baked bread once a week unless there was a special occasion then they may bake on another day. My visit was a special occasion for them. The bread they baked was called *aish shamsi* which meant the sun bread.

They mix the ingredients and cut the dough into small rounded discs.

They put those discs on a thick mud-made plate and left them under the sun for a couple of hours. They usually make small cuts at the four corners of each dough. During this time the dough would rise. Then they would transfer the dough into the oven.

They usually baked enough bread for the whole family that would cover them for one week. Each piece of bread was about one pound in weight. This bread was usually thick and one inch thick and seven inches in diameter. It was made of whole wheat. Some people call it *aish abu goroun* which meant the bread with horns. This was because of the shape of the cuts made at the corners before baking. It is tasty especially when fresh.

I saw my aunt for the first time. She was short and very slim. She wore a simple black dress because her husband died many years ago. I saw my two other cousins Rose, who was about ten years older than me. She broke her right leg when she was a child, but when they put plaster to fix it, they made the plaster very tight which resulted in her right leg becoming atrophic and the muscles becoming weak. For the rest of her life, she had to use metal support for her leg in order to walk. She learned to make dresses and she worked as a professional seamstress. Her other sister was Gameela who was a few years younger than Rose. She worked as a teacher. Fawzy worked as *wakeel muhami* which meant a lawyer's assistant. The whole family was happy that I came. Every few minutes one of them would say, "Sharaft. Nawart el-beit," which meant, "We are honored to have you with us. The house is brighter because you came." They started to ask about all my relatives in Sudan. They knew most of the old relatives and the young who came to visit them in Sohag. My aunt stopped the conversation and told them, "Victor is hungry now and we have to eat." We sat in the dining room and all the family members sat together. My aunt started to fill my dish with a huge amount of rice and *molokhia*. I told her to stop. But she continued and told me that "you are living alone in Assiut and you have to eat." Then she gave me two big cooked pigeons (pigeons were more of a delicacy than chicken). I told her that it was too much and I couldn't eat all of this. She started to say "Wehayat el-adra," which meant, "For the sake of the Virgin Mary." "Tiadamni," which meant, "Eat or otherwise you may lose me." They meant that the person would die. I was astonished because I couldn't eat that huge amount of food, and I found it very difficult to convince them and it was impossible to reduce the amount of food from my dish. As soon as I started eating, my aunt and cousins would automatically add more food to my plate. I discovered that they were very generous but to the extent that I started to be angry. I didn't like to leave food in my dish at the end, but it was impossible to do that. After dinner, they asked me to have a nap, and they offered me one of my cousin's pajamas. I told them it was now just 4:00 PM and I came to stay with them and not to sleep. In the evening Fawzy took me to visit my married cousin Magda. She was married and had four young girls. They were living a few blocks away from their house. They told me that another cousin Samy, who was working as a teacher, was on a study program in West Germany.

I spent Thursday evening and Friday till the afternoon with them. This was considered the weekend in Egypt as well as in Sudan. The vacation was only Friday. I enjoyed my visit. I felt that they were truly my aunt and cousins, but they were of a different culture and different traditions.

I repeated this visit about five or six times during my seven years in Assiut. During my other visits, I saw my cousin Samy and later on, I saw his wife after his marriage to one of his colleagues. My cousin Gameela also got married. And when I got married, their whole family attended my wedding ceremony in Assiut.

Chapter 15

The Journey from Assiut to Khartoum by Train and Ship

At Assiut University, we had two school vacations. The end-of-the-year vacation was about three months, starting from the end of June and continuing till mid-September. All the students leave for their home cities on this vacation. I used to fly by airplane back and forth to Khartoum. I discovered that the Sudanese Embassy in Cairo offered free second-class train tickets to all Sudanese students who were studying in Egypt. The trip by train was very nice. We would leave Assiut by Egyptian train to Aswan in southern Egypt. This would take about twelve hours by the quickest train. We usually had one more stop after Aswan which was called Al Sad El Aali, which meant the high dam station. This was the last stop of this train.

From there, we took a three-level ship owned by the Sudan Railway. The ship would take three days and two nights to reach Wadi Halfa in the north of Sudan. The ship usually stopped in Abu Simbel Temple.

This was an ancient Egyptian temple engraved in a mountain in 1244 BC. From the entrance until you reached the end of the temple, it was about sixty meters. The width was about thirty meters. At the deep end of the temple, there was a huge statue of Ramses. The tour guide told us that "the entranceway to the temple was built in such a way that on two days of the year, October 22 and February 22, sunlight shines into the inner sanctuary and lights up three statues seated on a bench, including one of the pharaohs. All the sides of the temple are decorated with drawings and writings with different very distinct colors." After the construction of the high dam in Aswan, they transferred the whole temple to another place because the old site was covered with water. I saw the temple before the transfer. When I went inside the temple, I felt the greatness of the Pharaohs, and I felt proud that those were my ancestors.

There were two ships that traveled between Egypt and Sudan. One of them was called *El Mareekh* and the other was called *El Zahra*. Both of them were of high quality, and the services were great. They had nice restaurants serving hot meals and cold drinks like lemonade with ice. Tea was served with biscuits on special china tea sets.

After we reached Wadi Halfa, we would have to take the Sudanese train to Khartoum, which would take thirty-six hours in the best conditions. All in all, the trip usually took about five entire days. I did this trip for a few years. After the beginning of the construction of the high dam in Aswan, the Egyptian authorities decided that it was not safe to let the Sudanese ships navigate inside the Egyptian territories and especially near the high dam. They asked the Sudanese ships to leave and replaced them with very small Egyptian ships. The Nile trip with the new ships became six days instead of three days. The ship was not convenient to use. They had no cabins to sleep in, and the drinking water was straight from the Nile. They put the water in a big *zeer* which was a baked clay pot, especially for drinking water. Many people used the zeer in Sudan, but they put clean water in it. I remember once I saw one passenger beside me fill his metal pot with water from the zeer and started to drink. I stopped him because I saw a small living fish swimming in his pot. At night when we slept, the rats jumped over us every now and then. The food was terrible. They served tabeekh without meat in scratched old metal dishes. The bread was dry and was of very bad quality. A few years after my graduation, I heard after my graduation that the Egyptian authorities bought slightly better ships but still a lot worse than the old Sudanese ships.

The Sudanese train from Wadi Halfa to Khartoum was another story.

The train that I used to take from Wadi Halfa to Khartoum was old. The first twelve hours after we left Halfa, we would pass by what was called Sahraa El-Atmore. This was simply a desert because the train left the River Nile and cut the distance in the shortest way. There were twelve small stations. The biggest was station number six which had six brick cottages. All the other stations had only two cottages. The train usually took a big half hour break at station six. All the stations were named in numbers from one to twelve.

If there was a sand storm, they had to send some workers (dereesa) using a manually operated trolley to inspect whether the lines were covered by sand. In this case, they had to remove the sand. Then the train could pass safely.

I remember that between stations six and seven, the train had to go uphill. Most of the trains would fail to do it the first time around. Just like when you go uphill with a weak old car it will go up and midway it will stop and go backward, and then you have to try again.

It was always hot and we had to open the train windows to get some air. This would bring a huge amount of dust. Even if you closed the windows and doors, the amount of dust was great to the extent that we had to get off at each station to wash our faces. It was common to get mechanical problems for the train.

Traveling by Airplanes

Our second school vacation was the mid-year vacation. It was in the winter, two weeks at the end of December and the beginning of January. Most of the Sudanese students spend it in Assiut. My father usually insisted that I come to Khartoum. I used the plane on this vacation. After the shift from the Sudanese ships to the bad Egyptian one, I started to use the plane on almost all my trips from Assiut to Khartoum and vice versa. To save time, especially during mid-year vacations, I usually finished my last exam and went back to my room, packed my suitcase, and took the 9:00 PM train from Assiut to Cairo. The train would reach Cairo at about 4:00 AM. I would go to Cairo railway station cafeteria and drink tea or *sahlab*. Early in the morning, I would go to Cairo Airway office. In the beginning, I used Egyptair, later I used Sudan Airway. Most of the planes traveled at night. I would confirm my reservation with the office and leave my suitcase with them. I would start walking to buy a few things that I needed from Cairo and eat les trois petits cochons in Al-Amerikeen. Finally, I would come back to take the bus to the airport. I remember one time I was very exhausted. I did all this journey and at last I sat at the Egyptair office in Cairo waiting for the bus to leave for the airport. I slept because I hadn't slept for more than forty-eight hours. One of the employees noticed me, woke me up, and told me that the bus was leaving now. I was the last passenger to get on the bus. I finished the routine check-in for the plane. As soon as I reached my seat on the plane, I slept. I woke up suddenly and found the plane had landed. I looked and discovered that this was neither Cairo Airport nor Khartoum airport. I remembered at that point that the plane was destined for Addis Ababa (Ethiopia) after Khartoum. I thought I slept and the plane left Khartoum and reached Addis Ababa. I asked the person next to me about where we were. He told me that we reached Khartoum airport, but there was a strong wind storm, so the pilot chose to go back to Wadi Halfa airport. I slept again and woke up when we landed in Khartoum.

Chapter 16

My Tours to Different Cities in Egypt

Assiut University Trips

In Assiut medical school, there were a lot of social activities. The trips were usually organized by the college. In my first year, we visited an ancient Egyptian area near Sohag called Tell El-Amarna which was about seventy miles to the south of Assiut. The leader of this trip was a professor of zoology, Dr. Nawar. I learned that he was a visiting professor at Khartoum University, and he was a friend of my older brother.

At the end of the first year of medicine, we went to Cairo to visit three of the main drug factories in Egypt. It was a very nice trip. We spent three days in Cairo.

They booked a second-class hotel for all of us. During this trip, my Egyptian friend Mahir invited me to eat les trois petits cochons in the well-known ice cream and coffee place El-Amerikeen.

This was a lovely high-class place where you could eat ice cream, drink tea, coffee or eat some cakes. There were some tables and seats to sit at. Most of the clients were of foreign origin who were living in Cairo for many years. Most of the people spoke French. In Cairo, at that time, the French language was considered the language of the high-class people. So the rich people and those of prominent, prestigious families sent their children to study French. Even people who had no

French education tried to add some French words in their speech when meeting someone new to give the first impression of a high-class family. Anyhow les trois petits cochons was just delicious ice cream. They put three different-flavored balls of ice cream, and then they add some marmalade, nuts, and syrups. It became my habit to buy it whenever I visit Cairo. Our visit to the drug factories was very informative, and I learned a lot from this visit.

Visiting the pyramids

This was the first time I saw the pyramids. I felt very little compared to this unimaginable pyramid. Each stone was huge, and immediately I started to think about how they moved all those stones. I also recognized the greatness of the pharaohs, my grandparents!

Victor at the Pyramid,Univestiy journey, Cairo 1963

Visiting the pyramids

In our second year in college, we went on a day trip to the zoo in a small town north of Assiut called Abu Teej. This trip was only social, and I remember that Leila brought her two sisters Nabeela and Suad. It was a nice trip, but the zoo was small and had very few animals, and most of them were domestic animals.

In our fourth year, we went to Aswan and Luxor in southern Egypt and spent three days. This was a nice trip and we visited Aswan High Dam, which was in the process of construction. We visited most of the ancient Egyptian monuments in these two cities.

Visiting Aswan

Aswan boat

Alkarnak Temple, Luxor

We also visited the tomb of Agha Khan, the leader of an Islamic sect Ismaeeleyeen. He was originally from India and his wife was French. The tour director told us that his wife used to send a new flower each day to be put on his tomb. His son became one of the high officials in the United Nations Organization. Till this day, I have no idea why he was buried in Aswan.

My tours to different cities in Egypt

I bought a kilometria, which was a booklet for transportation by train to any station. Each time you start a trip, it should be stamped at the ticket booth. They calculated how many kilometers you traveled and subtracted it from the total amount of two thousand kilometers that you paid for. I found that this was a cheap and convenient way to travel.

I left Assiut alone on a discovery adventure trip. I stopped in Beni Sweif then to Cairo, Sues, Ismailia, and then Port Saeed. In each city, I went to the nearest hotel, rented a room, and started to walk in the city. I usually took the address of the hotel, so I didn't get lost coming back. I stopped by many other cities like El Menya. I found nothing of interest to spend a night there.

Port Saeed was at the junction of the Suez Canal and the Mediterranean Sea.

On the other side was Port Fouad.

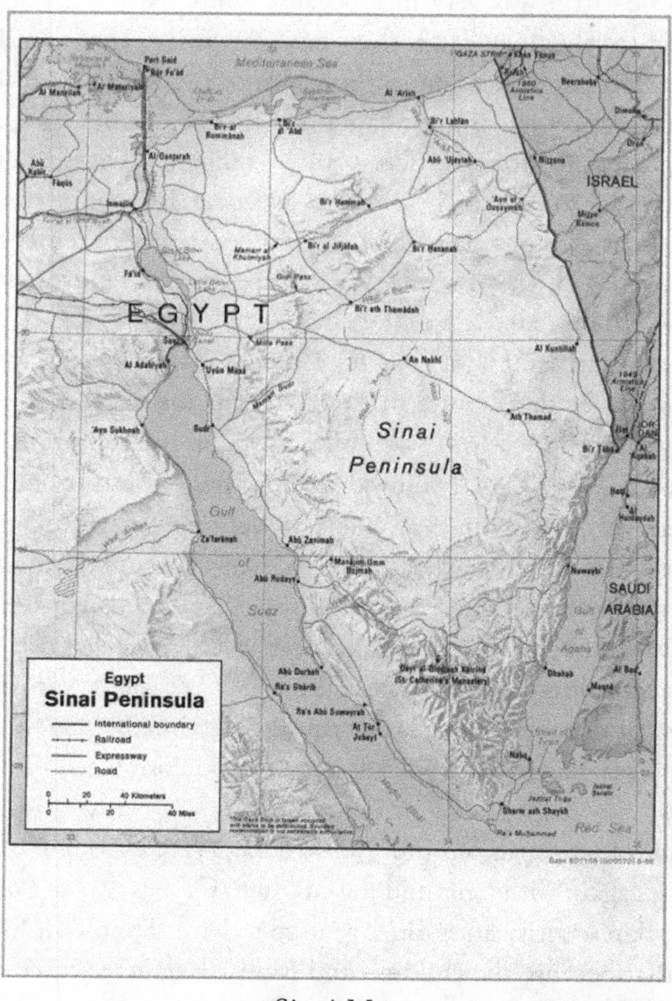

Sinai Map

The Suez Canal is an artificial sea-level waterway in Egypt, connecting the Mediterranean Sea to the Red Sea through the Isthmus of Suez.[1] It is often considered to define the border between Africa and Asia. Constructed by the Suez Canal Company between 1859 and 1869, it officially opened on November 17, 1869. There was no transportation to Port Fuad from Port Saeed other than a nice steamboat. To take the boat, you had to buy tickets. The price of the tickets at that time was two meleems from Port Saeed to Port Fuad and free on the way back. Ten meleems equaled one cent.

This boat trip was very nice because you crossed the Suez Canal and could see the huge cargo ships pass the Suez Canal. You felt that they were too big in relation to the width of the Suez Canal. Because the canal was very narrow, the captain of the ship would leave the ship to special captains from the Suez Canal Company to navigate the ship all through the Suez Canal from Port Saeed at the Mediterranean Sea to Suez at the Red Sea. Ismaileya is a city located between Port Saeed and Suez. In each city, I spent two or three days. I enjoyed Ismaileya the most. It had a special flavor.

I noticed in Ismaileya that they used the word borsa instead of gahwa for coffee shop. Borsa in Arabic means the stock market. I had no idea why they used it. It was written over all the gahawi in Ismailia and maybe in Suez City. I enjoyed visiting these cities very much.

Three years later, in 1967, the war between Israel and the Arab countries started, and Israel occupied the West Bank of the Suez Canal. Egypt evacuated the three main cities of Port Saeed, Ismaeelya, and Suez. I was unhappy when I learned that. Even Port Fuad became part of the occupied territories of Israel. This area became a war zone until 1973. Egypt regained control over this area again after 1974.

A few years later Egypt decided to convert Port Saeed into a duty-free city.

In one of our vacations in Egypt around 1979, I thought of visiting those cities again with Leila and the children. On our way to Port Saeed, the Egyptian security authorities refused to let us go to Port Saeed and told us that because the children and I were Sudanese, we couldn't go to Port Saeed. So we only went to Ismailia.

In 1966 on another school vacation, I decided to go on another trip to Alexandria. This time I decided to do it by hitchhiking. I asked some of my friends to join. The only one who agreed to join me was Sameer. We decided that we must not spend any money on transportation on this trip. We left Assiut walking to the highway. We carried the minimum things that we would need. Nobody stopped for us till we reached the police station. In Egypt, there was a police station at the entrance and exit of each big city. They were mainly security officers, and they could stop any car if they suspect anything wrong. We spoke with the police officers and told them about our intentions. The police officer told us that there was a regulation in Egypt that any truck couldn't carry passengers unless he had special permission from the police. He told us that he would help us. He simply stopped the first truck and asked the driver to take us to the next police station which was the entrance of the next big city. We stayed in some cities for one or two hours and stayed overnight in others. Some police officers refused to help us. They mentioned that we had to get special permission from the security headquarters in Cairo. In such cases, we walked in between the two cities, and we did that several times. When we got closer to Cairo, an elegant car stopped, and the driver who was a medical doctor invited us to go with him to his village home. He was a very rich person. We went with him. His house was inside a big farm that he owned. He offered us some light food and asked one of his servants to bring some figs from the tree. It was very delicious. We managed to go from Assiut to Alexandria and came back without paying any money for transportation.

We walked during this journey for long distances. It was nice, and we enjoyed it. On our way, we saw many cities. One of the cities was Tanta. It is between Cairo and Alexandria. They were celebrating the birthday of one of the famous religious leaders who was born and lived in Tanta. His name was El Sayed al-Badawi. They sold humus, which was roasted chickpeas. They called it humus El Sayed al-Badawi. We tried it. It was very delicious. Usually, all the visitors to Tanta would buy some of this humus to their relatives as a blessed item.

One of my short trips was by bike. On this trip, my Sudanese friend Gamal joined me. I thought of visiting Abnoub El Hamam because it was the birthplace of grandfathers of two of my sisters-in-law. We reached first Abnoub. It was a small town about fifteen miles to the south of Assiut. We asked about Abnoub El Hamam, they told us to take the unpaved road along a small canal. We biked on this road for about five miles. At last, we reached a small village which was Abnoub El Hamam. We had a small tour of our bikes. We noticed that everyone was watching us carefully. I guess it was unusual for them to see foreigners visiting their village. We stopped in a small shop and bought clementine. When we started to eat, we felt that if we stayed longer, something wrong would happen to us. There was a lot of grumbling and strange movements. We decided to leave immediately and quickly. This was during Ramadan fasting month, and no one was expected to eat at this time.

I noticed that the people in this village had green eyes and they were fair in skin color. One of the explanations was that during the invasion of Egypt by the French emperor Napoleon Bonaparte, some of his soldiers settled in Abnoub El Hamam. This was possible from mixed generations of the French and Egyptians. This may be true because most of the people living in the south of Cairo, Saayeda were dark in color and had dark-brown eyes, except the people from this village.

During my medical school period in Assiut, I visited almost every city in Egypt from south Aswan to northwest Alexandria and northeast Port Saeed. Egypt is a lovely country, and I encourage everyone to see every city and enjoy it. Each city is different from the other and even the traditions and the way of living.

References:

1- https://www.britannica.com/topic/Suez-Canal

Chapter 17

The Sudanese Students in Assiut University 1961–1968

In 1961 when we arrived in Assiut, we found four Sudanese students at Assiut University. Three of them came one year ahead of us, and one came a year before that. All of them lived in the same apartment. Our group was a big one made up of eighteen Sudanese students during that year. A good number came together by train. Because most of the students who applied to Egyptian universities were graduates of Egyptian schools in Sudan, most of them knew each other from Sudan.

I had one colleague who was with me in the same class for the last two years of high school. He went to the college of science in Assiut. I used to visit him regularly until he finished his third year in college. When he arrived at the border of Sudan and Egypt to finish his last year, the Egyptian security police refused to let him into Egypt. We heard that they accused him of joining the Muslim Brothers. He went back to Sudan and managed to join Khartoum University and finished his education there.

All the Sudanese students in Assiut were like one big family. We met regularly and visited each other. The majority of the students lived together in apartments in groups of three or four. So visiting one apartment meant seeing three or four people at the same time. Friday was my day off to visit my friends. We used to celebrate Sudan

Independence Day on the university premises and invite some of the top university officials.

We would bring literature about Sudan, maps, and some Sudanese souvenirs like jabana, marwaha.

Some of our colleagues were good singers, so they would sing, and others would play Sudanese music for them which were mostly national and political songs. We would share and buy cakes and drinks on such occasions. We used to enjoy such celebrations. I remember we made a big celebration when the people uprising in Sudan overthrew the military government in 1964. We used to celebrate the anniversary of this revolution every year. On the two big Muslim holidays, the Daheya and Ramadan, we used to share and buy food and cook it in one of the biggest Sudanese apartments and eat together. On such days we stayed together all day long, We played cards, chatted, ate, and drank tea. The number of teacups was not enough for such a large number, about twenty of us, so we had to take turns drinking tea. They usually gave me tea in the first round because I drank hot tea very quickly, so another person could use the cup after me.

Each year our number increased by four to ten new students. Around 1965, the Egyptian authorities decided not to admit any new Sudanese students to Assiut University. This policy continued until my graduation in 1968. Most of the Sudanese students were of a high standard and good quality; only a few of them were not. I saw one of them sleeping at the main entrance of the college of science building. He put his shoes under his head and slept. That was a busy place, and no one could imagine a respectable student sleeping that way. He came from a small village and used to sleep in any place.

The other odd person was a Coptic colleague, who declared that he was gay. At that time in Assiut, this was a great disgrace to all of us. All the Sudanese students met and decided to report him to the Sudanese Embassy in Cairo and asked them to send him back to Sudan. We succeeded, and he went back to Sudan.

Academics at Assiut University were difficult. The university was attached academically to Ain-Shams University in Cairo. Most of our professors came from there. Both Ein-Shams and Assiut Universities were well-known to be very strict in their exams. Our fourth-year pharmacology professor, who came from Ain-Shams University to give us lectures, was very arrogant. He told us in his first lecture, "The results of pharmacology in Ain-Shams last year were 13 percent, and I do not expect your results to be better than that." Our results at the end of the year in pharmacology were 11 percent and 30 percent in pathology. My opinion was that the professor failed, not the students, because he was unable to convey the material to the students. This was one of the reasons that many Sudanese students were not very successful in their studies. The other reasons were culture shock, homesickness, and financial problems. The system at Assiut University was to get a passing grade in all your subjects in your first year in order to pass. If you pass all of them except one, you could take that particular exam in September. If you did not pass, you would repeat the entire year. If you failed to pass the year again, you would be dismissed. Some students applied for exemptions due to medical problems or other reasons. If the university accepted their reasons, they could repeat the first year for the third time, and they called them external students. Unfortunately, many Sudanese students became external students. Some of the external students succeeded on their last chance and proceeded to the next year. One of them graduated from Assiut medical school and later on came to America he got his license in the USA,

Some of them were unable to pass, and they had to return to Sudan. There were at least six with this problem. One of them was very intelligent. He was in the college of agriculture. After he finished three years and was unable to pass the first year of college, the college dismissed him. He went to work in Libya for one year and managed to fake a certificate that he graduated from Assiut University, faculty of agriculture. He returned to Sudan and worked as an agricultural engineer. The Sudanese government sent him to do a master's degree in England. He went and passed his studies there and got his master's degree. He came to visit me in my clinic in Khartoum in 1984 and told me his story.

Among the Sudanese students in Assiut, there were about ten Coptic students. Some of them were good friends. One of them was Gamal, who was living in the same building as me. He was studying pharmacy. Adel was another friend, and he was my best friend. He was studying science. Most of the time, he lived with other Sudanese students, but we were together almost every day. We used to go together to the University Students' Meeting in the Coptic Orthodox church every Thursday evening. I liked those meetings. I used to go early to be able to find a seat. The meeting was an hour and a half long. It would start with singing from the hymnbook, followed by a sermon from a priest. One of the priests was excellent, and his name was Abl-Masseh El-Nikheily. This meeting was always very crowded; at least one thousand students attended each week. I never missed a single meeting during my university years. On Friday morning, I usually go to Mar-Girgis church. In Egypt and Sudan, the official holiday was Friday, and Sunday was a normal working day. There were two masses, and one finished at 10:00 AM, and the other started after that. I usually attended the first one. Both of them were very crowded. If you didn't come early, you had to stand outside the church because all the corridors and the entrances of the church would be packed with people. Sameer was a Sudanese Copt who came to join Assiut medical college one year after me. Because I repeated the first year, he was with me in the same class. Adel was living with Sameer in the same apartment. He was different from Adel in many things. They argued many times on many subjects from politics, social life, or even how to eat.

Sameer tried to be like the English people. He turned his radio on to BBC (English) all the time. He didn't like to read Egyptian magazines or Arabic books. He even preferred to add many English words in his regular speech. Sameer usually spoke about the new English songs and who won the cricket tournaments in England. He also would tell the stories of how his brother shot two gazelles with one bullet. After a few years, Sameer started to mix better with us. I used to play tennis with him. As expected, Sameer was very handsome. He usually wore tight pants and shirts. After graduation, Sameer became a full-time private practitioner and became rich. He told Leila and me once that when he reached his clinic, sometimes he thought that there was a demonstration. He meant that he had so many patients coming to his clinic.

Sometimes I went to the movies with Adel. He, at a particular time, was a regular movie-goer to the extent that if anyone wanted to know what films were playing in any of the three cinemas in Assiut, he could just ask Adel.

At our wedding ceremony in Assiut, all the Sudanese students who were still in Assiut attended. I was the only Sudanese student who married from Assiut.

The Sudanese students in Assiut attending our wedding 1970

For many years after our graduation we, the Assiut University graduates, used to meet together in Khartoum and remember the lovely days in Assiut.

Chapter 18

My Marriage Proposal 1986

I knew Leila from her first year in college, which was my second year in 1962.

Victor and Leila in Eglish class 1962

To me, she was always a beautiful colleague who was constantly smiling. I never saw her angry or arguing with anyone in college. She always spoke softly. Her hair was long and smooth. If you saw her, you would feel that she had a stable personality and had inner peace. She was decent with all her colleagues, even the wicked ones. But she knew how to stop them. Her simplicity was noticeable. I felt that she was different and special from the first day I saw her.

To get her picture, I asked the English teacher's permission to take pictures of the whole section after English class. This was her first year in college. I had an old camera. I took about six pictures and I still have them till now. I never mentioned anything to her. I considered that if I wasn't ready for marriage yet, it would be impolite to share my feelings. In reality, I passed the English class last year. I thought of attending again to learn more English and to get more chances to see Leila.

Leila was a good student, but she failed the exam in her fourth year. The reason was that two of the four subjects that year were tutored by two professors coming from Cairo. So they were not happy to come to Assiut. So our results were 11 percent, and the other professor was 13 percent.

During my last two years in college, I rarely saw Leila because we had completely different schedules. I never forgot her though, and her pictures were with me all the time.

At the end of my last year in college, I felt that now was the right time to act. I had no idea about her feelings, but what I was quite sure of were my feelings toward her. I knew nothing about her family. I had only seen her two sisters once at one of the college day trips.

On the field trip, Leila was on my left and her sister Suad on my right and Nabeela on the left of Leila.

Victor and Leila in field trip in Abu-Teeg , near Assiut 1965

I was quite sure that the family that produced Leila had to be a very good family. I decided to tell her that I liked her and I wanted to marry her and see if she would accept or not. I rarely saw her at that time. I had no idea about her schedule or where she was studying every day. Did she go to the university or the hospital rotations? Did she go alone or with some of her colleagues? I thought if I found her alone, it would be difficult to speak with her on the subject of marriage on the street or at college. I knew she would not be comfortable speaking to me on Assiut streets. In college, she didn't like to talk with any male colleague alone, especially that I wasn't in the same class anymore. At last, I thought that the best way was to give her a letter explaining my proposal and ask her to think about it and tell me later her decision. I wrote the letter and put it in an envelope, and then I thought how could I see her alone to give her the letter. It was my habit if I faced a difficult situation to ask God for help. When I ask God for help, I didn't hope that He would help me, rather I trust that He would help me if this was to my benefit. I asked God first to strengthen my faith to believe that whatever I asked of Him, I would receive. Then I asked Him to help me with that subject. I usually remember the Arabic hymn that says, "I believe in you, God, strengthen my faith and increase my trust in you." I knew to find Leila alone to give her the letter was almost impossible. That was why I found the only way was to ask for God's help. I wrote the letter in the morning and rode my bike and went to a Catholic church, Santa Teresa Church. I went inside the church and prayed to God and told Him if Leila was who you chose for me as a wife, please let me see her now when I go outside, and she must be alone. I took my bike and went outside the church. Before I tried to ride my bike, I found Leila coming in front of me and was alone. She was even on the same side of the street. I greeted her and gave her the letter without any explanations about what was inside. I felt from that minute that she was who God wanted me to marry.

After our marriage, Leila mentioned that she used to go to the hospital with her friend Nonna. On that particular day, Nonna did not pass by, and when Leila contacted her, she found that she was ill and couldn't go to the hospital with Leila.

Leila had to go alone. Now after fifty years of marriage, I must say that every day during those years, I felt that whatever I dreamt of as the ideal, most perfect imaginary wife was far less than Leila.

About a week later, I went to the hospital where Leila was doing her practice. I had no idea about her schedule. Again she was walking alone between two wards. I asked her about her decision. She told me that this was not her decision alone. Her father had to agree as well. She said she owns only 50 percent of the final acceptance. I asked her about the 50 percent. She smiled and I understood that she accepted my proposal.

A few days later, I phoned Leila at her home and asked if I could come for a visit. She consulted her father and he accepted. I went to visit them for the first time. She opened the door with her usual nice smile. I saw her father and it was a short visit. The next day I contacted again and asked for another visit. This time I mentioned to her father that I liked Leila and I wanted to marry her. He was friendly and I got the message that they had no objection.

After the results of my final exams, I sold all my belongings in Assiut, a bike, bed and mattress, a two-door metal cupboard, a chair, and a desk. I made arrangements with the buyers to come and collect what they bought on my last day in Assiut. I took the money and bought a gold ring with blue beads and a small cross with a gold chain for Leila. I phoned again and visited her. This time her father was not there. I gave her the ring and the cross. I left Assiut and promised Leila that I would write to her and would come for the marriage on my first allowable vacation from my work.

On my last day in Assiut, I was walking and met Leila's father. He greeted me and invited me to come with him for dinner. I told him there was no time. He insisted and I went and spent a nice time with them, and it was a good chance to see Leila before leaving Assiut.

When I arrived at Khartoum, I told my parents and family that I would marry one of my colleagues in Assiut. They laughed and considered that as a joke. I told them that I was serious, but nobody believed me. Then I remembered that I had the receipt of the ring and the cross. When they saw the receipt, they realized that I was serious. They were happy and they asked to see her pictures. I showed them our pictures from the first year in college. At that point, I recognized that I must have up-to-date pictures of Leila. In my first letter to Leila, I asked her to send me a new picture. I received the picture after about one month. This was how much time it took for regular air letters to go and return from Khartoum to Assiut.

My first vacation from work was on March 1, 1970, which was eighteen months after my graduation. I arranged our marriage to be at that time.

I felt that God truly loved me so much so that he chose Leila to be my wife. He arranged every step in my life to meet Leila, first to study at Egyptian schools in Sudan. Even when I changed to the Catholic schools, He arranged that I wasn't happy and returned to the Egyptian schools again. I was unconvinced to go to medical school. I tried to change to science in my first year and to the college of engineering in my third year, but I was unsuccessful. He helped me in a miraculous way to convey the message to Leila that I wanted to marry her. At the same time, He gave me a clear message that Leila was the one that He arranged to be my wife. I was quite sure that God gave Leila and her parents the acceptance even though the tradition in Assiut was that the parents of the groom had to go with him when he proposed. Also, it was miraculous that they accepted without seeing or even asking about my family. Actually, after I left Assiut, her father asked his colleague Bagi Sadaga, who later became a famous respected pastor about me and my family. Bagi worked in Sudan as an English teacher for some years, and he knew my brother George and my cousin Amal Edward. Bagi answered Leila's father that my family was a good family and that I was a good person, and if he had a daughter, he wouldn't hesitate to accept me as a husband for her.

Chapter 19

Starting My Medical Career 1968–1970

I finished my medical school's final exams in Assiut around June 1968. The results were announced a few weeks later. I passed all my exams and got a grade of *Good* in every subject. This was very satisfactory to me, especially that I found out that only 57 out of 114 students who sat for the exam passed it.

I immediately started the process of issuing the legal papers that certified that I graduated and finished medical school. I discovered that this was a long and tedious process. First I had to write out the transcript and type it in Arabic, and if I needed it translated to English, then do that then type it. Then all those papers had to be signed by different personnel in the student affairs office, then by the dean's office, and finally by the president of the university. This was OK because this could still be done in Assiut, but I discovered that I had to go to Cairo to endorse the certificates from what was called the High Commission of Education in Cairo, then from the Egyptian ministry of foreign affairs and lastly from the Sudanese Embassy in Cairo. I finally left Assiut ready with all my bags to go from there to Khartoum. I spent about a week in Cairo to finish all the legal papers. I booked my flight to Khartoum, and when at last I reached the airport to take the plane, they said that I carried bags weighing ninety kilograms and the allowable weight was only twenty kilograms. When I explained to the director of Sudan Airway that I just graduated from college and I was carrying all my books back home, he did not charge me any money for the excess weight.

I arrived in Khartoum on August 3, 1968. The very next day I went to the Ministry of Health in Khartoum and applied to work as a medical doctor. They accepted my application and asked me to start working at the beginning of the week which was Saturday 8/8/1968.

The first year was called *housemanship* which was equivalent to an internship in the USA. It consisted of four three-month mandatory shifts, one in each department of medicine, surgery, and obstetrics and gynecology. The fourth rotation, we could choose one of the following departments: anesthesia, ENT, psychiatry, pediatrics, or ophthalmology. I chose Ophthalmology.

The ophthalmology rotation was my first rotation. I was stationed in Khartoum North Hospital. When I went there for the first time, I saw an ophthalmologist named Dr. Haroun. He was very friendly. He showed me the department—his office, his clinic, the medical assistant clinic, the refraction department, the operating theater, the male and female wards. He told me that work started at 8:00 AM and finished at 2:00 PM. There were evening rounds at 5:30 PM. I told him that I lived in Khartoum 2 and the distance between my house and the hospital was about forty-five minutes each way. He immediately told me, "There is no need for you to come for the evening rounds. I will come and do it for you because I live near the hospital."

I started observing him, seeing patients on the first day. The next day they arranged a desk for me and booked some patients for me. This was scary because I felt that I was still not confident enough to see patients on my own. The big problem for me was memorizing the names of medications and doses. Some days Dr. Haroun was busy, and I found it not nice to go to him to ask every few minutes. I discovered that the medical assistants were very helpful. They were certified nurses and had a course as ophthalmic assistants for three years. They were authorized to treat all the external eye diseases and to refer the difficult cases to the ophthalmologist. Actually this was a good system. They screened all the cases and only referred about 10 percent of the cases to the ophthalmologist. Some of them were very good and could diagnose glaucoma, cataracts, and even strabismus. This gave the ophthalmologist the time to see the genuine difficult cases properly and to do the operations and the ward rounds. I started to ask the medical assistants and learn from them. They were very cooperative and gave me a lot of information. At the same time, they felt that I was humble. Most of the house officers before me considered themselves as more knowledgeable than the medical assistants and just gave them instructions. My entire three months period in this department was a nice one, and I had a very good relationship with all the staff. I did many pterygium excision operations and assisted in many other operations. At the end of the first week, they told me that I was on duty to cover the emergency department of the hospital for the next weekend. This meant that I saw all the emergency cases coming to the hospital for anything, not just eyes. I learned that I would be the only doctor in the hospital between 2:00 PM Thursday till 8:00 AM Saturday. There were other doctors on call. I could call the surgery house officer on call if there was a surgical case and I was too busy and couldn't do it. There was also another house officer for obstetrics. There was a medical assistant to help me between 2:00 PM–10:00 PM. I found that ophthalmology was much easier than the emergency clinic especially that I had no previous experience. I brought a book with the names of the drugs and doses with me on my first emergency duty. I discovered that I had to write all the treatments in Arabic. They only used the brand names of the drugs, for example, Seclopin for injectable penicillin. They just wrote 2 cc for example instead of the number of units which was used in any scientific book. The number of patients was unbelievable. They were standing in line for me. In medical school they taught us that we had to take the history from the patient, first his complaint then the history of his present illness then the past history of any illnesses starting from childhood till the present time, family history, history of allergies. After all this, we had to start the exam, and we had to examine every part of the body. This meant one hour for every patient. When I started to examine the first patient within a few minutes, I noticed the number of patients in line was increasing in length. I discovered that I had to skip many things in history and the exam. Actually to be more accurate, I had to ask the patient for his problem and just try to guess what was wrong and maximally to have a quick look at his throat or to put the stethoscope on his chest to be sure that his heart was still beating regularly. To complicate things, some patients didn't speak Arabic and nobody could translate. For most of the patients even if they knew Arabic, it was very difficult to get history from them. One of the medical assistants noticed that I was trying my best to get an accurate history. He told me to just give them anything because most of them came to spend their time before going to the movies. All the treatments in Sudan's hospitals were free. Some of the patients tried to help. I remember one of them without saying a word, spat on the floor in front of me to show me that he had a cough and he had bloody sputum. This was clearly a very infectious case of tuberculosis.

In the middle of this busy clinic, a nurse came from one of the wards and told me that one of the patients could not pass water and was in pain. I had to leave the clinic to go to the ward to see him. When I came back, I found a huge number of patients, and no organized line. All of them were just crowding the entrance, and I couldn't enter the exam room. The attending nurse tried to convince the crowd to let me in because I was the doctor on duty who will see them. Everybody started to ask if I was really the doctor and why I was away from the clinic. I didn't have time to explain that I was seeing other patients in the ward and that I was the only doctor in the hospital at the moment. The nurse tried to explain this while I started to see the patients. I heard them saying why was there only one doctor in the hospital. I found myself examining the patients as quickly as possible and just listening to the patients' complaints and tried to guess the diagnosis and dispensed what I thought was the right treatment. I found no time to even look at my book with the drug names. I gave every patient who needed antibiotics Seclopin, and every patient who had a cough a cough syrup.

At 10:30 PM, the clinic was still crowded. A policeman walked into the clinic and gave me a printed paper. I noticed that he was holding a person in his hand. I read the paper and this was form 8, which was the form the doctor has to fill after he evaluated the degree of drunkenness. I started to speak to the person and noticed that he was completely drunk to the extent that he was unable to stand steady. In the form, the doctor had to answer three main questions: does the person smell of alcohol, is he drunk, can he drive a car safely or not? I discovered that this evaluation depended completely on the doctor, and there was no scientific way to do it. In the USA and maybe in Europe they use a special bag that the patient has to blow and in it is a device that measures the amount of alcohol. I remember once I was called to witness in a court because I wrote in one of the forms that the person couldn't drive the car safely. The police revoked his driver's license because of my report. The person was a chemist and in the court, he asked me if I checked his blood alcohol level. My answer was no. The judge accepted my testimony and withdrew his driver's license. He used to work with my brother. He complained to my brother that because of my report and my statement at court, he lost his driver's license. This action was to save his life and others. He was forced to take public transportation. I learned from my brother that he later quit drinking.

About 2:00 AM, the nurse told me that since there were no more patients, I could go to the doctors' room in the doctors' sleeping quarters. I went and I was unable to sleep. After about fifteen minutes, another nurse came from the medical ward and told me that one of the patients in the medical ward was deteriorating. I went with him, and when I reached the ward, I found the patient was already dead. After some time I discovered that this was the nurse's habit to call the doctor after the patient died and tell the doctor that the patient's condition was deteriorating, so nobody blamed them that they did not call the doctor in time. I found that they prepared the death certificate for me to sign, which I did.

When I went back to the doctor's quarters, I found the emergency nurse waiting for me and told me that he managed to keep the patients waiting till they became five patients, so I could see them together. I have to mention that the emergency building was separate from the wards and each ward was far away from the other, and I had to walk in the cold or the rain from one place to the other. The doctors' quarters were outside the hospital, and I had to cross the street to reach it.

At last, I finished thirty-six hours of continuous work in the emergency department. At 8:00 AM on Saturday, I discovered that I had to immediately start my regular day in the ophthalmology department. (In Sudan, the weekend was only Friday.) I started working and explained to the medical assistants that I just finished thirty-six continuous hours of work. They were nice and they examined most of my patients for me. At the end of the day, I went back home completely exhausted.

Three months went by quickly, and I became more experienced in ophthalmology. My second rotation was in the general surgery department. Dr. Haroun went with me to the surgeon and introduced me to him. I remember that he told him that Victor was going to change from fine surgery which was ophthalmology to rough surgery. In the surgical department, I learned appendicectomy, piles removal, and many small surgeries by myself. In the surgery department, we had to do the evening rounds every evening and be on call for a whole week every three weeks. There were three house officers, and each covered the emergency department for a continuous week. During this week, we couldn't leave the doctors' quarters for the whole week. Some weekends we had to cover the emergency department as well. Once one of my colleagues, Mustafa, was on call for surgery and at the same time on duty for the emergency department that weekend. He simply didn't show on a Thursday afternoon. The nurses asked everybody and looked in his room at the doctors' quarters where he usually lived, but nobody had any idea where he was. The hospital authorities contacted his relatives, and still, he was not there. One of us covered for him for those thirty-six hours. On Saturday morning he came back to the doctors' quarters. We discovered that he cashed his monthly salary and went to a prostitute and spent all his money.

At that time in Sudan, the prostitutes had their own well-known houses.

Proverbs 29:3 says, "Whoever loves wisdom makes his father rejoice, But a companion of harlots wastes his wealth."

He was a very nice person and a good friend. After we finished the surgery shift, we had to go to the medicine rotation in Obeid. My colleague had the same rotation.

Chapter 20

Working in Obeid, Western Sudan

Obeid is the largest city in western Sudan and has characteristically yellow sand. That is the reason it is called the Bride of the Sand. This was my first visit to El-Obeid. My parents lived in Obeid for many years, and two of my brothers as well as my sister were born there.

El-Obeid was famous for its production of Arabic gum, peanuts, and raising cattle. The people speak Arabic.

I went to Obeid by train. The journey took me about twenty-four hours. I found that the hospital booked a room for me in the doctors' quarters. It was about two blocks from the hospital. Life in Obeid was much quieter than in Khartoum. You could walk almost anywhere in the city without a problem.

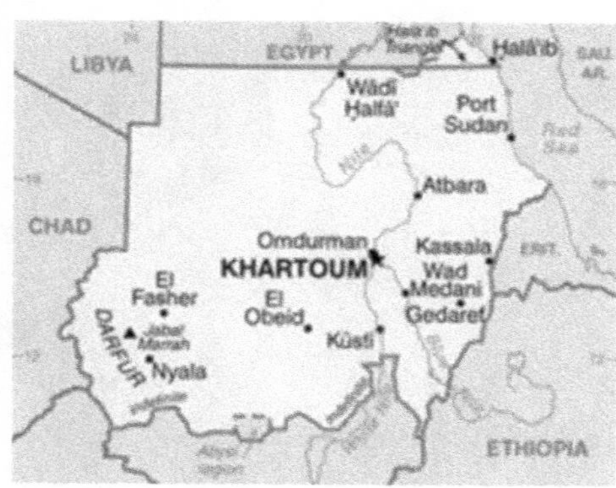

Map of Obeid

Work was less busy than Khartoum North Hospital. The physicians were quiet and well organized. We used to work more in the outpatient department. I remember once I was working in the outpatient department in the evening, and three people came walking in together. They told me that one of them felt short of breath while coming from the cinema. I asked him to lie down on the couch and asked one of the nurses to go and bring some injections for him. I put my stethoscope on and heard his heartbeat twice, and then his heart stopped. I tried to do anything, but I was unable to stimulate his heart to work again. The nurse came, but it was too late.

Another day I was working in the morning and prescribed penicillin and wrote in the prescription "sensitivity test first." The nurse ignored my instructions and gave the patient the injection without testing if the patient was sensitive or not. A few minutes later, the nurse came to me and told me that the patient was not normal. The patient developed a severe allergic reaction and had great difficulty breathing. We gave her intravenous fluids and many injections. The anesthesiologist came and put a tube in her throat to help her breathe. She developed severe diarrhea, and she passed a long tapeworm Taenia saginata. This was a tapeworm that was endemic in that area and lived in the intestine of the patients and cause anemia and abdominal pains. These worms were very difficult to treat. It was about ten meters long. She was lucky to get rid of this worm. After about three hours, she was fine again and went home without her Taenia saginata.

The evening was long because we finish the work in the hospital at 2:00 PM. We returned to the doctors' quarter to take our dinner. Before and after dinner, most of the doctors play cards, gambling. They continued until the time of the evening rounds. I usually take a nap, and at 5:30 PM I do my evening ward rounds. I used to go with Mustafa to the Greek club. It was a nice, quiet club. We spend about three hours chatting and eating our supper. They serve good-quality food. I usually drank tea and Mustafa drank alcoholic drinks. He usually drank one complete bottle of Cherry which was a special cheap type of alcoholic drink. He never changed with all what he drank. At the end of the night, we returned to the doctors' quarters. Some nights when we returned, we found a party in the doctors' quarters. The other doctors joined together and bought a lamb and asked our cook to prepare food for them. They brought some prostitutes and asked them to sing, and as expected, they drank and ate till after midnight.

Obeid Catholic Church

The Obeid Catholic Church had a very elegant building. I never saw such a beautiful church even in Khartoum.

In Boston, one of my Sudanese friends told me that he was a student in high school in Obeid at that time. He mentioned that I gave them a lecture. He was a student in the Catholic school in Obeid. I couldn't remember that. But I usually like to give presentations and lectures wherever I go.

Also, I used to attend Sunday service in the Coptic Orthodox church.

After I finished the medical shift in Obeid. I returned to Khartoum North Hospital to do my last shift in obstetrics and gynecology.

Khartoum North Obstetrics and Gynecology

In this shift, I did a C section and many other operations. I became more confident in dealing with patients. In obstetrics, they have expert *dayat*. Those are qualified nurses that have the training and usually long experience in deliveries. So this was not my headache. I had a very good relationship with them.

I finished the housemanship period (internship) successfully. Each supervising consultant had to write a report about the under training doctor. If the report was not good, you had to repeat this shift. Now I was a qualified medical doctor. I could open my own private clinic.

As soon as I finished my work in obstetrics, the Ministry of Health asked me to work in Kassala, eastern part of Sudan.

Chapter 21

Kassala, Eastern Sudan, Different Tribes

In Sudan, I worked for the Ministry of Health. I had no right to choose where I could work. The Ministry of Health made a list of the doctors that would work in each city. The trend was to transfer every doctor about every two years from one city to another. They claimed that this would give the same chance to each doctor. Actually some cities were terrible, and others were good, especially if the private clinics brought a good income. I found that I would be working in Kassala. It is the regional capital of eastern Sudan. I went to my new station by train. It took thirty-six hours by train from Khartoum. This was my first visit to Kassala. The town was surrounded by green fruit gardens. Immediately to the east of the city, there were very high mountains. The mountains had a rounded top. They were called Taka Mountains.

I stayed in the doctors' quarter for a few days then joined the optometrist in hiring a house. I knew that this would be temporary because I planned my wedding in a few months. I stayed in that house for less than a month and then I rented a house with two separate apartments. In one I started my new private clinic, and in the other, I established it as the house. There was a grocery shop just across the street. The owner of this shop came and tried to make an agreement with me, that he asked the patients to come to my clinic and for everyone, I'd pay him twenty-five cents. I refused the whole idea from the beginning.

The hospital was dirtier than El-Obeid Hospital. They asked me to work in the outpatient department first. All the medical officers (general doctors) worked in the outpatient department in the morning between 7:00 AM–10:00 AM. There was a breakfast break for one hour. After breakfast, all the doctors went to work in their different departments except for the doctor who worked in the outpatient department. He would continue seeing outpatient cases. The number of patients in the morning was huge. I remember one of our colleagues, Fouad, used to carry a pack of papers and pass in front of the patients who were sitting in the line waiting to be seen. He asked the patient about his name and his complaint then wrote the prescription for him. It took him about ten minutes to see at least fifty patients. Till now I had no idea how he could manage this. He had a very successful private clinic in the evening. In his private clinic, he had a sign with blinking colored letters. During my work in the outpatient, I used the help of the translators that the hospital provided. We had three appointed translators, two for the male outpatient and one for the female outpatient. There were two translators on the male side because one was for translation of the Hadandawa language and the other for the Beni Amer language. The translator on the female side was able to translate both languages. Actually this particular translator was not good. I noticed that almost in all the patients that he translated, I found that their complaints were not matching with their signs. After a few weeks, I started to learn some of the common words in those two languages, especially those related to the symptoms. I discovered that the translator was just telling the doctors some common symptoms for each patient without conveying what the patient was trying to say.

In Kassala, there were three major tribes that lived there. The largest tribe was the Hadandawa. They were light black in color. They did not speak Arabic. They spoke their own language. It was like all the other local languages in Sudan; it was just a spoken, unwritten language.

Hadandawa tent

They were a herding tribe. The men leave their hair long and put a wooden fork in it permanently.

Also, all men carry a special curved knife. Those were very courageous men who lived in very tough land and dry, hot weather with minimum resources of food. They lived in the eastern part of Sudan from Port Sudan in the northeast at the Red Sea to Kassala in the southeast.

The second tribe was the Beni Amir. They spoke another language different from the Hadandawa. The females had a characteristic odor. I didn't like it. I think it was a special type of local perfume.

The third big tribe was the Rashaayda. They were not black like the other two tribes. They looked like Arabs from Saudi Arabia. They came from Saudi Arabia 300 years ago. They were like the Saudis and their hair was dark and smooth, not curly like the other tribes. They lived in tents made of wool. Most of them were very rich.

They specialized in raising camels. They usually wore very dirty clothes.

Rashidi wool tent

Once one of our colleagues in his clinic examined one of them and found that his clothes were very dirty, so he told him, "I will not charge you money for this visit, and you can use the money to buy new clothes." This Rashidi immediately pulled out from his pocket a huge amount of money and told the doctor, "I have the money to buy your clinic. We do not wash our clothes because the water is always very difficult to find where we live. So we used not to wash our clothes."

I found it very difficult to examine the Rashidi female patients if the exam involved opening her mouth. It was a great shame to open her mouth in front of anybody. She could expose any part of her body without hesitation but not to open her mouth.

Rashidi people were very intelligent. Once a mother came with her six kids. They had food poisoning after eating a diseased or dead camel. I was outside and when I came in, she made a slight movement with her hand, and I noticed all the kids immediately lay down pretending they were very sick.

In Kassala, there were a good number of people from another tribe, which was *Shayegia*. This tribe usually resided in the north of Sudan in and around the city of Kareema. They speak Arabic. They used to make huge scars on their cheeks. All the old males and females Shayegias had these typical face scars on each cheek.

Now the young stopped this tradition. Some Shaigiya settled in Kassala for many years. Most of them owned the big fruit gardens and sold the fruits in the Kassala market and even sent it to Khartoum. They mainly grew oranges, grapefruit, banana, guava, and mangoes. The Shaigiya rarely came to the hospital outpatient. They usually went to private clinics.

In Kassala, there was a big Indian community. They came from India about fifty years ago. All of them still visit India regularly. They lived in one area of Kassala in an area known as the Indian district. They worked as merchants for cloth fabrics. They were Hindus, so they did not eat meat or eggs. The females dressed in the classic Indian sari.

During my period in Kassala hospital, I worked in the obstetric and medical departments as well. I remember the obstetrician was a strange person. He once operated on one of the patients and finished the operation at about 2:30 PM. During the operation, the patient died. The usual thing was to inform her relatives immediately. He asked the nurses to take the patient to the ward and not to inform the relatives. When I came in the evening to do the evening round, I found the patient was still there, and the relatives had no idea that she died during the operation. I spoke with the relatives and informed them about the death. The people in Sudan never get angry with the doctors if the patient died. They considered death to be God's will.

I used to eat in the doctors' quarters my breakfast at 10:00 AM and dinner at 2:30 PM. During Ramadan fasting month, all Muslims were supposed to fast from dawn to sunset. I was the only Christian doctor at that time in Kassala. I thought I would miss my breakfast. I found that the breakfast meal was served at the regular time as usual. Most of the doctors ate it regularly. In addition, many married doctors came and take their breakfast with us, so they pretended in front of their families that they were fasting. The dinner time changed from 2:30 PM to 6:00 PM which was the time for Ramadan breakfast.

As with most of the doctor's quarters in all cities in Sudan, it was the place for alcohol drinking, gambling, and prostitutes. I was the only doctor who did not drink in the group, in Kassala, Obeid, and North Khartoum. In reality there was another doctor who did not drink. He was a good Muslim.

I worked in Kassala for about a year before my wedding in March 1970.

During this period, communication with Leila was difficult. There was no cell phone or internet, and it was impossible to use regular phones. The only communication was regular mail. It took three to four weeks each way.

Chapter 22

Witness the Execution: Death Penalty by Hanging

One day I was on call. A prison officer came to me in the afternoon and told me that they would hang a person sentenced to death. He mentioned that this would be at 4:00 AM. I had to attend to verify that the person was dead and sign the death certificate. He assured me that a prison car would come and pick me from the doctors' quarters and return me. This was the first time for me to attend such a terrible event.

At about 3:30 AM, the prison car came and drove me to the prison. When I entered the prison, the officer greeted me and led me to his office. He then gave me a death certificate and asked me to sign it. I immediately told him, "How can I sign this and the person is still alive?" He smiled and told me, "He will be dead in about fifteen minutes. I wanted to save your time, so you can leave immediately after the hanging process." After I thought for a few minutes, I signed. Then we went to the place where they did the hanging. It was a huge place, about 40 feet wide and 500 feet long. The hanging pole was almost in the middle. Standing beside the walls was a large number of prison guards. The guards were standing one beside the other, covering all the walls. The place was dark, but there were enough lights to see what was happening. After I entered the place, I noticed a small side door opened. I saw three prison guards holding a person with a black cloth bag covering his face. They entered and held the person with them near the hanging pole. A person, I assumed, was a judge in a hearable voice read the death sentence. The prison guards took the person toward the hanging pole. The pole was a simple wooden one and from it was hanging the knotted rope. There was an elevated wooden platform about one foot higher than the ground. At last, they put the person's head in the rope tie. Suddenly, part of the wooden platform dropped and the person's body dropped halfway to a hole underneath the platform. There was no movement or any sound. After about three minutes the prison officer asked me to go and check if the person was dead or not. The prison guards pulled the body from the hole and laid him on the floor. I went and put my stethoscope on the person's chest to hear if his heart was beating. The place was very quiet. I heard his heart beating. I started to think could this be true, could he still be alive? Then I noticed that my own heart was beating very loudly. I tried to concentrate to be sure whether that was my heart and not his heart. Then I thought it was better for me to hear the breathing noise. After a few minutes, I was convinced that the person was dead. I nodded my head, announcing that he was dead. I went out immediately and the prison officer followed me and took me back to the doctors' quarters. I was unable to sleep at all this night. I started to think about the death penalty. What was his crime? Most probably he killed somebody. Now we decided to kill him. So we did what we punished him for doing. At last, I thanked God that I was not a judge.

In the USA the last person who was executed by hanging was in 1909.

Internationally, the debate between ethics and justice is recently discussed in many medical associations.

The participation of a medical doctor in the process of capital punishment is incompatible with the physician's role as a healer.

Till now I remember that day and feel that this was the worst day in my medical career.

Every day as a medical doctor, I am trying to heal someone, but to go to participate in the killing of a person was not good and against all my ethics.

Chapter 23

My Wife Leila's Childhood

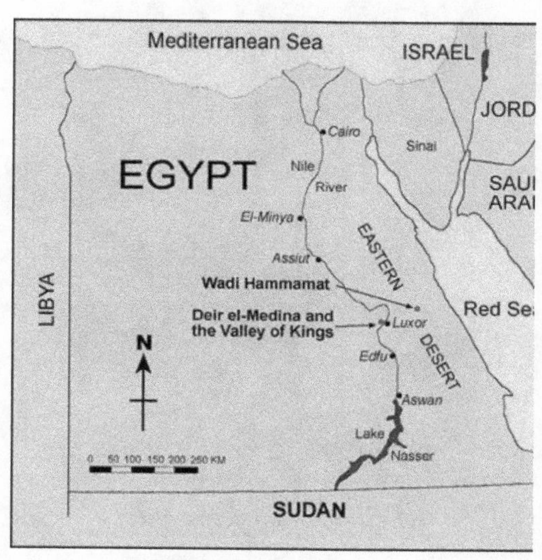

Map of Assiut, Egypt

My Wife Leila

I first met Leila at Assiut University in 1962. All these stories about her I collected from her and her family. Leila was born in Assiut, Egypt, on Sunday, February 3, 1946. Her father Hezkial was an English teacher in the American Mission Schools in Assiut. Most of Leila's life was spent in their huge apartment in the center of Assiut. The apartment was one of eight in a building that belonged to the American Mission in Assiut. These were large apartments with wide balconies.

All the other apartments were occupied by teachers at the same school. All of those families were very closely connected to each other. The wives visited each other in the mornings and at least twenty of their children played together in that building.

Leila at two years old

Each age group played together. Leila had two girls from her group in the same class from elementary school until college. Samia and Shadia. Samia was in the same class in medical school as Leila, and Shadia went to pharmacy school in the same university. The older kids were responsible for the younger ones. The mothers rarely needed to watch their children when they played.

The missionary's elementary school was right next to the building and had a huge yard. This yard was empty after school hours, so in the summer all the kids in the building played there safely for hours.

Leila went to the Pressly Memorial Institute, an American missionary school for girls. At that time, there were large numbers of crows in the area of Leila's school. They were very aggressive. Leila remembered it well, sitting in the schoolyard, eating her lunch. and the crow flew down quickly and stole the sandwich from her hand. It was not a happy memory.

Leila had a beautiful voice. Her American teachers encouraged her and her two younger sisters to sing English and Arabic hymns. They used to sing together in church and in some of the American gatherings. Leila joined the choir in most of the churches in Egypt, Sudan, and the USA.

Leila's father was an elder in the evangelical church. He used to take all his children to church regularly. Leila used to be in church from her childhood.

Students in Leila's school practiced for the spring festival all year long. Leila's school had a special class for singing and folk dances. Every year, the school celebrated the beginning of spring by doing the spring festival. The students sang and danced. The school picked the queen of the year. She had to be a high school student who had the best grades, character, and social activities. Some activities every year was to choose the best singer. Students could sing songs other than hymns like "Que Sera, Sera." The best singer was selected to be the best for the year.

Leila loved to help her family. She used to polish all her father's shoes every week. Apparently, our characters did not change. Till now Leila loves to serve all of us.

When she was eight years old, as her habit she was doing her homework while lying on her bed and she fell asleep before finishing her math, her mother gave the homework to her father, who simply wrote the answers in her homework book. The teacher asked Leila, "Is this your handwriting?" She said no, it was her father's. The teacher asked Leila to stand with her hands up at the front of the class. Leila came home crying. Her parents gave her a ring to cheer her up and told her, "This is a gift from us because you are giving a bath to your brothers Nazeeh and Maged."

The next morning the same teacher asked Leila, "Who gave you a ring?" Leila told her, "My parents gave me the ring because I am bathing my brothers." The teacher asked all the class to recognize the achievements that Leila did.

Leila self-learned knitting and crochet. She used to knit pullovers (sweaters) for herself and all her siblings. Before the winter, she would unknit the old pullovers, wash the yarn, and reknit new sweaters with different colors and patterns.

Leila used to do etamine and embroidery.

Leila graduation from Middle school

Leila during her middle school graduation

In high school, Leila had army training, and she was able to use the guns. She received a certificate showing that Leila passed her military training

At home, they had a helper to clean the house and a lady to do the laundry and the baking. At the time of our wedding, the man who cleaned the house was Ratib. He came three times a week to clean the floors and to do some of the errands.

The laundry lady was Om Fathy. Everyone called her Khalty Om Fathy. In Arabic khalty means aunt and om means mother. This means that her older son was Fathy. In Assiut, it was disrespectful to call a lady with her first given name, especially if she was old. So they would call them by their older son's names. Om Fathy was a unique woman. By the time we got married, she was around sixty-five. She dressed as most of the old women in Assiut, in black. She covered her hair with a black scarf. She came twice a week, but on certain occasions like at our wedding, she came every day. They had a washing machine but no dryer. In hot weather, dryers were not needed. Om Fathy worked with Leila's family for more than twenty years. She was a Muslim. She used to pray the Islamic prayers in Leila's house. She considered herself one of the family. The Egyptian Christians fast for fifteen days for St. Mary. They do not eat meat or any animal products like milk and cheese. Om Fathy used to fast this period. She told us, "Mary is not only yours, but she is for the Muslims as well." Leila loved Om Fathy, and whenever we came to visit Assiut, Leila brought a gift to Om Fathy. She considered her as one of her family.

Leila during her high school graduation

Leila's family

Leila's father Hezkial Bestourous

Leila's father was born in Deir El-Janadla which was a small town about twenty miles south of Assiut. He still has his brother's family living there. He started his elementary school in Deir El-Janadla. He then moved to Assiut to finish his elementary school and then middle high and high school in Assiut American College. This was a school built by American missionaries around 1880. The Americans hired some high-quality Egyptian teachers, but there were many American teachers, and all the directors were Americans. In the 1960s, the Egyptian government asked the Americans to leave, but till now the schools are under the power of the evangelical church in Assiut. There are three main schools, an elementary school, a middle school for boys, and a school with all grades for girls.

Leila's father was very intelligent. He won many awards in speech and sports. He was in the official basketball team for southern Egypt, and he was a good swimmer. He finished high school and took special courses in English. Then he studied on his own and passed some exams from Cambridge University in England in English and English literature. He was appointed as an English teacher for the high school of the Assiut American College. After a few years, he became the head of the English department. He was interested in history, and he taught history as well.

He translated many books from English to Arabic. Most of them were Christian books. He wrote a book about Lillian Trasher, the American missionary who built an orphanage home in Assiut. Thousands of copies were printed of this book. All the income went to the orphanage.

He loved Egyptian proverbs. He collected hundreds of them. He used to challenge any person to start any proverb, and he could finish it. If he could not, he would pay that person ten cents. It was rare for him to pay anyone because he knew almost all of them. He collected 1,492 Arabic proverbs and translated them to English and put the transliteration in English, so anyone could say the proverb. The book was written in Hezkial's handwriting on sheets of paper. In 2005, twenty-one years after his death, Leila managed to publish this book in the USA.

The book's name is *The People's Proverbs of Egypt*.

It is available on Amazon.

Leila's father's proverb book

Leila's father was very active socially. He was a leader in a committee for the fight against drinking and smoking. It was the habit for all the government officials in Egypt to accept cigarettes from every person coming for any business. Leila's father told me that he was against smoking, so he used to carry with him a number of pens and would give every official a pen. I saw him doing that many times. He usually explained that cigarettes were not good for health.

He believed in God and he trusted Him in all his life. He was an elder in the evangelical church in Assiut. He used to speak in public events and sometimes in the church. He was always persuading others to accept people from other religions. He usually repeated his story when he was a child and while swimming in the River Nile. Suddenly a current took him away and he was about to drown. A Muslim man saw him and came and saved him. He made it a habit to go and visit that person on all the Muslim holidays. He also mentioned to me that the Muslims were the cousins of the Jews because the mother of Ibrahim's son Ishmael was Egyptian. And the Egyptians were cousins of the Muslims because Ishmael married an Egyptian girl.

He had many friends. I was astonished when he visited us in Sudan. All his friends came to see him, and every day he was with one different friend. In his last visit to us in Sudan, he died suddenly of a heart attack in 1984.

Leila's parents with my family in Assiut
Our family with Leila's parents

Leila's mother, Edna Fam

Leila's mother Edna Tadrus Hawash was born in Abnoub, a small town to the south of Assiut. She was a housewife. She was a beautiful woman. She cared about her clothes and her jewelry. She would never accept to wear something that was not matching. She was dedicated to her home and children. She was the last one to sleep and the first to wake up. She would never hesitate to wake up in the middle of the night to wake her son or daughter to finish their homework. She always had her special way to communicate with her grandchildren. All of them loved her very much. She took care of her big house. After their wedding, and for most of their life, they lived in one of the large apartments in the teachers' building of the Assiut American schools. This was the same apartment that they lived in during our wedding and fifteen years earlier and twenty years later. It had six huge rooms. Each room was about twenty feet long, twenty feet wide, and fifteen feet in height. The rooms were arranged three on one side and another three on the opposite side. Between the two rows of rooms, there was a very long ten-foot corridor. Outside of each row of rooms, there was a big balcony about twelve feet wide and sixty feet long. Leila's mother took care of this apartment for about thirty-five years until she moved to a smaller one in 1992.

Leila has three brothers and two sisters.

Chapter 24

Our Wedding on March 1, 1970

I chose Leila to be my wife because I felt that she was the best girl I ever saw, and I always felt comfortable whenever I saw or spoke to her. I believe that God chose her for me. I was even more sure of that when He gave me a clear sign when I tried to convey my message to her. I explained this in detail in the chapter, "My Marriage Proposal."

When I started my job as a medical doctor in Sudan, I asked my employer at the Ministry of Health, about my first vacation. They told me that the first vacation was usually 18 months for new employees. I could take forty days of vacation. I chose Sunday, the first of March 1970, as our wedding ceremony date. I contacted Leila, and she agreed to the date. My parents went to London a few months earlier because my father had severe dizziness attacks. I asked them to buy the wedding dress for Leila from London. I printed the invitation cards in Khartoum.

My father, mother, and my sister Thuraya decided to go with me to Assiut to attend the wedding. This was the first time for all of them to see Leila or her family. We spent a few days in Cairo then arrived in Assiut three days before the wedding. We stayed at the Windsor Hotel which was the same building where I was living during my school days. We arrived late at night. Early in the morning, I went to Leila's house. I knocked on the door, and Leila opened the door with her nice smile and comforting face. I could not believe my eyes. Could this nice person be my wife and live with me in just a few days. Actually till now after fifty years of my marriage, I still feel that I am just dreaming that Leila is my wife. I feel that I am in a wonderful dream.

I went in and greeted all her family. I asked Leila to come with me to the hotel to see my family. She went with me. My parents and Thuraya were happy to meet her. Thuraya went with us to Leila's home to see her family. The distance between the hotel and Leila's house was less than five minutes' walk. Leila's parents came and visited my parents in the hotel. We bought the favor bags to give to the people coming to the ceremony. We booked the church for 8:00 PM.

While enjoying our time together at Leila's home, we heard a knock on the door. A man said he was a police officer. From his uniform, we knew that he was the secret police. He asked for Leila's father. He told him, "You are inviting foreigners in Assiut without the permission of the authorities."

I went with Leila's father to the police headquarters. I told them that I came legally through Cairo Airport and registered in Cairo and told them where in Assiut I was going and gave them the address, which they had then. The officer told me that I had to go to Cairo and get permission to stay in Assiut. I replied, "I am not going to do this since I was in Cairo, and nobody told me to do that." The officer was rude and insisted that I could not stay in Assiut without this permission. I was very clear. I did nothing wrong, I came to marry, and I would stay for five days and leave. I would not waste my time going to Cairo to get this permission. They could do whatever they liked.

Leila's father told me, "OK, I could go to Cairo and get the permission for you." My reply was "No one will go because if there is a required registration in Cairo, it is their responsibility to mention that when we were in Cairo." At last, another officer came and said, "OK, you can stay till Sunday, and after the ceremony leave immediately." I insisted that I would stay for five days as I planned, then I would leave. The head of the department came and agreed that I could stay the five days.

Before the wedding day, Leila's friend Hilda offered to use her brother's car on the wedding night. So he drove us to church, the photography shop, and back to Leila's house.

Leila's father said that the two families would come after the wedding ceremony to his house to have dinner. Other than the police incident, everything went smoothly. I went with Leila to Baladia Club for one afternoon and the cinema on another evening. The rest of the time we mainly spent in Leila's home. Her sisters Nabeela, Suad, along with Nabeela's friend Suhaila, used to sing some popular wedding songs like "Edalaa Ya Arees." My family and her family and some of Leila's friends were always together in Leila's house. Her mother prepared the food and a continuous supply of tea.

Everything happened quickly, and the wedding day came. In the evening, I went to Leila's house. Leila put on her wedding dress. She looked wonderful, very beautiful as usual.

Our wedding in March 1970

The car was big, and Hilda's brother decorated it nicely. We took some pictures in Studio Khashaba then we went to the church. It was

Mari Girgis Church. The church was a big one, but it was full. The church's outer door led to a yard covered by tiles about fifty feet long, and then there were wide stairs that led to the church's entrance door. I found Leila's friends stood there carrying palm branches decorated with flowers and made arches.

We passed through those arches from the church's outer door until we entered the church's inner entrance. That was creative and created a very nice feeling for us.

Entering the church

The church was full of friends and relatives. All Leila's relatives, her father's friends, and colleagues attended.

With both families

From my side, my cousins came from Sohag and all the Sudanese students in Assiut. Some of my Egyptian friends who were still in Assiut and the owner of the restaurant where I used to eat in Assiut were also there. Also, the porter of the building where I used to live was there. Everybody was happy for us, and I was delighted.

The ceremony went well except that the areef who was the head singer was singing very loudly. He, like most of the people who worked like him, was blind. In addition to his voice, he used the nagous, which was a pair of silver concave discs. He hit them together in a special way to make the required music. He was standing just behind us.

In the car leaving the church

We hired a photographer to take pictures of the ceremony.

After the ceremony, we went to Leila's house. Her father prepared a first-class dinner for us, my family, including the cousins who came from Sohag, and Leila's family including her uncle and his family who came from Deir El-Janadla.

After dinner, I went with Leila to the hotel to stay for the next two days in Assiut. This was a new hotel, about three minutes walk from Leila's house and seven minutes from the hotel where my parents and Thuraya stayed. In the morning we ate cheese omelet, drank orange juice and tea. We went to Leila's parent's house and bought *malana*, green chickpeas, on our way there. It was usually sold as a group of green plants with green leaves and small beans covered in tiny green cases. We usually only ate the beans and threw away the rest. We spent a lovely few days in Assiut before we left for Cairo.

In Cairo we went to register our marriage, to get an official marriage certificate to facilitate the issuance of a passport for Leila. One of Leila's relatives, Magdi Nafid, helped us. First, we went to El Shahr El Eqaree. This was the office that recorded marriage and divorce certificates. It was a crowded office with many ladies carrying their children. Apparently, they were in the process of divorce. When we showed the official our marriage certificate from the church in Assiut, he asked when our engagement was. We told him that we did the engagement and the marriage at the same time. He said that this was wrong. We couldn't be married without an engagement first at least two weeks prior. I tried to convince him that the Coptic Orthodox church did the marriage, and if this was improper, how would they perform the ceremony? He said the laws of the Coptic Orthodox Church specify that there must be a period of two weeks between the engagement and the wedding. I told him even if they did it incorrectly, how could we do an engagement now after we already got married for a few days. His answer was "That is your problem. I have the laws and I can't disobey the law." At last Magdi Nafid told him that this law was the law of the Catholic church and the law for the Coptics was law number so and so. Magdi had a degree in law. The official was unable to argue any more. He said where the witnesses were? I need two witnesses. Magdi was a witness, and there were some people outside that worked as witnesses for anybody who had no witness. We went outside and hired a person. His name was Mohamed Fargali, and we paid him one dollar. I thought that the official was just going to look at the marriage certificate and issue the official one, but he asked me if I accept Leila as a future wife and the same questions for Leila. At last, the two witnesses signed and we signed. After that, we paid the official fees and the fees for the hired witness. The rest of the papers were more straightforward because of Magdi Nafid and his friends. After a few days in Cairo, we took the flight to Khartoum.

Chapter 25

Our Honeymoon 1970

The first five days after our wedding, we spent time in Assiut. We enjoyed our time at the same hotel. We used to eat our breakfast at the hotel; it was always cheese omelet, orange juice, and tea. We used to spend the rest of the day at Leila's family's house. We were busy getting all of Leila's university certificates and getting them certified by asking almost each of all the university officials to sign them. This was not bad because we went to the same university together. I remember once we sat in the university cafeteria to drink Coke and to have my shoes shined. The shoe shiner told us that we must be brother and sister because we had the same features. I was surprised to hear that because Leila was not related to me at all. Maybe we tend to be attracted to a person with similar features or characters.

We left Assiut for Cairo to finish the other papers and mainly to get the official marriage certificate. We spent ten days in Cairo, and they were almost all business. Leila's father came to Cairo to sign that he agreed to our marriage. At last, we got the official marriage certificate which had the official Islamic header sentence Bism Allah El Rahman El Raheem. It didn't matter the religion of the married couple, all the official marriage certificates must be headed like that. I took Leila to eat my favorite ice cream in Cairo, which was les trois petits cochons in the fancy coffee place Al-Amerikeen. Apparently I was fond of America even back then.

We took the plane to Khartoum. Leila was tense when the engine of the airplane went to the highest gear before taking off because this was her first flight ever.

I held her hand and told her that this was normal. I felt the importance of sharing the feeling between husband and wife. This was one of the important bases for a successful marriage.

When the plane landed in Khartoum, we felt the difference in temperature. Egypt at that season was cold and Khartoum was as usual very hot. We took off all our jackets between the airplane and the airport. You would feel it was too hot to wear more than a shirt.

We stayed in my parents' house.

Leila at the junction of Blue and White Niles

My friend Adel and his wife Merevat came to visit us. They were married three months before us. We spent a nice time with them.

We visited the historical places in Om-Durman, mainly Beit El-Khaleefa.

This was an important building in the history of Sudan. It was built around 1885 and was the headquarters of the Mahadi's government at that time. The two-floor building was built out of mud. It had many rooms filled with war uniforms, swords, shields, and spears. Those were the weapons they used when they conquered the British army. They also had some of the weapons that they snatched from the British army, mainly guns and a pistol. The guide showed us the bathroom and the drainage system. This was just a tube taking the wastewater to the yard outside. I remembered this when I visited London for the first time in 1973. In London I saw the subway system the Underground, and I discovered that it was built in the 1880s. I found that what the guide considered advanced technology in Beit El-Khalifa was nothing compared to the subway in London. But we had to acknowledge that everything was relative. For Sudan, at that time it was very advanced.

In Khartoum, we were busy because all our relatives came to visit us. We received many presents. This was the tradition at that time. We received similar gifts from different people, for example, we received three tea sets with the Romeo and Juliet decorations.

All the items were nice. One of the practical gifts was a butane gas cooker with two burners and could be used on any table. We used this one till we went to London in 1972.

Leila was amazing. She memorized all my relatives' names very quickly. Everybody loved her because of her humble personality. She was the first medical doctor in the family. In a short time, she developed strong relationships with all my relatives. All the direct relatives invited us for dinners in their houses.

Leila applied to work at the Ministry of Health in Sudan. This was the only place that any doctor could start his medical career. She was appointed to work in Khartoum Hospital starting May 1, 1970. They promised to transfer me to work in Khartoum on that same day.

After ten days of our arrival in Khartoum, there was a limited war between the military government led by Jafar Nimeiri and the Mahadi family. This fight was in central Sudan far away from Kassala and Khartoum. The war took only about one day. The Ministry of Health announced that all the doctors had to report to their stations to see if they were needed. I asked the director of the Kassala medical area if they needed me. His answer was to come immediately. I had to cut my honeymoon short.

I went to the Ministry of Health to get my train tickets to Kassala. I booked the first available train to Kassala. This meant that we spent only fifteen days in Khartoum.

For Leila, Sudan was completely different from Egypt. Most of the people were darker in color. The Sudanese accent was another problem. The third obstacle was the slow pace of life in Sudan. In the streets of Egypt, everyone walked quickly. When you go to any shop in Egypt, the owner would quickly come and greet you and offer his services. In Sudan, the owner of the shop would leave you to choose whatever you like, and when you want to pay, then he may come to help. In Sudan, at that time you couldn't negotiate the price of any item. You had to pay the price without negotiations. In Egypt, almost all the prices were negotiable except for a few stores owned by the government.

Economically Sudan was different from Egypt at that time. The Egyptian pound was equal to 0.8 Sudanese pound. In 1970 the salary of a first-year medical doctor was 58 pounds compared to 14 for our Egyptian colleagues. For the second year, the Sudanese doctor's salary was 62 and the Egyptians was 24.

Egypt was famous for its fertile green land around the River Nile. The fruits and vegetables were available and cheaper than in Sudan. On the other hand, in Sudan the cows and cattle were raised, so the meat was cheap.

I discovered that Leila was a godly lady. When she came to Sudan, she had no relatives at all. She just considered my relatives as her new family. She loved them, became very social with them, and enjoyed being with them. She reminded me of the story of Ruth in the Bible. As God blessed Ruth, He blessed Leila as well when He gave us four children and eight grandchildren. Leila was the one who reminded me to visit my relatives. Till now she is the one who writes the letters to them and Christmas cards.

We took the train from Khartoum to Kassala. For me, I did this trip many times, but for Leila, this was a completely new experience in a new world. The Ministry of Health gave us tickets for the first class on the train, but we paid the difference and used the sleeping class. In the sleeping class, there were eight rooms in each car in addition to a room for the jarasson who was the person responsible for cleaning the rooms each morning and bringing the tea, breakfast, lunch, and dinner. The services were good. The room had two bunk beds. In the room, there was a sink to wash your face and teeth in the morning. There were two common bathrooms in each car. The food was fairly good. For example, they served fried eggs, toast, and marmalade, tea, and biscuits for breakfast. Lemonade was served in a huge glass cup with a long spoon at midday when it was very hot. For lunch, which was the main meal in Sudan, you could order fried fish and chips in addition to some vegetables and canned fruits for dessert. They served all food and drinks in china plates and teacups with the letters SR which was the initials of Sudan Railways, even the spoons, forks, and knives had these initials engraved in them. We used to enjoy being on the train because of the great service. The trip took about thirty-six hours, but Leila did not complain. She was amazed at how everybody was so relaxed and not worried about when the train would arrive.

For the first time, Leila saw the huts, ghattati, when we reached the El-Gedaref area.

Chapter 26

Starting Our life as a Family in Kassala in 1970

The train arrived at Kassala at night. Kassala, like most of the small Sudanese cities, was very quiet at night. We took a taxi from the train station to our house. I think it was a big shock for Leila. In Egypt, newlywed couples usually rent an apartment and furnish it with the most modern furniture. The couple spent months discussing what would be the color of the curtains and would it match with the color of each room furniture. Our new home was very bare with no curtains and not even any furniture in the Egyptian sense. I did not buy the classic bridal bedroom. Actually, I never thought of that. My idea was to delay this until we settled in our permanent house.

Our house in Kassala was divided into two parts, separated by a wall. There were two rooms, a veranda, and a bathroom in each part. The outer part was my private clinic. I used this clinic only every evening from 5:00 PM to 8:00 PM. The wall between the clinic and the house was not complete, there was a gap. We called it the door. In the house, there was the bedroom and next to it another room, and in front of both of them was the veranda. The bathroom and the kitchen were outside in the yard. This meant that in the winter or if there was rain, you had to go through the rain or cold weather to reach them. This house was considered a typical Sudanese house. Usually, the clinic part was called the men's house, and the other part was called the women's house. The men's house was usually used for the visitors. When we say visitors in Sudan, we mean men. Men usually visited separately. The man invited his friends for breakfast or dinner on Friday or any day. The men would stay in the men's house, and the wife would prepare the food in the women's house, and usually her friends and neighbors would come to help her. The food would go to the men first, and after they eat the women could start eating. They usually put the food in a large tray and send it to the men's house. A servant carried the food to the men, or if there was no servant, the wife would shout her husband's name from the women's house to come and take the tray. If there were older children, they could transport food. This tradition was almost the same in all parts of Sudan. The poor and rich, educated people, or illiterate did the same things. The only differences would be the type of food, the quantities, and the quality of the plates and silverware they used. The typical breakfast on Friday for visitors would consist of the following items. First, the *marrara* which was small pieces of raw lamb liver mixed with onions and soaked in lemon and hot red pepper powder. This marrara was very delicious and I liked it, and we ate it with our hands and without bread. It is considered an appetizer. Next would come to the main dish, which varied but almost always contained lugma which was a type of semi-cooked dough and was served with heavy minced meat gravy, which was called *mulah*. The third dish was fried or roasted lamb meat. Sometimes they served them as two separate dishes. The fourth dish would be the foul which was fava beans, and it was served with oil, lemon, and spices. Fried eggs were one plate in some breakfasts especially if the invitation was a surprise for the wife as in many instances. Fried sausages, fried liver, or sometimes fried cow's brain were also commonly used. The dessert was usually shaareya which was very thin spaghetti cooked in water and sugar. At the end was tea served in small glass cups. If the invitation was for lunch, the main meal in Sudan, the items would be the same, but there would be one or two additional main dishes. Fatta was a dish with pieces of bread and cooked rice mixed with cooked meat, and everything was soaked in meat soup. They served the fatta in a big, deep tray. Four or five people would eat from the same tray. Most of the time they ate the fatta with their hands, but sometimes they used spoons. The next popular dish was *kirsha*. This was a tomato sauce of a mixture of pieces of lungs, stomach, and intestines. I never ate it. I felt it was not nice to eat. Also, there was a dish called kawaria which was lamb joints in its soup. I never liked that either. Then a popular dish was *molokhia*, a thick soup of green leaves like spinach. This was used in Sudan as well as in Egypt. It was usually mixed with rice. The molokhia was prepared in chicken or meat stock. The meat or the chicken was served fried separately. The molokhia and rice were the only dishes that truly required the use of a spoon.

Instead of bread in Sudan, they used *kissra*. It is a thin layer of sorghum dough that was cooked on a heated flat metal plate. All the Sudanese families used to prepare kissra every day. If it was left till the next day, it would ferment. Nowadays, most families buy it ready-made. It is sold as a folded pack. When you unfold it, each one is a round disc about one foot in diameter.

The usual tradition in Sudan and even more so in smaller towns was when visitors come, the family would buy a lamb and the servant would slaughter it, and the wife would prepare the food. This was the reason that they served the marrara fresh. Very few times we did that in our house because Leila and I didn't like the mess of slaughtering the lamb in the house yard.

Our bedroom was just two metal single beds, a two-door cupboard, and a dressing table. Our sitting room had six metal chairs weaved with plastic ribbons and a small metal table. The dining room had a metal table and six chairs just like the sitting room chairs but without hands. I bought some kitchen utensils before Leila's arrival. Leila managed to start her new home with what was available. She never asked me to buy anything. She started to clean the house, the rooms, and the yard. The next day when we got up in the morning, Leila was shocked when she found that everything in the house was covered by a thick layer of dust. And I mean EVERYTHING was covered, the floor, the beds, the chairs, the cleaned plates, our faces, hair, and even Leila's glasses. I explained to Leila that there was a windstorm at night, and this was the aftermath of it. In all cities in Sudan, except the south of Sudan, windstorms were common most of the year but more during the months of March and April. You couldn't prevent the dust from coming inside the rooms or any other place because the windows were not tight enough, and the wind came in a strong gusty force. I left the house to go to the hospital. In the hospital, all my colleagues asked me, "Why you came before the end of your vacation?" I explained that this was the order of the medical director there. They told me that we had no emergency in Kassala. I went to ask the hospital director where I had to start working. He asked me to work in the medical department. The medical director of the hospital had the title Hakim Basha. This was a Turkish word. Hakim meant a medical doctor and basha meant high-grade ruler.

I returned home during breakfast time from 9:00 AM to 10:00 AM. I found Leila waiting for me with her nice smile. She cleaned the house again and prepared breakfast. She boiled some eggs and then fried them. She prepared fresh vegetable salad and Feta cheese. She put everything in a nicely decorated way. Even the tea was ready. I was not expecting this at all. I discovered that to be with Leila was a great blessing. At 10:00 AM for the first time, I was very reluctant to go back to the hospital. I felt that now I had a nice home to stay in and a lovely wife that I didn't want to leave. From that day I felt that I could prepare food, but the way Leila prepared it was completely different. I felt that it was not the food ingredients but the person who prepared it, the way it was presented, and the smile of the person who was eating the food with you. I felt that now I had started a new joyful part of my life. Until this day, every day I feel joy and happiness when I eat what Leila prepares and more when she eats with me or even just sits in front of me.

Leila spent one month in Kassala. There was a windstorm every day for about twenty days that month. Some days the dust would be stagnant in the air for many hours. Leila used to keep the plates, and when she brought the food, she had to wipe them again.

In Kassala, at that time, I had a cousin living in Kassala, Fawzy and his wife Muneera and their six-year-old daughter Rita. Fawzy was the director of Bata which was a famous shoe store. Fawzy and his family came to visit us. They were very friendly. Muneera became a good friend to Leila. She explained to Leila many of the traditions and the way the people thought and behaved. They invited us to their house several times.

Our next-door neighbor's wife visited Leila when I was in the hospital on Leila's third day. She gave her some special perfume for the newlywed bride called Khumra. When I came home, Leila showed me the Khumra and asked me if she could use it. My answer was a big no. I hated that perfume. I discovered only now why that perfume caused a disgusting feeling in me. That type of perfume was usually believed by laypeople to stimulate the sexual desire in men. This was the reason that it was usually used by the new brides. I discovered now that the prostitutes who came to my colleagues in the doctor's quarters usually wore that perfume. Some of those prostitutes stayed till they took their breakfast with us in the morning. That was the reason that I hated the smell of that perfume. When I smelled that perfume on any patient, I felt that I wanted to leave the patient and get away. Leila told Muneera about the Khumra. Muneera told her that this was a very precious perfume and if Leila was sure that she wasn't going to use it, she would be happy to take it.

Leila's first cooking problem happened once when I simply bought two living pigeons and molokhia. Leila knew how to cook the pigeons and the molokhia, but the problem was how to kill the pigeons. Leila was embarrassed to tell me that she was unable to do that. When I left for the hospital, she tried but found that it was impossible for her to kill the pigeons. She opened the house door and waited till a man came driving his donkey. I think he was selling vegetables. Leila stopped him and asked him if he could help her by killing those two pigeons. The man agreed and did the job. When I came home I found the food was ready and well prepared. She told me about the story.

On Leila's first Sunday, we went to the newly opened church. It was a Coptic Orthodox church. There was no church in Kassala before. The Christians collected contributions and rented a house for the priest to live in. In the same house, they used the veranda as a church. They put some chairs and put a small table in the front as an altar. While the priest was doing the service, one of his chickens came to join the service.

Everybody tried to push her away, but she insisted on staying. It was fun and a nice change from the routine church service.

It was the habit in all the small towns for every family to raise some chickens. This provided the family with free eggs and chickens to eat. One of our friends from the church called Tanious invited us for dinner at his house. We met his wife and his six young children. His older child was about nine years old. His wife prepared very good food. While we were sitting, we were surrounded by some ducks and chickens. It was not the habit of Sudanese families to raise ducks. This family was Naggadeya. Naggadeya came from a small town in southern Egypt near Luxor. This town was called Nagada. Some of the Naggadeya stayed in Sudan for three generations, and some came just the last ten years. Most of them worked in trading mainly in fabrics. Many of them became rich and were good businessmen. "Tanious" had a shop for kitchen utensils. He was doing well. He was active in the church. He was one of the few who built the new church. The Naggadeya maintained their Egyptian traditions. Because they were Christians and of different ethnic origins, they didn't mix well with the other Sudanese families.

Starting a new church was a great blessing for Kassala. The absence of a church let some of the Christians forget about Christianity to the extent that some were fasting during the Muslim holy month of Ramadan.

Some of my colleagues' wives invited Leila to their houses. The only colleague that invited us as a family was Fouad. His wife was from Yugoslavia. He was an artist as well as a doctor. He used to paint and also make house decorations from simple materials.

Once an Indian lady came to my clinic with her relatives and asked me if Leila could examine her. In a small community like Kassala, everyone heard that my wife was a medical doctor, so I asked Leila and she agreed. The Indian community was very conservative. Leila at that time had no license to work because she did not finish the internship training period. The lady was living with her in-laws. Her husband went out of town for the last eight months. She missed her period for four months. When she went to the obstetrician, he simply told her in-laws that she was pregnant. They did not let the obstetrician examine her. This created many questions because her husband was away for eight months. When Leila examined her, she found that she was not pregnant. The missing period was just a side effect of her psychological condition. Her five years old daughter died after falling from a wall, and her husband was away. After Leila declared that she was not pregnant, everybody was happy, and they thanked Leila and me very much.

A month passed rapidly. Leila had to go to Khartoum to start her internship on the first day of May 1970. I received a letter from the Ministry of Health telling me that I could transfer to Khartoum starting from the first of May 1970. I went to the head of the medical services in the province of Kassala. When he saw the letter, he told me that he was not going to release me till all four doctors who were transferred to Kassala arrived. I argued with him and told him if every head of a medical service did the same, no one would move. His answer was "I don't care." I explained to him that Leila had to start her job at the beginning of the month. He told me, "She could go alone and stay with your family until you finish here and join her." I asked him how long this would take. His answer was, "Maybe a month or two or a year or two." I was very upset. I decided not to leave Leila to travel alone. I went to him again and told him that I decided to send Leila and our luggage to Khartoum and I would stay here in Kassala. So he issued the tickets for Leila and our furniture and luggage. I packed everything and I bought a ticket for myself. All my colleagues knew that I was leaving. They came to the train station to say goodbye. While waiting for the train to leave, I found the porter of the hospital came carrying a letter from the head of the medical services, telling me not to leave my job without permission. One of the other colleagues when he saw the letter became angry with this behavior and took the letter and tore it in pieces.

When we arrived in Khartoum, I went next morning to the Ministry of Health. The person in charge showed me a telegraph that came from the head of the health services in Kassala. In this telegraph, he mentioned that I left my work without permission, and I had to return immediately, and if I didn't come, the authorities would prevent me from opening a private clinic. I had no idea why he had all this hatred.

The Ministry of Health officials in Khartoum, after knowing my situation, told me to forget about Kassala and go to my new station in Khartoum.

Chapter 27
Living in Khartoum 1970–1971

We used the train from Kassala to Khartoum. We enjoyed the journey as usual. In Khartoum, we lived in my parents' house in Khartoum 2. Leila started her internship year in the anesthesia department. She was amazed when she saw all the workers, the doctors, nurses, and porters eat their breakfast from one big foul dish. In Egypt, the doctor never stayed with the nurses in the same room. In Sudan, people were humble and lived a simple life. The Sudanese accent caused some confusion for Leila in the first few weeks. When she was doing the anesthesia of one of the patients, her supervisor asked her, "Fatarti," which in Sudan meant, "Are you tired?" In Egypt, it meant, "Did you eat breakfast?" Her boss asked her this question several times, and each time her reply was no. When she mentioned what happened, I told her that he meant, "Are you tired?"

After about three months, we moved from my parents' house to a lovely home in Khartoum University. This house was for rent for three months, the university vacation house. It was a large house with a garden that had a direct water supply from the Blue Nile. It had lovely flowers completely surrounding it.

We bought our first car, a Volkswagen Beetle. It was a second-hand car, a 1962 model, which meant it was nine years old. In Sudan, cars were used until the engine failed. There was no rust in Sudan because the weather was dry.

Our next residency was an apartment on the second floor in El Zuhour Fatahat area, which meant blooming flowers. Ironically, there were no flowers in that area. The apartment had three bedrooms, a kitchen, and a bathroom. The ventilation of this apartment was excellent. The airstream would pass so quickly and smoothly whenever you opened the windows from one side to the other. This was the best feature in any apartment because the weather was extremely hot, and there was never a guarantee of electricity supply.

Leila's second rotation was surgery. In this rotation, she had to sleep at the hospital when she was on call. The first night she was unable to sleep at all. There was a room for her to sleep in, but the door had no lock on it. The male nurses would simply open the door without bothering to knock. Leila was frightened. For a while, I used to stay with her at the hospital.

In October 1970, we heard the news of the death of Jamal Abd El-Nasser, the president of Egypt. Leila was upset because she felt that Nasser represented Egypt. Maybe it was, to some extent, but very likely there was some homesickness.

In December 1970, my father died. For the last year, he could not balance his gait well. Whenever he stood, he immediately lost his balance and fell down. He was very sharp and alert and knew everything around him. It was a pity to see him in this condition. I put some wheels in one of our chairs to push him. He suddenly died without any apparent cause. His funeral was packed with a great number of relatives and friends.

Life went on, and Leila finished her internship. She worked in Khartoum, teaching in the hospital in all her shifts. After the internship, Leila worked at the blood bank in Khartoum Hospital. In this position, Leila felt more relaxed. We felt God's love for us when we discovered that Leila's blood group was Rh-negative, and my blood group ias Rh-positive. In such cases, the children were usually Rh-positive. The usual story was that the first child would be healthy. The mother's blood then creates antibodies against the Rh-positive from the first child's blood. All the consequent children would be delivered healthy and die within a few days. The proper treatment was to immediately give the mother after the first delivery, a specific injection to prevent the development of the antibodies in her blood. This process had to be repeated with each childbirth. This is the reason that we now have four healthy children. I feel that nothing happens by chance or accident to us. He prepares every step in our life in great detail to give us the best. In short, "He cares."

On Christmas Day, the tradition of our family was to visit each other. Leila suggested that we sing some Christmas carols in each home we visited. We found great acceptance, and everyone sang with us.

Christmas caroling became our tradition in every city we lived in. We found that our Christmas carols brought a lot of joy to every home we visited.

Every Christmas holiday, Leila would bring all the family's kids to act out the Christmas play. She continued this tradition every Christmas till now. My daughter in California now is doing the same tradition with her children and her neighbors' children.

I worked in a health center in Sagana. This was a third-class area in Khartoum. The name means the prison guards. Apparently, there was a prison in this area. The health center was new. There were two medical assistants to help examine the patients. There was a small operating theater for minor surgeries. There was a pharmacy and a pharmacy assistant. Shortly after I started working in this health center, I discovered that the pharmacy assistant was stealing the drugs. I warned him and asked the Ministry of Health to replace him. To fire any employee in Sudan was very difficult. The senior nurse was doing many circumcisions in the operating theater. This was illegal. I asked him to stop. I discovered later that he shifted his operations to the weekends when I was not watching.

Next to the health center was Maljaa Al-Ajazza. This was a nursing home. It was an old mud building. Once, the authorities in this nursing home asked me to come and examine one of their patients. I went and I was shocked by the inferior condition of this place. I could not describe in words how dirty the rooms and beds were. I started to visit this health center on a regular basis. I tried to give some ideas to help improve the hygiene of that miserable place. One of the patients living there was an old Lebanese lady. This nursing home was not under my authority but belonged to the city of Al-Sagana.

In the health center, there was a clerk to record the data. One day I found twelve new employees coming with a letter from the Ministry of Health. The letter informed me that all those twelve new employees would be working on recording the data. Of course, there was no work for them. There were no desks or even chairs for them to sit in. I discovered those parts of Al-Hindy boys. Al-Hindy was a minister of finance in Sudan. The government was democratically elected. To get the votes in the coming elections, this finance minister appointed thousands of young people to work in the government. The government was obligated to distribute them in different places even if there was no need for them. I tried to get rid of them, but the Ministry of Health refused to take them back.

Our first anniversary

I applied for a position of residency in ophthalmology. Ten doctors competed, but they selected another colleague and me. The Ministry of Health regulations required that any doctor couldn't start his residency without working six months in one of the more troubled areas in Sudan, Manteggat Shidda. Accordingly, they transferred Leila and me to Wau in South Sudan.

We had no idea if we could find a house in Wau to live in and when. We decided that Leila would go for a vacation to Assiut. During that time I would go to Wau and prepare a house for us. Leila took the plane to Cairo, and from there, the train to Assiut. I terminated our rental agreement for the apartment. I sent our furniture to Wau by train, and I took the plane to Wau.

This was the first time for me to be without Leila. I tried to find any other alternative arrangement, but there were none.

Chapter 28

Working in South Sudan Wau 1971–1972

I took the plane from Khartoum to Wau. When the plane reached the Wau region, I noticed that the ground was green. Now I was in a tropical area. Tropical forests cover the whole region. The rainy season lasted nine to ten months every year compared to about two weeks or less in Khartoum. When the plane landed in Wau Airport, I noticed that the soil was firm and red. After the rain, there would be no mud. You could walk on the dry ground immediately after the rain. In Wau the weather was much cooler than in Khartoum. I thought that the tropical region would be warmer. The rain and the dense forests made all the difference. When the hospital car drove me toward the city, I could see mango trees lining both sides of every street, and I could see beautiful wildflowers growing underneath the mango trees. There were no paved roads in Wau, still the streets were much smoother than the paved ones in Khartoum. I stayed in the doctors' quarters. I had four new colleagues. Two of them were originally from South Sudan. As in other parts of Sudan, the drinking and the prostitutes were already there. I went to Wau market. I found a few stores, but they had almost everything. All the stores were owned either by people from the north or what everybody called the Bazrameet. Those were a mixed race from the Greeks and southerners. Their color was really a mix of the dark African color of the southerners and the white of the

European Greeks. I saw one family whose father was white Greek, he married a southerner from Wau. He told me that they came here about fifty years ago. They were unable to bring Greek women with them, and they stayed in Wau for many years. They had no alternative other than to marry southern Sudanese girls. Their children marry from the Bazrameet' group. Both the southern Sudanese and the Greeks did not like to marry a Bazrameet.

Most of the people in Southern Sudan were Christians. The Catholic missionaries worked hard for many years, so most of the Christians were Catholics. There were a few Episcopal churches, apparently from the influence of the English ruling of Sudan for about sixty years.

When I went to the hospital, they told me that the holiday was Sunday instead of Friday, unlike in north Sudan. The Muslims could leave earlier on Fridays for their prayers. Also, all the prescriptions were written in English and not in Arabic, again very different from north Sudan. I felt that the standard of work in Wau hospital was better than in the north.

The hospital was not far from the doctors' quarters. I could walk to the hospital. The hospital was nice and relatively clean. I met some of my new colleagues. There was a colleague who was married to another colleague. Her name was Fatma. Her husband was a fanatic Muslim. He used to prevent her from sitting with us. This was against the fanatic Muslim beliefs. This was completely odd because at that time nobody expected such behavior from a doctor. We were only ten doctors, so I was expecting good communications.

I started working in the medical department. One day after the breakfast break, I went to the male ward. To my astonishment, I found one of the workers, who was responsible for distributing the food to the patients, was sleeping in the middle of the ward in between the patients' beds. I discovered that he was completely drunk. I heard his story. He lived in one of the nurses' houses around the hospital. When he would go to his home for breakfast, he usually drank *mareesa*, the locally made alcoholic beverage. Mareesa was prepared from sorghum, and they considered it as a drink and food at the same time. This worker apparently was an alcoholic. He was the head nurse. He had been to disciplinary courts eighteen times for coming to the hospital drunk. After the third time, they decided to dismiss him, but they discovered that he was responsible financially for his eight children and his parents and three young brothers. As a compromise, they demoted him to a nurse then down to a simple food distributor. I feel that drinking alcohol, especially in big quantities, is part of the devil's plan to destroy any person. How can I drink what I know would ruin my career, health, and family.

One Saturday I was on call to cover all the hospital emergencies. I was in the hospital seeing some emergency cases. A policeman came with form number eight. I knew this form was to determine the state of alcohol intoxication. To my astonishment, I found the name written on the form was that of one of my colleagues in the doctors' quarters. His name was Matthew. The policeman told me that Matthew was driving the hospital truck after he drank a lot. He completely fell asleep while driving, and the truck hit the door of a house. I went to see him. I found him in a state of deep sleep or you could call it a sort of coma. I tried to wake him by shaking him, but there was no response. I then gave him injections of Coramine which we usually use in such cases. I found at last the best solution was to admit him to the hospital. I wrote in the form that he was admitted to the hospital, and the final report would be after the treatment. I learned that alcohol could completely destroy a person's life. It could also cause financial loss, "damage to the truck and the house." and problems to others like me when I was in a difficult situation facing this crisis. I thought that Matthew would learn from this and would never drink again. Sadly, this didn't happen. The next day he resumed his drinking as usual. I remember I asked Matthew once if he went to church? He laughed and told me about his only visit to church. He went and took communion in a Catholic church. The priest gave him the whole cup to take one sip as others. He discovered that this was good alcohol, so he drank it all.

In Wau, I asked about a house for us to live in when Leila arrived after her vacation in Egypt. They offered us a government-owned house.

Leila and our house in Wau 1972

Leila in our_house in Wau

It was a very nice one. It was located over a small mountain. There were two houses over this mountain. From our new house, we could see the whole city below. The house had three bedrooms. We had no children at that time. It had a special summer room made of a thin layer of tiny metal mosquito net. This room was very cool as if you were sitting in the yard. The sitting room was built so the front part was protruding toward the mountain cliff and was supported by long pillars to the ground. The walls of this part of the sitting room were just glass. When you sat in the sitting room, you felt as if you were sitting in an airplane. Outside in the yard, there were two rooms and a bathroom, and a kitchen for the servants. In the yard, we had four big mango trees. All the trees were full of unripe mangoes. Unfortunately, we left Wau before they ripened.

Leila finished her vacation in Assiut. I must say that the communications were not that great. There were no telephone lines between Wau and Assiut. The postal services were much better than now. I missed Leila a lot. This was my first time to be away from her for more than eight hours. I received our new house and our furniture from Khartoum.

Our second wedding anniversary

I prepared everything for Leila's arrival. I went to Wau Airport to meet Leila. I was delighted when I saw her coming out of the plane. She was always beautiful and smiling. After the arrival of Leila, my life changed. I was living in the doctors' quarters, all my colleagues were drunk, and the prostitutes were almost living with us every day. I never drank or came near a prostitute, but I was not happy even to live in such places.

Leila in Wau was a working doctor, not like Kassala, when she was just a housewife. This was good for me because I could see her during working hours. In Wau we were not that busy. I had the feeling that I was on vacation. We spent a nice time in Wau. The hospital car would come in the morning and take us to the hospital. At breakfast time between 9:00 AM and 10:00 AM, I usually took one of the hospital's big trucks and drove to our house and returned to the hospital at 10:00 AM.

Victor taking breakfast under a mango tree

All the hospital trucks were old, and it was difficult sometimes for the truck to climb the mountain to our house. Leila used to prepare breakfast and put it on a table in the yard under one of the mango trees. This was one of the happiest times in my life. Most of the time in the evenings, we stayed alone at home. In Wau, I taught Leila how to play the tawla. When Leila won, she would be happy and continue to play till the food burnt. If Leila lost a game, she would get upset and stop playing. There was no TV in Wau, and the local radio programs were very limited. We were unable to hear the national radio broadcast of Sudan. Most of the stations that you could hear were coming from Congo. Most of the songs were what they called Trim. Those were songs with a rapid monotonous beat. The southern Sudanese usually had many parties and danced at these parties to the Trim songs.

Life was totally different in the south than in the north. The tribes of the south were more black than the north.

Leila picking mangoes from our garden

The Arabic language was not in use in the south. The people communicated in their own tribal languages and in English. The Bible was written in those tribal languages. You could even buy a dictionary of the Dinka language which was the language of the majority of people in and around the Wau area. The people in Wau dressed in regular European clothes, a shirt and pants.

Most of the southerners were Christians, but some of them married more than one wife. They usually married one in church and the others only through the tribal ceremony. When a man wanted to marry a girl, he had to give her father a number of cows. The richer the man was, the more cows he had to give to his father-in-law. If the woman failed to get pregnant, the husband has the right to get back half of the cows he gave.

Leila as usual quickly created new friends and visited them. One of them was the wife of the dentist. She was Indian. We were invited to the house of another colleague. He was Egyptian. I remember that they gave us tea to drink. Their two-year-old daughter came and simply put her dirty finger in Leila's cup. The parents saw what happened but did nothing. Leila was unable to drink the tea.

Leila and Victor are leaving Wau.

I spent six months in Wau and Leila stayed about four and a half months. We were unable to go out of the town because of the civil war. Nobody could travel outside the town safely. If anybody wanted to go from one town to another, they had to join the Touf. To assure the safety of the travelers, the government asked all the cars that needed to travel from Wau to the other towns to be ready, for example on Tuesday. They didn't finalize the time until the last minute. This was to avoid the timed bombs that the rebels used to put in the path of the Touf. A military armed truck would lead the Touf and another one would follow at the end. I remember one of my colleagues assigned to work for three months in a town called El Tonj. He prepared the hospital car with all the needed medicines and equipment. On the day of departure, he was not feeling well. He decided to let the hospital car go without him, and he would follow in the next Touf. By the end of the day, we heard that the hospital car exploded by a road bomb. All the people who were in the car died. My colleague was very scared and upset, but he left to El Tonj two weeks later. I was not selected to work in one of the other towns near Wau because I was married.

South Sudan was a rich country. The land was tropical, and you could plant anything, and there was a lot of oil. The problem was the war that continued from 1955 until now. The war destroyed the economy, and more importantly, the self-esteem of the people.

The educated Southern Sudanese people felt that they had no fair chance to compete in north Sudan because of the discrimination and in the south because of the war. Hundreds of well-educated Southern Sudanese left their country to work in high posts all over the world.

Chapter 29

Residency in Ophthalmology, Khartoum 1972

We returned to Khartoum so I could start my residency in ophthalmology at Khartoum Eye Hospital. I went to the hospital and met with the director of the hospital who at the same time was the senior ophthalmologist, Dr. Abd El-Gadir. I found him a very brilliant fifty-five-year-old, tall, slim person. I learned later that he was the ambassador of Sudan to the Soviet Union for two years. He was a good teacher. If he saw any interesting case, he would ask me to come and see it. He started the tradition of clinical meetings in Khartoum Eye Hospital. He used to select the cases to be presented and reminded everybody to attend. His knowledge was not only in ophthalmology but in other subjects such as astronomy, history, and literature. He had the habit of reading at least six hours a day. He knew which football team won in England. He read all the new books out. He never missed a novel. He was very knowledgeable about music.

The residency in ophthalmology was three years and a half. The first year was in Khartoum Eye Hospital. Then a year and a half was in London. We had to attend a six-month full-time course in ophthalmology at the Institute of Ophthalmology, London University. The rest of the time, we were allowed to work or to get clinical attachment (fellowship) to any eye department in London. During this period, we had to pass the diploma in ophthalmology exam of the Royal College of Physicians of London and the Royal College of Surgeons of England. After we returned to Sudan, we spent the last year getting the final training in eye surgeries at Khartoum Eye Hospital.

Khartoum Eye Hospital was the only specialized hospital for eye diseases in Sudan. It had 120 beds for patients. At that time, there were about eight ophthalmologists, four to six residents, and about five house officers. There were also about six refractionists and about six medical assistants. There were three clinics. One for the medical assistants to screen all the patients. They treated all the external eye diseases and referred other cases to the second clinic which was the residents' clinic. In that clinic, the residents and the house officers saw the patients and treated what they could manage. The difficult cases would be seen by the consultants' clinic. Usually there were two ophthalmologists in the specialists' clinic. They saw the difficult cases with the residents and taught the residents about those patients. They also followed up with their patients after surgery. All cases that needed refraction would go to the refraction department. The refractionist did the refraction. They studied for three years after high school. There was also an orthoptic department for cases of strabismus and related problems. There were three refractionists who had training in orthoptics and did all the exams and vision training.

I found the work in Khartoum Eye Hospital was well organized. I was very impressed by the friendly atmosphere at the hospital. All the doctors would go and eat their breakfast together in the hospital cafeteria. The second ophthalmologist after Dr. Abd El-Gadir was Dr. Genawi. Dr. Ginawi was a very nice person as well. He treated us as his colleagues and not as young residents. Dr. Hussein Ahmed Hussein was still practicing ophthalmology. He was a graduate of Khartoum University in 1932. He was the first Sudanese ophthalmologist. He was about seventy years old when I was a resident. His attitude toward us was just like a father to his beloved children. We never called him doctor, but usually we addressed him as Amm which meant uncle. He was very humble and used to give us encouragement. I remember him telling me that what we knew there in Sudan was far more than the residents in London. He told me about his training in England and how he saw a surgeon there doing his operations as "camel bite", which meant he was a bad surgeon. Dr. Hussein told me that in his family, they had the habit of naming the firstborn boy with the same name as his grandfather. This was the reason that Dr. Hussein's name was Hussein Ahmed Hussein Ahmed, and this was repeated ten times. In Sudan and Egypt, the first name was the person's name, the middle name was the father's first name, the last name (third name) was the grandfather's name. For the Sudanese passport, they usually put four names. The fourth name was the great grandfather's name. After marriage the wife keeps her maiden name. I think this system of naming was better than the European and American way of names in which they use surnames. In Egypt and Sudan, we used Dr. followed by the first name. So in Sudan I was Dr. Victor. In the USA I was Dr. Zaki. I chose Zaki as my last name because of Dr. Abd El-Gadir's advice before I left for England. He told me that Boutros, which was my third name, was difficult to pronounce and write, and Zaki was easy. So I put Zaki as my last name and Boutros as my middle name.

When I went to England in 1973, I had a problem with the Home Office, the immigration authorities in England. I put in all my applications to the Institute of Ophthalmology in London, my last name as Zaki. In my passport, they wrote my name Victor Zaki Boutros Harmina. The Home Office sent me a letter that I missed the registration with them. They sent the letter with the name Harmina. I registered with them with the name Zaki. I explained to them that I am the same person. In America, the confusion was more. In my marriage certificate, the last name was Boutros, the passport was Harmina, and in all my other documents, Zaki was the one used. To complicate things in my passport, Zaki was written Zekkie, and Boutros was written Buttros. In Sudan they ask you to fill the forms in Arabic, and the person who writes the passport writes the name in English the way he thinks is right. Apparently Americans are more familiar with different names. They let you choose the name you want to use in America, and at the same time, they put a space for all other used names. Most people after immigrating to America change their names. This change of names was more often seen in Jews coming from Eastern Europe and Russia but also seen in Chinese giving their children American names. Last week, I saw a sixty-year-old Chinese patient whose name was Danny Wong.

In Khartoum Eye Hospital, I learned a lot about ophthalmology in a practical way and on patients.

We rented an apartment in El Zuhour Fatahat' next to our old friends and neighbors Tadrous and Yvonne. It was a two-bedroom apartment with a small yard. After less than two weeks in that apartment, we had a problem that Leila decided not to stay in that apartment at all. We used to walk from our apartment for about one hour. On a particular evening, we went for our walk at around 7:00 PM. When we came back, we discovered that thieves had entered our apartment and took most of our valuables. They took our radio-cassette recorder, most of my pants and shirts, our alarm clock, and a small amount of cash. The strange thing was the timing. Our street was not the main one, but it was usually full of people walking at that time. The only explanation was the presence of some construction workers at our next-door neighbor's house. They were building a second floor, and they were able to watch our apartment. We left that apartment and moved to another one in Khartoum 2, next to my cousin Ayad and his wife Kokab. It was just in front of my mother's house. Actually this apartment was very good. It was clean and bigger than the first one. Also its location was nearer to Khartoum. It was one big house and as usual divided into two separate apartments one for us and the bigger one where Ayad's family was living. After we settled, we invited Leila's parents to come and visit us. This was the first time for them to visit Sudan. We spent a nice time with them. All my relatives came to visit them. Leila's father had many friends from Assiut living in Sudan. One of them was a lawyer called Emil. He was very rich. He studied high school in Assiut with Leila's father. It was strange that it had been about forty years since he left Assiut, but his relationship with Amm Hezkial was still strong. He came and visited us, and he invited us to have dinner at his house. There were also many other friends who came to visit them and invited us to their homes.

As I said before that Khartoum was very hot. That was the reason that we used to sleep in the yard. Leila's father was not convinced to sleep in the yard on his first night in Khartoum. He told me that he would sleep in the room. After about one hour, we heard him moving his bed toward the room's door. Gradually he moved his bed outside into the yard. By the second night, he decided to sleep in the yard and continued to sleep in the yard on all his visits to us in Sudan. I remember the first night for them in Khartoum, our neighbor Kokab sneezed. Because the two apartments were separated just by a wall, Amm Hezkial thought that Leila sneezed so he said, "Bless you, Leila." We laughed and told him that it was not Leila but our neighbor Kokab.

Amm Hezkial was a very active person. He never used to stay idle. He used to go to the market of Khartoum 2 and buy all that we needed while we were at work. He used to tell me that this item was cheaper in Sudan and the other item was cheaper in Egypt.

Leila worked at this period in Khartoum Hospital in the dermatology department. She started to like dermatology. She decided to study dermatology in London during my period of study there. Leila sent all her papers from Sudan to ask about the dermatology study in London. She was the first person from Sudan to do this course. Leila kept her Egyptian citizenship. She decided not to apply for the Sudanese nationality. This was the reason that she was unable to get a scholarship from the Sudanese government to study in London. She paid for all her studies in London from her own pocket. This was the same reason that she had to apply for a permit to stay in Sudan every year and a permit to work in Sudan and to renew them every year. Because Leila was a wife of a Sudanese citizen, she had the right to get Sudanese citizenship, but she preferred not to get it.

Our life went on smoothly during this period. Life in Sudan in general was easy, and everything was available and cheap. At that time we used to use the telephone to order a butane gas cylinder (tank) for the stovetop. The gas company would send a person to the house to change the cylinder tank and test it before he left. It could be compared to the time in 1990, immediately before we left Sudan for America, we used to stay in a line for hours just to give the gas company the gas tank and get a receipt. After a week or two, we had to go again and wait a few more hours to get the filled tank. There was almost no electricity shortage in Khartoum in 1970–1972 compared to about twenty hours a day of no electricity in 1990. The bread, sugar, rice, and flour were abundantly available compared to 1990 where everything was not available and in the black market. The dollar was equal to 0.33 Sudanese pounds. Later in 1990 the dollar equaled about 1,500 Sudanese pounds.

Before we left for England to start our studies there, we sold most of our belongings in Khartoum. I remember that we asked a *dallal* who was a person who specialized in selling second-hand things to come and evaluate our furniture. He offered to buy everything. He bought everything for very little, but we thought that this was better than ask people to come and buy each item separately. We booked a student's house in London. Leila decided to pass by Assiut to see her family for two weeks. I went straight to London, and Leila went to Egypt.

Chapter 30

Living in London, England, 1973–1974

I took the plane to London in February 1973. This was my first visit to England and Europe. I was excited to see London. I heard a lot about it from my parents, brothers, and sister, all of whom visited and lived in England for some time. My parents spent some of their vacations in London. My brother George spent one year in London for one of his programs. Joseph and his wife Widad lived for two years in London to get his master's degree in food analysis. Baheeg spent about four months studying English and accounting in London. Thuraya went with her husband Bushra on almost all their vacations to London. Nabeel went to England around 1966 to work there and stayed in a town in the north till 1974, then he moved to London. Just by chance on the same plane to London was my cousin Sameer. He was an electronics engineer, and he was going to London to finish his PhD. He was doing his studies in a town near London. He decided to stay a night with me in London then head out to his town.

Leila and Lillian Penson Hall

I booked a student's dorm for me and Leila to live in. The building was Lillian Penson Hall. It was a six-floor building. The rooms were either for one student or a student and his spouse. In the basement, there was a first-class restaurant that served delicious, hot meals at a reduced price. We used to eat almost all our meals there. There were coin laundry machines. Our room was a small one with a fold-up bed that could be pushed to the wall. We had a private bathroom. There was a desk and a bookshelf. There were three TV rooms in the building, each one had a big TV turned to one of the three channels at that time. Channel 1 was almost the official one with the news and some documentary films. Channel 2 was less conservative and had more films. The third channel was the ITN, which was a private one and presented the news in a different way. We used to spend most of our nights there for the first month. Within a few weeks, Leila became an expert in different TV programs. In Sudan we had only one channel, and it only worked for five hours each night. In addition, there were study rooms. Actually Lillian Penson Hall was well built to give the student what they needed. Its location was in Paddington near the Underground station, the subway. It was about a fifteen-minute walk to Oxford Street and the center of London. I spent the first few days using my own technique of walking to recognize the different places. I used to walk from Paddington to Tottenham Court Road and return. This was about two hours of continuous walking. As usual, I quickly learned my way around London. The astonishing thing that attracted my attention in London was how clean the streets were. The sidewalks were well maintained. I remember that once I found a blinking light was on one of the sidewalks. After a few minutes, I discovered that the reason was a very tiny level difference between two adjacent tiles on the sidewalk. In Sudan there were no sidewalks except for a few main streets in the center of Khartoum market. On those sidewalks in Khartoum, a missing tile was not a big deal. In London all the streets were very clean, not a single small paper on any street. In Sudan and Egypt, all the streets were full of trash. I learned that self-discipline was the key. If each person had self-control and didn't litter, the streets would be clean. The same principle was applied in our homes. If each person puts their things in their place, the house will be clean. How can you teach people to do that? We used to throw what we didn't need from the car window in Sudan, but I couldn't do that in London. This meant that we could change if we wanted to.

In London I found that public toilets were very useful and clean. In all the underground stations, there were public toilets. This was much better than in America where there were no public toilets except in big restaurants. I also found in London there were signs in all the streets. In Sudan you could hardly find a sign to indicate the name of the street. I found no difficulty in moving to London. My difficulty was the language. I found that it was difficult for me to understand the way the people spoke. They spoke very quickly. I asked about the Sudanese Embassy. I showed the address to the subway information center. He told me to go to Knight's Bridge Underground station. He repeated Knight's Bridge several times, but I was unable to recognize it. At last, I asked him to show it on the map. By the end of our two years in London, I had improved a lot in this area.

Victor and Leila, Hyde Park, London 1973

Victor and Leila in Hyde Park

I discovered that in London, everybody only cared about themselves. If someone in the street fell, nobody would come and try to help. This was strange to me. In Sudan and Egypt, if anything happened to you, all the passersby in the street would come and help.

I went to the Institute of Ophthalmology on Judd Street near Kings Cross Underground station. This was about seven stops with the Underground, the circle line. I used to buy weekly passes.

Leila spent seven days in Assiut. During those days, her sister Nabeela gave birth to her daughter Hoda. Leila came to London airport. I was waiting for her. There were some problems with the immigration papers. Leila was impressed by London just like me. She liked Lillian Penson Hall, the food at the restaurant, and the laundry. As usual, as soon as she came, she started to organize my books and clothes. By the time Leila came, I was already busy with my studies at the institute. Leila started to find her way in London by herself. She went to the Institute of Dermatology in London, where she would study. She got her permit to practice medicine in England. She started to find temporary jobs in medicine. Her first job was a temporary one in orthopedics in a hospital called Hackney Hospital. She was surprised to find many Egyptian doctors working there. After her first period, they asked her to work for another period. Then she found a position at the hospital, which was attached to the Institute of Dermatology. She worked for the first period and then for another longer period. She worked with one of the main professors who would teach her during the program. She learned a lot. She became an expert on how to go to different areas in London to places that I never went to or heard of. She also learned about the hospitals in England and their system. In between jobs, Leila used to walk and visit different places, parks, museums, and historical places. Until we finished our period in London, I used to ask Leila for directions.

We found a cubicle for selfie pictures. You insert ten cents and press the button, and the picture would come out.

Selfie picture for ten cents

After I finished the course at the Institute of Ophthalmology, I took another short course in orthoptics which was related to eye muscle balance. I applied for jobs to work in ophthalmology. The first job that I applied for was at the Middlesex Hospital in London. I went for the interview. There were four applicants. At the end of the interview, they told me, "Sorry we decided to take another candidate." After two days I received a letter from them telling me that there was a problem with the first person, and they decided to select me. Every time I remember, I realize how God arranges everything in a very special way. Middlesex Hospital was a teaching hospital.

Victor visiting The Middlrsex Hospital, London 1980

The Middlesex Hospital

It was the hospital of Middlesex medical school. It was one of the best known medical schools in London at that time. They offered me an apartment inside the hospital premises. The apartment had two bedrooms, a living room, and kitchen. It was located in downtown London, three minutes walk from Oxford circus. The hospital was a huge one with many doctors. I discovered that all the doctors, about five hundred, were British except three. One was of Indian origin but graduated from Middlesex medical school. The second was from Iran, who got his FRCS in surgery and worked as a house surgeon in the plastics department. The third person was me, and I worked as a house surgeon in the ophthalmology department. In the eye department, there were two ophthalmologists. The first one was Sir Allen Goldsmith. He got the title Sir because he was the Queen's ophthalmologist and eye surgeon. He was about sixty-five years old but very active. He used to do one-day operations at the Middlesex Hospital and another day in another private hospital. He used to ask me to go with him to assist him in the private hospital. I remember that I used to go with him to his house in Harley Street'. I ate lunch with him, his wife, and his friend Sir Duke Elder.

Both of them were very famous ophthalmologists, and their clinics were in the same building where Sir Allen lived. Sir Duke Elder was famous because he wrote *System of Ophthalmology.* They were thirteen volumes of the textbook; each volume was about three hundred pages. It described all the diseases of the eye in great detail and was considered the reference in ophthalmology at that time. He wrote other books in ophthalmology as well. He was short in stature and very sociable. I remember he asked me about Leila, and I told him that she was studying at the Institute of Dermatology. He laughed and told me, "Tell her that all their diseases are untreatable, and they give steroids to all their patients." I replied, "We in ophthalmology have some untreatable diseases as well." He laughed again and said, "Do not tell her that." He mentioned that he visited South Sudan and told me about his visit there. I was astonished when I ate with them for the first time when Sir Allen's wife brought lunch. It was three big lettuce leaves, one small boiled potato, and two slices of cold cuts. For me coming from Sudan, this amount of food was very small. Our idea in Sudan was if you were rich, you ate more, but now my thinking changed, and at last, I understood their opinion of eating such food.

The first time after I assisted Sir Allen in the private operation, he gave me a check. This was new to me. I considered that helping him was not a big deal, and he was good to me and I could help him without fees. I refused to take the check. When my friend Ffyttche who was the senior registrar heard this, he was very upset. He explained to me that this was my right. He insisted on bringing my money back, and he did. After that I used to take the check and say thank you. Sir Allen asked me to assist another famous cornea surgeon who was not working at the Middlesex Hospital. This surgeon asked me to assist him because his wife who was an ophthalmologist was away for some time. All those private operations were done at a private hospital away from Middlesex Hospital.

Sir Allen Goldsmith invited Leila and me for dinner in his home.

Sir Allen wrote me a letter after I left England and went to Sudan before he died in 1976.

The second ophthalmologist was Mr. MacFaul. He was excellent and trusted me a lot. He became the head of the department when Sir

Allen retired in early 1974. He invited Leila and me to his house for dinner and gave us a book about beautiful places to visit in England.

After Sir Allen retired, a new ophthalmologist came to replace him. This ophthalmologist was Mr. Hamilton. We noticed when he went for the first time that his initials were A. M. Hamilton. When he introduced himself, he said Peter Hamilton. The head of the operating theater was an old Scottish lady. She said it must be that they chose an ugly name for him because his mother had many children who died. When they choose a bad name, they were hoping that the new child would survive.

Victor at Christmas celebration in the eye department in Middlesex Hospital

Mr. Hamilton became very famous after a few years and now later became one of the authorities in diabetic retinopathy. In 1990 I met him at a conference in Cairo. He was introducing a new laser machine called Ioid Laser. This was a small machine that could be attached to any slit lamp and be used as any other laser. When I was working in Khartoum, I used to send some of my diabetic patients to him in London.

The senior registrar was Mr. Ffyttche. He was a good friend. He used to tell jokes all the time. I remember he saw one patient from an

Arabian country. He asked me to come and translate for him. He told me, "I want to know in Arabic one important sentence, which is 'Pay the bill!'" Once I was invited to the Middlesex Dinner. This dinner was done once every year. It was held at Savoy Hotel, one of the elegant hotels in London. When you drive into the hotel, you have to drive on the right side of the street, which was the wrong way in London. On the invitation, it was written that a party dress was required. When I asked Tim Fffyttche about that, he told me, "You have to wear the classic black suit and a white bow tie." I told him I did not have it. He advised me to rent one, and he gave me a bow tie. For me this was humiliating to rent a suit. In Sudan, this was unknown. Actually in Sudan nobody wore suits except at their wedding or some elderly people during Christmas church service. I went and rented the suit. The invitation was just for the employees and not their spouses. Even the ophthalmologists came alone without their wives. Tim Fffyttche took me in his car to the party. This was the first time for me to attend such parties. When we reached the entrance of the hall, the attendant who was wearing a tuxedo asked me for my name. When I told him, he announced my name with a microphone in a loud voice, "Dr. Victor Zaki." This was the tradition for this particular event. They announced the name of every person as they entered. We had some drinks outside the hall before dinner. Then they asked us to come for dinner. Each department had a table. The name of each of us was written in front of our chair. The head of the department Sir Allen Goldsmith was at the head of the table. First they started with the wine. They brought the bottle of wine and showed it to Sir Goldsmith. He read the labels first, then tasted it, then he said OK. After that, they started to serve us. The food was great, and the way they served, it was special. At the end of the dinner, they started the toast. The mayor and the director of the Middlesex Hospital saluted, "Her Majesty the Queen." Then they saluted other people or the hospital, I can't remember. I enjoyed the party. It was a good chance for me to see the traditions of such parties. At the end of the party, Mr. Ffyttche gave me a ride home. I gave him his bow tie and thanked him for his advice. The next morning, I returned the rented suit.

The eye department at the Middlesex Hospital was a friendly place to work in. Every two weeks, I used to work in the outpatient department. My main work was in the wards and assisting in the operating rooms. The rounds with each consultant were nice. We attended the round and then went to the head nurse's office to drink tea and eat cakes. At ten in the morning, it was coffee time, and at 4:00 PM, it was tea time and cakes were mandatory in each case. The consultant, the senior registrar, and the house surgeon, myself, used to meet at the head nurse's room. The head nurse prepared the tea, brought it with cakes, and joined us in this mini tea party. The consultant was always first to leave, and as soon as he left, they started to gossip about him. Then the senior registrar would go, and the gossip would be about the senior registrar. It was good that I always stayed until the end. Actually, the head nurse of the operating theater usually joined us at those tea parties.

After leaving the ward, most of the patients gave some presents. For the consultants, they gave bottles of wine or whisky. Some patients gave me the same gifts. I usually gave them to Mr. Ffyttche; he liked to drink. They usually brought chocolates to the nurses. They usually opened them and kept them in the ward. Everybody ate chocolates all day. I can't remember a single day that there were no chocolates in the ward. At that time in England, chocolates were of high quality and caliber. I can still remember till now that delicious taste of English chocolate. Back then, nobody cared about cholesterol or fat.

Middlesex Hospital was huge. Inside the hospital, there was a bank, a chapel, a small grocery store, and a flower shop. There was a big restaurant for the doctors at a reduced cost. I was not used to the different types of meals they served. Once I picked one from the menu and ordered it. It was a good, well-cooked piece of steak, and on top of it, they put grapefruit syrup. I was unable to eat it. I just couldn't eat meat with sweet things.

At Christmas time, the BBC choir and the music band came to play Christmas songs in the hospital yard. Most of the patients came out and heard the songs; some nurses pushed their patients with wheelchairs to the yard. It was beautiful; they sang in four different voices.

Sir Allen Goldsmith's wife was a volunteer at the hospital. She used to bring flowers every morning and put them in a vase at the hospital's main entrance.

My assignment at Middlesex Hospital was for six months. Near the end of this period, I found an added time assignment for the next six months. I thought that I would be happy at this job. Leila was studying near my place. I asked the personnel officer of the hospital if I could reapply for the same position for another six months. He said yes. He advised me to ask the consultant about that. When I went back to the ward, the consultant told me that he heard that I asked about working for another six months. I told him yes, I asked. He told me to go and sign the papers right away for the next six months. Actually the consultants and all the staff trusted me in everything.

Part of my work was to cover the general surgical emergency department for four hours once every two weeks. One day, I was at the emergency department, and they told me that a person came with a head injury after a car accident. I went to see the patient. To my surprise, the patient was one of my high school colleagues from Sudan. His name was Mohammed El-Zubeir. He was hit by a car and had a fracture of one of the facial bones. He was astonished to see me. He told me his story. After we finished high school, he went to Yugoslavia to study engineering. He married an Italian classmate of his. After graduation from college, they went and lived in Sweden. During their yearly vacation, they decided to visit England. On their first day in London, he was hit by a car and brought by the ambulance to our hospital. By chance, I was the doctor on duty at that time. There was a language barrier. His wife could not speak English or Arabic. She wanted to call Sweden to communicate with their medical insurance company. I took her to our apartment to use our telephone.

Our apartment was very comfortable. It was on the main hospital premises but two blocks from the main hospital where the eye ward was. There was a special underground tunnel that I could use to go from my apartment to the ward. Even in winter, I used to wear my lab coat and go from the apartment to the ward and back. I used to carry my beeper and go shopping around the hospital.

I worked at Middlesex Hospital for a whole year. It was one of the best times of our life. Leila's studies were at the Institute of Dermatology in Piccadilly Circus. She sometimes used the subway to get there. If she was in a hurry, she preferred to walk because she got there faster.

During our stay in that apartment, we had some visitors. My sister Thuraya and her husband Bushra came on one of their annual vacations. My brother Nabeel stayed with us for a few weeks when he took a new job in London and left his old job in a small town in the north of England. Leila's brother Magid came to visit us from Assiut. He was a student at the university in Assiut. He spent a few weeks with us.

During our period in London, we were able to do a tour of Europe for two weeks. I will give the details of this tour in the next chapter.

In London, I got my degree in ophthalmology. I worked for one complete year in one of the best hospitals in England. I got a lot of experience in ophthalmology, English language, and got a good idea about British culture. Leila studied and got her degree in dermatology, got practical experience in medicine from working in a London hospital, and she learned a lot about London and became an expert in all the parks and museums.

During our stay in London, we saw many movies at movie theaters in London. We saw *The Sound of Music* and *My Fair Lady* for the second time. I saw both of them in Assiut while I was a student. We saw some plays live at the theaters. We saw *Jesus Christ Superstar* and *Godspell* and some others.

I remember in *Godspell*, all the actors came in between the viewers and gave each viewer a tiny glass cup of wine. We were planning to attend *The Mouse Trap*. This play was on continuous showing for thirty-two years. Maybe they changed actors every few years. Anyway, we were unable to attend because we had to book two weeks in advance. My schedule was changing every week, so we missed that play.

Leila and Victor, London 1973

Victor and Leila at an amusement park in London

On weekends, we used to go to a park or a museum. In the beginning, we were fond of seeing the speakers in the Speaker's Corner at Hyde Park. This was a few minutes' walk from Lillian Penson Hall and our apartment in Middlesex Hospital. At the Speaker's Corner, any person could stand and give a speech. Some people may stand and hear him. Usually most of the speakers brought a chair and stood on it. There were usually some people arguing with the speaker, and in almost many cases, they shouted. The police usually were around this area but will never interfere except if there was an actual fight. The English people and government are always proud that they have freedom of speech. Our favorite picnic was to take our lunch and eat it in one of the parks. Most of the London parks have lakes with ducks. All the parks are almost deserted in winter.

I remember once Leila and Thuraya, who was visiting London at that time, got lost in Hyde Park. They were in the park and stayed till it was late in the evening. Daylight started to fade out. They discovered this a bit late. They took one direction, but apparently it was the wrong one. At last the park police came and helped them to find their way out. They closed all the parks at night. The police checked that nobody was in the park after closing. On another day, Leila and Thuraya went to the supermarket. They bought many things and ice cream. They were apparently attracted by many shops in between. On the way back to the house, they discovered that the ice cream was dripping from the bag. I think they saved some of the ice cream but not much.

We used to go to the Coptic Orthodox church in London every Sunday. We went with the church group on day trips to different places. Once we went to Brighton, which was a city in the south of London and had a nice beach. We went with another group to Gloucester that was to the southwest of London and had some Roman antiques. We visited Cambridge with its famous university. Most of the streets in Cambridge were brick. Leila went for a couple of days with her college to Oxford.

We had some Sudanese friends in London. One of them was John and his wife Mary and their two-year-old daughter Grace. Their daughter was brilliant. She used to watch TV with her parents. Once there was an Irish speaker. She immediately told her mother, "Why this person cannot speak English well." She recognized that he had an accent.

Our friends Gamal and his wife Hoda visited us on one of their annual vacations. We went with them to an amusement park. We spent a very nice time with them. Gamal usually liked to tell jokes.

One of my colleagues in Sudan was Mona; she used to come to our flat and study with me. We used to laugh about her umbrella that flipped with any wind.

Leila's first pregnancy (Tony)

During the last three months of our period in London, we bought many things that we may need in Sudan. We bought a butane gas cooker, a fridge, and all dining sets. Even the silverware, we bought from London. Leila was good at making yogurt at home, so she bought a yogurt maker. We used this one for one year in London. When Leila tried to use it in Sudan, it did not work.

The room temperature in Sudan was always higher than the temperature of the machine.

Leila was keen to stay in London. She said both of us could work in London, and we could have a nice life. I objected to this idea. I was convinced that since the Sudan government paid for me to do this course, I had to go and work there for some years. I told her we could come back after a few years and settle in England. I felt it was an obligation to my country.

Chapter 31

Our Tour in Europe 1974

Leila was studying as a full-time student at the Institute of Dermatology, London University. She had a two-week vacation. One of her colleagues from Thailand told her that he and his wife planned to do a tour in Europe during the college vacation. He said that he bought a new BMW car and wanted us to join them on this tour.

He mentioned that he wanted us to share with them the cost of the gas only. I took my annual vacation from my work in the Middlesex Hospital. We started the tour in April 1974. Leila's friend drove the entire journey. His wife was reading the maps for him. Leila and I were sitting in the back seats, relaxed and enjoying the lovely scenery of the tour.

The tour was nice because we never worried about finding a taxi or train. Leila's colleague was driving us from one hotel in one city to another hotel in another city. Even the tours inside each city were mostly in his car. It was very convenient.

We started our tour in London. We drove east toward the sea that separated England from Belgium. We took a ship to Belgium. We went into the ship by our car, and on the ship, we went out of the car. The immigration and custom authorities did their jobs while we were inside the car. We drove immediately toward Brussels, the capital of Belgium. We saw the Atomium, which was a museum in the shape of an atom.

It had different huge balls, each representing the neutron and the electrons. We arrived late, so we did not enter the museum. From Belgium, we proceeded to Holland. Amsterdam was the capital.

Atomium in Brussels, Belgium

It was a very pleasant city. It had many canals, and you could use the car to see all those canals. Also you could use small boats to pass through all those canals.

Amsterdam, Holland

We saw a hotel for cats only. I am not sure if the owners of the cats can join them as companions or not. We noticed some parts of the city that were part of the sea. They built dams and evacuated the water. Then they replaced the water with nice buildings. I remembered at that moment, the empty land in Sudan. I was amazed by the number of bikes in Holland. Almost everybody had a bike.

I like Amsterdam. You feel happy there. We lost our way in Holland. We found ourselves going through small streets. At the end, we stopped at a small house. We knocked on the door. An old man and his wife came out. We tried to speak to them in English, but they could not understand. They know only their local language. At last, they showed us with their hands the German direction to the highway.

We left Amsterdam on our way to Germany. At that time, it was West Germany.

Leila in German coffey place 1974

Leila in Germany

At the borders of Germany, the immigration authorities were very tough with Leila and me. At that time, the Munich Olympics was just over. At this Olympics, some Palestinians killed eight Israeli athletes. So the Germans were very strict with all the Arabs entering Germany. We went first to Bonn, the capital. It was a small town adjacent to Cologne. We spent one day in those two cities. Cologne had a huge cathedral facing the river. We passed small cities in between and at last we reached Munich. In Germany, it is called Munchen. I have no idea why it has a certain name in Germany and the rest of the world is using another name. I remember the beautiful flowers it had on the streets.

We visited the Olympic stadium and village. The stadium was covered by huge transparent plastic tents. This would ensure the passage of the sun rays but not the rain. Those huge plastic covers were attached to strong large metal pillars. Those tents were not covering the sides. They look just like huge suspended roofs.

Leila in the Olympic Village, Germany

A village in Austria

Our next stop was Austria.

We enjoyed Austria more than any other country in Europe. First, it was a small country, and all the cities were not big. The capital of Vienna had the characteristic royal-style buildings. There was a famous historical palace in the center of the city. The palace had a huge garden well-decorated with flowers and many fountains. Each fountain contained many statues. Maybe one of the factors that I was impressed with Vienna was a famous song by the Egyptian singer Asmahan which was called "Laialy El Ons Fi Vienna." The meaning of the song is a nice enjoyable evening in Vienna.

Victor and Leila on top of snowy mountain in Austria 1974

Snow mountain in Austria

In Austria we visited as well the city of Salzburg. If I have to choose only one city in Europe to visit, I will select Salzburg. It is a small town adjacent to high mountains. You feel that the city is just created for tourists. We visited a palace with huge gardens, which was built by one of the Catholic bishops about 1680. Apparently, he was an artist and engineer. He made channels for the water to pass through most of the palace. This water stream was used to move small characters. Those characters were in one place, forming a group of soldiers marching and one of them was raising a flag. On another level, there were some people in a market place. One of them was sharpening knives; some ladies were shopping. The nice thing was that all of them were moving. In part of this palace, we were passing in one place and looking at the nicely decorated walls. On those walls there were shapes of different animal heads all around. Suddenly all those heads started to sprinkle water toward us. They said that this was one of the bishop's tricks for his visitors. We went to the top of the mountain by suspended cable cars. Those cars each carry about ten people. It was frightening. This was the first time for us to try such a ride. At the top of the mountain, the people were skiing. For the first time, we saw the snow. This was in April. It was sunny and we did not believe that this was real snow. We did not ski, but we played with the snow and took some pictures. Some of the streets in Salzburg were narrow and just for pedestrians. This gave me the sensation that I was at home and not worried about passing cars.

After Austria, we visited Italy. As soon as we reached Italy, we saw one of the army soldiers waving to give him a ride. Also we saw people eating pumpkin seeds. We felt at once that now we were near Egypt. The first city we went to was Venice. It is a unique city. We had to park the car outside the town. No cars were allowed inside the city because the streets were water channels. There were sidewalks for the people to walk and many bridges to cross the watery streets. The water in those streets was deep, and it had strong waves because it was connected directly to the Mediterranean Sea. All the streets were full of their characteristic, well-decorated small boats. In Arabic, we call them jandool.

Venice, Italy

They looked nice, and they were painted black with different-colored decorations. The front and the tail were long and curved inward. I felt unsafe to use them because they were very narrow, and the water's waves were strong. In the center of the city was St. Marcus Cathedral. It was a big church built many centuries ago in which they kept the head of St. Mark. St. Mark was killed in Alexandria, Egypt, in the first century. Some of the Italian sailors took his head to Venice and built this church in his name. In the late 1960s there was some agreement between the Coptic Orthodox church in Egypt and the Vatican. They agreed to transfer the head of St. Mark to Egypt to be kept with his body, and they did. In the center of Venice City and just in front of St. Marcus Cathedral was a huge space covered by colorful tiles. All around this space were many coffee shops and tourist shops. The area was full of tourists visiting Venice. At the other end of this space was a giant tower that we went up to have a good view of the city.

We bought some slides from a tourist shop. We felt that we had to bargain with them. We bought the slides at about half the price they started with, but we felt that they still cheated us.

The next day we went on a guided tour by a machine boat to Morano Borano and Torchello. Morano was a very famous glass factory. We saw how they created different shapes from the raw glass. They put different colors and make different shapes. Everything in this factory was done manually. We bought a few glassworks from there.

When we returned to the hotel, we discovered that the car's side mirror was stolen. Leila's friend was very upset. He said that it was better not to go to any other Italian city because we may lose the whole car.

We climbed by car in the Alps mountains on our way to Switzerland. There were no protecting walls on those curves, and you could see the ground a hundred of meters away. Our driver was driving very fast on those curves. When we told him to slow down, he said that he was used to driving in his country's similar mountains. This was his first time to drive in Italy. It was scary. We survived this part of the trip.

At last, we reached the borders of Italy. The Italian officer checked our passports, and suddenly, he said that Leila stayed longer than her visa permitted. I tried to explain to him that we came together, and definitely, he read it wrong. The communication was difficult. He doid not understand English, and we were unable to communicate in Italian. At last, I started to shout at him; he then said, "OK, go."

The next immigration officer was speaking with his girlfriend. He simply waved to us to go without checking our passports. After one hour, we found another immigration station. We were astonished because we were supposed to be in Switzerland. We discovered that we entered France when the immigration officer with his girlfriend waved to us. Now we are exiting France. By chance, our visa to France was multiple visas. Then we entered Switzerland. We visited Losan and Geneva. There was a huge lake in Geneva and a fountain in its center. Also, there were many shops for watches. We bought a small clock with a bird that came out of his house and went back continuously. It was a pendulum clock. Switzerland was the most expensive country on our tour. Our last country was France. We only visited Paris in France. It was a nice city with many coffee shops, especially in the Latin area. It reminded me of Cairo. We visited the Louvre Museum. There we saw the famous *Mona Lisa*. We also entered the Notre Dame Cathedral. We passed by the Arc De Triumph in the capital center. We took the elevators to the Eiffel Tower. It gives you a good view of all Paris. We felt that there was no point in going to the top part of the Eiffel Tower because you have to climb many stairs.

At last, we drove to the north part of France to the English Channel. The tunnel that connected France and England was not present at that time. We took a special boat that moved by pushing air to the water. It created a pad of air between the boat and the water. It was called Telefrique. It was a huge boat that carried many cars and passengers.

We enjoyed our tour very much. Leila discovered that she was pregnant during this tour. Leila started to be nauseated when she saw her Thai friend eat. Actually, he ate a lot. He was very fond of hotdogs and boiled eggs. He used to eat about eight to ten boiled eggs after his regular breakfast. I remember in France, we had a problem with communication. I was able to convey the messages with my little French vocabulary. I forgot or maybe, I subconsciously tried to forget the meaning of eggs in French. Our Thai friend was very keen to get his regular dose of boiled eggs. He started to imitate the sound of the hen while laying her eggs. He used his hands and body to show the restaurant owner that he meant eggs. He was very funny. He managed to get his eggs. Leila was very upset because of the way he used to eat the boiled eggs and the hotdogs. This nauseated her.

We spent two weeks on our tour. It was a great tour. The only problem was the Thai guy and the way he ate the hotdogs and the boiled eggs. I must say that this Thai couple was very good, and we matched with them nicely in everything except for the way he ate.

During these two weeks of vacation, I asked one of my Sudanese colleagues to replace me in the Middlesex Hospital. He came from Sudan at the same time as me to do the specialization in ophthalmology in London. He could not find a permanent job like me, so he was doing locums, which meant to work for a week or two to cover for doctors in their vacations. I thanked God that He prepared this job for me. Now I felt that God was giving us special care. He arranged for me to work in the Middlesex Hospital, provided us with a two-bedroom flat in the center of London. God even provided us with almost a free tour in Europe.

Chapter 32
From London to Egypt 1974

We finished our studies in London and had a nice time in there. I got my specialization from England in ophthalmology, and Leila got her in dermatology diploma.

We decided to stop by Egypt on our way to Sudan. Leila's family was in Assiut, in the southern part of Egypt. Leila was four months pregnant with Tony. Leila bought all the baby's clothes and even the bottles, a chemical sterilizing system, and a pushchair. Our luggage was over the limit. The airline officer told us that he would consider all the baby's belongings free to travel. When we reached Cairo, we took a taxi to Cairo's central railway station. It was called Bab El-Hadeed, which meant the iron door. We used to pass this railway station every time we visited Assiut. This time we found that the station was extremely dirty. The dirt was all over the windows, doors, and walls. Even the people, most of them wore dirty clothes. We felt that nobody ever cleaned this station since they built it. Apparently, we saw the dirt because we were comparing London stations to Cairo station. Everything was relative. Leila went to the bathroom. She found a fat lady responsible for cleaning the bathroom. The lady told Leila, "You cannot use the bathroom unless you give me the ticket." Leila went out to search for the place to buy the ticket." She went to the train ticket window. When she asked for a ticket to the bathroom, the person laughed. Then he asked Leila,

"Are you from another country?" He explained that the lady meant that Leila must give her one or two cents as a tip to use the bathroom. Everybody in Egypt knew this expression.

We bought the train tickets for the first train going to Assiut. When the train arrived, the crowd was great. We found that we may not be able to enter the train because of the crowd. Apparently, we looked like strangers. Many luggage carriers came to help us. Each one started to carry one bag and went in one direction. I stopped them and told them only one would carry all our bags. In Cairo and all other Egyptian railway stations, those bag carriers were organized by the government. They must wear blue uniforms. Each carrier must have a brass number. The carrier usually gives the passenger the number, and when he finishes his job, he will get back his brass number. The station officials put a big sign with the fees for carrying a bag. No bag carrier accepts those fees. You must pay five to six times the listed fees. All the passengers argue with the carrier about the fees. At last, we managed to enter the train with their help. Even if you booked your seat in advance, there is no guarantee that you will find a seat. On many occasions, there was more than one ticket for the same seat. The bag carrier is the only one that will go first and secure the seat for you. So most of the people will ask the bag carriers to help them in spite of the fact that they can carry their bags. The reason is to secure the seat, find a way to enter the train, and avoid their aggressive behavior if you are not using them. We bought second-class tickets. Before our period in London, we used to go in the second-class car. This was considered special and of a high standard in the 1960s. Only doctors, engineers, and high-ranking government officials go in this second-class carriages. This time despite booking our seats, we found that many passengers were standing around us. The types of people were now entirely different. This time most of the passengers were farmers. Leila asked me, "Are you sure that this is the second class?" We looked at the tickets, and they were second-class tickets. Everything changed during the last two years, which we spent in England. Maybe it was a combination of changes in Egypt and in our expectations after being in London for two years. We felt that all the other passengers were looking at us as foreigners. Leila started to hide everything valuable because she felt they might try to rob us. On that trip, we decided to use the first class for all our future train trips.

We reached the Assiut station. We found that there were more buildings in the Assiut University area. The railway station was recently renovated. It looked cleaner than Cairo station. We found Leila's father and brothers waiting for us. The bag carriers in Assiut did the same thing with us as their colleagues in Cairo. Leila's father rebuked them and told them, "Those are my guests and I will pay the fees for them." The hantour was still there. The hantour owner recognized that we were foreigners. The carriage owners selected the foreigners first because they expected them to pay more. They would not argue with them about the fees because they had no idea about the up-to-date fees. So if the usual cost was fifty cents, they would ask for five dollars.

We went to Leila's parents' house. We were very tired. It was a long journey. Our home in London to Heathrow Airport in London was the beginning of the journey. The end was in Assiut. In addition to the physical exhaustion, there was the tension of adjusting to the culture. I usually feel that the most stressful thing during my visits to Egypt was dealing with the taxi drivers and the luggage carriers. I would be very relaxed if I could avoid those annoying people.

We spent a few days in Assiut. It was a good transition period on our way to Sudan. In Assiut, we heard for the first time about the death of some of our colleagues in college in the war of 1973 between Arabs and Israel. In this war, the Egyptian army did very well. They managed to pass the Bar-Lev Line. This was an huge artificial sand wall built by the Israelis along the east bank of the Suez Canal. This sand wall was a very good barrier. If the Egyptians managed to cross the Suez Canal, they could not climb this sand wall by their tanks. So the Egyptians brought huge water pumps. The function of those pumps was to push the water from the Suez Canal to the sand wall of the Bar-Lev Line. They created passages in the sand wall for their tanks to pass. They sent at the beginning some of their individuals to climb the sand walls and attack the surrounding Israeli troops in those locations. It was a complete surprise to the Israelites. At that time, I remember the London newspapers mentioned that the Egyptians ate the hot meals of the Israelis. After creating the passages through the sand walls, the Egyptian army put their preassembled floating bridges across the Suez Canal. In a few hours, all the Egyptian troops passed the Bar-Lev Line. This was a great victory for the Egyptians and an unexpected defeat for the Israelis. The war went well for a few days for the Egyptians. Then America came to help the Israelis. They started to supply them with new tanks, air fighters, and the most-needed pictures of all the positions of the Egyptian troops. With the American aid, the Israelis managed to pass through a weak point to the West Bank of the Suez Canal. They trapped a small number of the Egyptian troops in Suez City. At that point, the president of Egypt, Anwar El-Sadat asked for a peace agreement. He said that Egypt could not fight against America. He was wise.

I remember during the war I argued with one of the patients in the Middlesex Hospital in London. The patient was a lord. He told me the Egyptian soldiers would lose. He said the reason was that the Egyptian soldiers were not brave; they hid inside the tank, so they could not see well. In contrast, the Israeli soldiers stood with their heads outside the tank and saw better, so they would win the war.

We had a nice time in Assiut with Leila's family. We also met most of our old friends in college. We found a good number of them were teaching at Assiut medical school. We discovered that all the Muslim colleagues were selected to teach. None of the Christians was able to join the university's teaching team even if they were grade-A students.

It was summertime. In Assiut, I like the summer. Many of the food stores put outside their shops icebox containers filled with soft drinks, Coca-Cola, Sprite, and other local drinks. Others sold ice cream. There were specialized stores that sold only sugarcane juice. They had electric machines to squeeze the sugarcane stalks. The customer usually watched this squeezing process. If the sugarcane juice was left for more than five minutes, the taste would be different and not acceptable. Those stores generally had many customers waiting to get some of the sugarcane juice. I like this juice. I used to drink it all my student years and every time I visit Egypt. The price of a big cup was one cent only. In Sudan, we do not have sugarcane juice.

Assiut in the summer was very hot and dry. In Assiut, it was rare to get rain. It may rain every three or four years once. In Leila's parents' house, we usually did not feel the hot weather. It had big rooms with very high ceilings. When we opened the windows, it was much cooler than the rest of Assiut. Besides, they had huge balconies that we used to sit on and enjoy the open air. The only problem was the mosquitoes. In Assiut, mosquitoes were present everywhere. In Leila's parents' house, they use mosquito nets for every bed. There was no malaria in Assiut and all Egypt. In Sudan, malaria was an endemic disease in all areas.

After a few days in Assiut, we went to El-Menia, visiting Leila's sister Nabeela with her husband Sobhi and their daughter Hoda.

Egypt always gave me special feelings. It is a unique country. It has its special features, characteristic culture, and very sociable people.

We proceeded after El-Menia to Cairo on our way to Khartoum. We usually did not stay in Cairo for more than a few hours. We never stayed in hotels in Cairo. The reason was the difficulty to find a room in any of Cairo's hotels without booking in advance.

Chapter 33

Back to Khartoum after Two Years in London

Spending a few days in Egypt before going to Khartoum was a good transition. When we reached Khartoum airport, it was raining. The weather was cooler than in Assiut and Cairo. In Sudan, the rainy season is during autumn. The rain starts in June and ends in late September. Some years there will be heavy rains, and in others it is moderate. In most cases the weather becomes very hot and followed by severe sandstorms, and at last, the rain will follow. The rain will last for a few hours only. The rain usually changes the hot weather to a cool one. This cool weather lasts for a few days, and then the very hot weather will take over to start a new cycle. The sandstorms are very characteristic of Sudan. We usually see sandstorms most of the year, more so from March till September. Some of the sandstorms were very heavy. I remember in heavy ones we had to turn the lights on during the daytime. In Sudan, the habit was to sleep in the yard or on the roof of the house. The roofs were not sloping like in America or England. If there is a sand storm, we usually try to cover ourselves and continue sleeping. In most cases, we had to carry our beds and go inside. The reason is that the strong wind will take away the covers. If we managed to stay outside, the next morning we would be completely covered with a heavy layer of fine dust. Sometimes we resisted to go inside the rooms, but the rain would follow the sandstorm, the layer of dust would convert to mud. Staying inside the room would just reduce the amount of dust from the sandstorm. In the morning you had to wash your face before doing anything because it is completely covered by dust, very fine dust. Cleaning the house was a big problem during the sandstorm season. It was not just the floor but practically everything in the house. Most of the house cleaners, called servants in Sudan, usually leave during this season. Sometimes the sandstorms come every day. There is no way to ignore the cleaning of the house after the storm. Without cleaning, you cannot eat, drink, or sit because the dust is covering every object in the house. After an annual vacation, when we come back, the dust will be accumulating from many storms. We usually change the bedsheets and sleep. When we get up, then we start the difficult job of cleaning the house. Luckily enough, we usually had a servant working with us most of the time.

When we arrived in Khartoum, both of us were specialized doctors. We thought that we could afford a high standard of living in Sudan. Our first task was to find a house to live in. We started to search by asking relatives and friends. Then we asked the real estate agents, called dallaleen or dallal for a single one. Our salaries at that time were about 120 Sudanese pounds for each of us. The rent of an average house in the Khartoum New Extension, Al-Imtedad, was above our combined salaries. We dropped the idea of renting a complete house and thought of renting a flat. We saw a few of them, but none was suitable to live in. I remember one of them was small with a very dim bathroom, which had no windows. When we mentioned that, the broker simply pulled one of the bricks from the wall of the bathroom to solve the problem. My friend Adil was aware of our search. One day he told me that his father-in-law had a flat which was on the second floor of their house. It had three rooms and a big hall, in addition to a verandah and uncovered a wide area about fifteen by fifteen meters, and they called it terrace. Their problem was that they want reliable tenants. We rented their apartment for sixty Sudanese pounds a month. It was in Al-Imtedad. We were very lucky to have this flat. First, the price was very reasonable. More important than this was that we found them to be very good friends. They were very friendly and like our family. We spent all our time in Khartoum in their flat till we moved after about eighteen months to another city, Halfa Al-Jadeeda. Actually, after spending seven and a half years in Halfa Al-Jadeeda, we returned to Khartoum. God arranged that this same flat was vacant, so we rented it again.

This family moved in 1993 to Canada. We visited them in Canada in 1996, and they came to visit us in Boston in 1997.

I returned to Khartoum Eye Hospital to work as a junior eye specialist. I started to do more eye surgeries. Dr. Haroun was my boss when I was doing the internship in ophthalmology. He was leaving for one year to do a special course in Austria. He asked me to work for him in his private clinic. It was a good chance for me to get used to the private clinics. At the same time, it gave me some extra income.

Khartoum Eye Hospital was one of the best hospitals in Sudan. This was because of the good leaders that it had. First there was Dr. Hussein Ahmed Hussein who was the first Sudanese ophthalmologist. He retired at that time, but he usually came every day to the hospital. He used to work in the clinic twice a week. He never missed any clinical meetings. He was about eighty years old. Many times I used to give him a ride to his home. He was very pleasant to speak with. The director of the hospital and at the same time, the senior ophthalmologist, was Dr. Abd-Elgadir. He was an excellent doctor. He made a lot of improvements in the ophthalmology departments all over Sudan and in Khartoum Eye Hospital. He gave me a lot of encouragement in all my career. He used to treat each doctor as a personal friend. I learned a lot during this period in ophthalmology and social relations. I was very happy with all the conditions in Khartoum Eye Hospital.

Leila joined Khartoum Hospital department of dermatology. This was located in the center of Khartoum. It had two stories. On the lower floor, there was an outpatient clinic and male in-patient wards. On the top floor, there were female wards and the offices of the doctors. Leila worked in this department before our period in London. Leila is very observant. She can detect any unusual thing very easily. For example, sometimes, when we are walking in the street, she may notice that the man who just passed has one leg shorter than the other. For me, I may not be able to recognize that even after she mentioned it to me. This is the reason that Leila was a very good dermatologist.

Our first few days in Khartoum was very difficult. The reason was the change of traffic in Sudan from driving to the left side of the street to the right side of the street in 1974. During the change, we were in England. When we started driving in Khartoum after returning to Khartoum, it was very confusing. When you are accustomed to driving on this street to the left all your life, it will become automatic to go to this side of the street. I felt this more when the street had no other cars. It took me about one week or more to adapt to the new way of driving. It is strange that only England, India, and Sudan were adopting to driving to the left side of the street. Sudan and India were British colonies. Sudan discovered that all the car manufacturers put extra fees to put the driving wheel on the right side instead of the left side. The first five to seven years after the change, all the old cars had their driving wheels on the left and driving on the right. For our last five years in Sudan (1985–1990), we had one car with a driving wheel to the left, and the other car had the wheel on the right side. The car with the right-side driving wheel was a Land Rover. We bought this Land Rover second hand from a pilot who brought it from England. Leila used to go to Khartoum during the last weeks of her pregnancies for her deliveries when we were living in Halfa Al-Jadeeda. The reason was that Leila had a blood group Rh-negative, and my blood group was Rh-positive. So Leila had to take immediately after each delivery a certain injection. Those injections were not available in Halfa Al-Jadeeda.

Also the care in Khartoum was much better than in Halfa. During our stay in Khartoum, waiting for Leila's delivery in 1976, we saw a Land Rover car with a sign For Sale. We thought that this was the most suitable car for Halfa El-Jadeeda. Actually, even in many parts of Khartoum, this was the only car that you could drive safely in the rainy season. I drove the new car from Khartoum to Halfa Al-Jadeeda. Leila took the airplane. This was the time of delivery of Sandra in August 1976. We had the Land Rover car from 1976 till we left Sudan in 1990. We drove it several times from Halfa El-Jadeeda to Khartoum. This was a nine-hour drive. Also once we drove to Kassala, which was about three hours from Halfa El-Jadeeda.

During this period in Khartoum, we had good friends. Adel and Gamal were my friends at Assiut University. With their wives Mervat and Huda, we used to visit regularly and go to picnics. Sometimes we go to picnics with some of our big families. Also, we used to invite the other Sudanese students from Assiut University. Most of them were bachelors at that time like Sameer, Farouk, Atteya, and many others. I remember once we arranged a meeting for all the Sudanese students of Assiut University in Khartoum. We met in the military officers club in Khartoum. One of our colleagues was an engineer in the military forces, so he arranged this nice place. There were at least one hundred and twenty people. The students came with their wives and children. It was very nice to see many of them after a few years. We were unable to repeat this again because most of us moved to different cities in Sudan or outside Sudan.

The policy of the Ministry of Health in Sudan was to transfer all the doctors every few years from one city to another. After spending one year and three months in Khartoum, they decided to transfer Leila and me to work in Halfa Al-Jadeeda. We moved to Halfa Al-Jadeeda in November 1975.

Chapter 34

The Journey between Khartoum and Halfa Al-Jadeeda 1975–1983

Halfa Al-Jadeeda is about 800 miles from Khartoum. When we moved to Halfa Al-Jadeeda for the first time in 1975, the most convenient way of transportation was the train. We had to take a train from Khartoum to Khashm El-Girba. Then another local train that traveled between Khashm El-Girba and Halfa Al-Jadeeda. The distance between Halfa Al-Jadeeda and Khashm El-Girba was about forty-five minutes by car. By train, it was usually in the best conditions for two hours. I remember once it took us six hours to make this trip by train. When I asked about the reason, they told me that the railway accountant was giving the salaries of the railway employees working in between. This was the reason that most of the people used their cars to avoid unexplained delays. For us, I usually try to avoid using the hospital cars for our annual vacation trips. In the rainy season, the train was the only way. The journey between Halfa Al-Jadeeda and Khartoum usually took about twenty-two hours. In the rainy season, it might take several days.

I remember once we traveled from Khartoum and reached Khashm El-Girba after two days. The headmaster of Khashm El-Girba station told me that there was an American lady with her daughter traveling to Halfa Al-Jadeeda for the first time. He asked us to help her to find a place to stay when she reached Halfa Al-Jadeeda. She was from a Middle

Eastern origin. She was an anthropologist. Her daughter was six years old. When we met her, she mentioned that her food supply was out. She calculated the distance, and she was expecting the journey from Khartoum to Halfa Al-Jadeeda to take about six hours. We already spent two days on the train from Khartoum to Khashm El-Girba. The train usually traveled once a week. At the end of our period in Halfa Al-Jadeeda in 1976 and after that, the train journeys stopped completely.

The second way to travel between Khartoum and Halfa Al-Jadeeda was by bus. From 1976 to 1980 there was only one way. This was a direct way on the unpaved road, Bottanna way. It usually took about ten hours with one stop in between for fifteen minutes.

We used the bus on many of our trips to Khartoum. All the buses stop in the rainy season. Because of the unpaved road, the journey was very tough. The bus shook the passengers all the time. You could not drink on the bus or read. I remember in one of those journeys, one of my friends was sitting in the third row at the back. The bus went through a rough part of the road, and my friend found himself flying up. His head hit the roof of the bus. A hole was created in the bus ceiling. My friend was in great pain. When he reached Khartoum, the doctor discovered that he crushed three of his backbones, lumbar vertebrae. He never returned to his work after that.

There were no toilets on the bus. The bus used to stop once during the ten-hour journey. The bus stop was a small cottage and attached to it was a partially shaded verandah. There were no toilets at this bus stop. The passengers usually walked a few feet away and used the ground as toilet. You could buy food and tea from this stop. The food was freshly cooked. When you saw the pot they cooked the food in and the plates they used, you'd decide immediately not to eat. We never ate at this station. Once I decided to drink tea. I paid the money. The owner of the place started to pour the tea for me. He put a strainer full of tea leaves over the empty cup. When he began to pour the tea from the big teapot, I stopped him. I told him that the tea which was coming from the teapot was dark enough for me. I did not want more tea leaves. His answer was a little surprising for me. He said that what was coming from the teapot was just water without any tea. I discovered that their water was almost brown. This was due to the presence of many impurities in it. Of course, I drank the tea. Since the water was hot, it was safe.

I remember once we were traveling between Khartoum and Halfa Al-Jadeeda by bus. As I mentioned, there were no towns or villages in between except for the poor bus stop. On that journey, the bus suddenly stopped. When I asked, they told me, "The bus lost all the engine oil." The reason was when they changed the engine oil in Khartoum, they did not close the drainage knob securely. With the shaking of the bus, the drainage knob gradually loosened then it dropped completely. There was nothing seen all around except for a few bushes; each was about one foot long. Two or three groups of passengers started to go in different directions.

The hope of one of the groups was to find a village. After about one hour, one group found a small village. The village residents came with their small truck. They insisted on cooking meals for all the bus passengers. The bus had about fifty-five passengers. The village was a very small one. The people of the village were very poor. The habit in such places was to spend all that they had to give food to the visitors even if they did not know them. In about half an hour, they brought the food, and everybody started to eat and drink. In the meantime, a group went to search for the missing oil drainage knob. Luckily enough, they found it. From the village they found oil for the bus. In about three hours, the bus was back on the road.

Those buses usually travel once a day each way. At a certain time, there was another company who had another bus the same way as the other.

In about 1976, the government with the help of many other countries managed to construct a new highway. This highway was between Khartoum the capital and Port Sudan, the port on the Red Sea. This was the only paved highway in Sudan. It had one lane in each way. The maximum speed on most of the highway was 55 kilometers per hour. This was equivalent to 35 miles per hour. For Sudan this was considered very high speed. I think inside Khartoum, the permissible high speed was about 30 kilometers per hour which was less than 20 miles per hour. In most of the streets, it was only 15 miles per hour.

With the newly paved highway between Khartoum and Port Sudan, the buses shifted their passage to use the newly paved highway. So the bus used to go on an unpaved road from Halfa Al-Jadeeda to Khashm El-Girba. Then the bus joined the paved highway from Khashm El-Girba to Khartoum. The journey with the bus in a new way used to take about ten hours. The journey this way was much more comfortable than the unpaved Bottanna way. There were two stops on the way with some toilet facilities. You could buy in those new bus stops bottled soda, sandwiches, and tea made with clean water. The buses were still the same ones that were used in the old Bottanna way. The buses had no air conditioner.

In Sudan, the weather was always very hot. The temperature was usually above 100 F. In the summer, it could reach above 120 F. So the bus journey was still not comfortable because of the hot weather. The bus windows must be open to bring air. With the open windows, a good amount of dust would come in as well. The amount of dust in the paved road was much less than in the unpaved Bottanna way.

In 1976 we bought a Land Rover, a four-wheel car. The first journey was from Khartoum, where we purchased it, to Halfa Al-Jadeeda. Leila was not fit for that journey. She just gave birth to Sandra. So Leila took the plane to Halfa Al-Jadeeda and I drove. On our later journeys, Leila and the children joined me in the car journey. We found that the journey was too long. So we started to stop in Al-Gedaref, which was about four hours from Halfa Al-Jadeeda. In Al-Gedaref we had friends. Our friends were the priest of the evangelical church of Al-Gedaref Morad and his family. We get to know him first through the Catholic priest in Halfa Al-Jadeeda. The Catholic church in Halfa Al-Jadeeda was next to the Coptic Orthodox church. There were three priests in the Catholic church. One of them was from France, and the second was from England and the third from Belgium. All of them were good friends. They used to visit us at our house. One of them used to go to the area of the sugar factory. He used to do Sunday service for the Christian employees there. He noticed that some of the Christians did not attend the service. When he asked them, they told him that they belong to the evangelical church. There was no evangelical church in the Halfa Al-Jadeeda area. So the Catholic priest went to Al-Gedaref where there was an evangelical church and priest. He convinced the evangelical priest to come with him to Halfa Al-Jadeeda in his car. He took him to the sugar factory area. The evangelical priest Morad did the service. In the end, he brought him to our house for a visit. Then he drove him back to Al-Gedaref. This was the first time for us to know Rev. Morad. We discovered that he had part of his studies in Assiut American school. He mentioned that he knew Leila's father Hezkial.

The three Catholic priests were very godly people. I remember at a certain time there was a shortage of car gas. One of them insisted on using a bike to go to the sugar factory area to do a regular Sunday service. The distance was about 15 miles, and the road was unpaved and very rough. The French priest told me that he served in Algeria in a Muslim-populated area. He spent 30 years in that area. He said that he was happy because he gained one person to Christ.

The English priest told me about one of his journeys to Al-Gedaref. It was the beginning of the rainy season. The bus he took was a local bus that traveled only between Halfa Al-Jadeeda and Al-Gedaref. In the middle of the journey, it started to rain heavily, and the bus was stuck in the mud. They stayed in that place one day. There was no water on the bus. The only source of water was the collection of rainwater in the mud. All the passengers started to take some water from over the mud and drank it. The English priest said to himself, "I am British. I will not drink that dirty water." After many hours, he felt very weak because of the dehydration. In the end, he filled his hand with water and drank it. He said that he developed after that severe diarrhea. He went to the doctor and took different medications. He was very sick for two weeks.

Our main problem with the car journey was the shortage of petrol. At that time it was impossible to go to any gas station and fill the car with gas. You have to get permission for a limited amount of gas from the authorities. So in all such journeys, we had to fill a big barrel with gas and put it inside the car. We stopped a few times during the journey to fill the car from the barrel. If the gas ran out, we could not replace it. There was no way to buy any gas for the car in any city.

Once, we were traveling from Khartoum to Halfa Al-Jadeeda. We took the train from Khartoum. When we reached Al-Gedaref, the train stopped because of heavy rain. We contacted the military authorities in Al-Gedaref. They gave us one of their huge trucks to take us to Khashm El-Girba. To get in the truck was a problem. The truck was about three feet high from the ground. In Khashm El-Girba they took us to the house of the director of the military area. Leila discovered that the wife of that high-rank military person had a fight with her husband. When we came in, Leila found the wife putting her clothes in a suitcase ready to leave her husband permanently. This was the first time for us to see those people. The lady complained that her husband came very late every night. She thought that he spent his nights with prostitutes. At the same time, the husband told me that he stayed at his office every night studying for his master's degree. Leila started to talk with the wife and explained that her husband was studying every night. After a few minutes, the lady changed her mind. She put her clothes back, and then she prepared dinner for us. Later they became good friends with us and visited us a few times in Halfa Al-Jadeeda. I remember that I was uncomfortable when he took his pistol and put it on the table in our house. I do not like pistols in my house. In rural areas of Sudan, you have to help people, and some people will help you, without knowing them.

Chapter 35

New Halfa, the Largest Planned Mass Movement of People

The story of New Halfa started when Egypt built the high dam of Aswan in 1960. It was a very good project with great benefits to Egypt.

The dam started gradually to collect a huge amount of water, the Nasser Lake.

The level of water was very high. Many villages in southern Egypt and northern Sudan were completely and permanently immersed in water. More importantly the largest Sudanese city in northern Sudan, Wadi Halfa, was buried underwater. I saw this city before the flood and after. The last thing I saw was the tip of the minaret of the big mosque. I was very sad.

A big project started in 1961 to create a new home for those displaced people.

The Sudanese government decided to use a large area in the eastern part of Sudan.

The New Halfa Project was a 164,000-acre site constructed in 1964 to house 50,000 Nubians displaced from Wadi Halfa and the villages around it. Also it was to accommodate the nomads who were living in this area.

There was a great difference in the weather between Wadi Halfa where there was hardly any rain to New Halfa where there was a lot of rain.

Difficulty to travel in New Halfa during rainy season

New Halfa during heavy rain

Until I left New Halfa in 1983, the only paved road was 1/8 of a mile inside the hospital.

For the Nubians, this was a great shock to see the lightning and hear the thunder and then the heavy rain in addition to missing their homeland.

New Halfa map

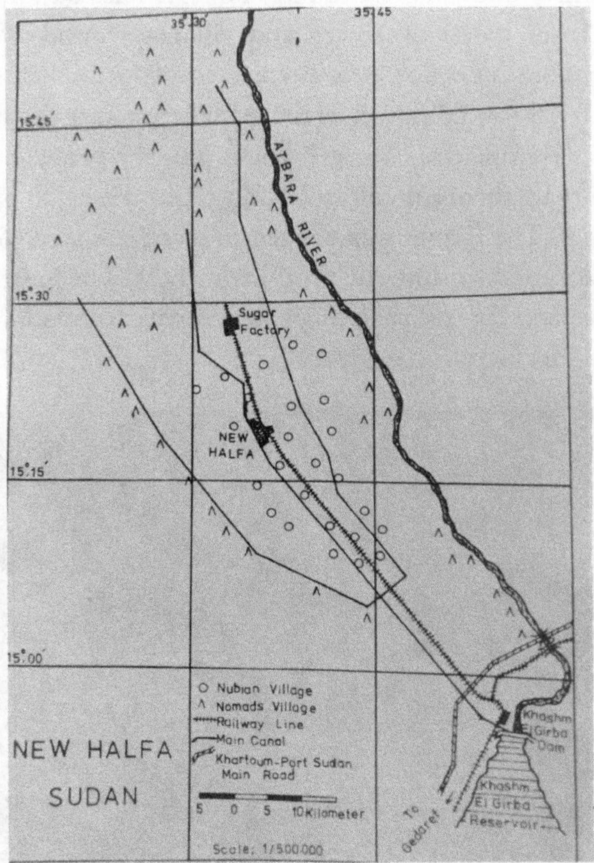

Moving from Wadi Halfa to Halfa Al-Jadeeda

It is a city in the eastern part of Sudan. It was built about 1962 to replace the old city Wadi Halfa. They moved all the people from that area to the eastern part of Sudan. It was the largest planned mass mobilization of people from one area to another in Africa. The distance between Wadi Halfa and Halfa Al-Jadeeda was about one thousand and two hundred miles. It took the authorities a few months to complete this difficult job.

The area where they built Halfa Al-Jadeeda was an area where many herding tribes lived. They then built a new town and called it

Halfa Al-Jadeeda for the people coming from Wadi Halfa City. Also, they built thirty-one villages around Halfa Al-Jadeeda for the people who came from the small towns and villages around Wadi Halfa. Each family got a new house as a replacement for their lost house in Wadi Halfa. All the houses in Halfa Al-Jadeeda and the new thirty-one villages were made of concrete blocks. For the people living in the villages, they gave them agricultural land to cultivate. Each piece of land was four acres. The farmer was obliged to plant one acre with peanut, the second acre with cotton, the third with wheat. The fourth to be left without any plant for one year. They would have to rotate regularly to keep the land fertile.

A Nubian village house

For the nomad tribes who were in the area before this transition, they gave them land to cultivate as well. They also gave them villages around their new lands. These villages were composed of huts only.

A nomad village

This transition was difficult for the Halfaweyeen who came from Wadi Halfa. Their original land was adjacent to the River Nile. Some of them were farmers but for very small lands. They were doing everything manually. In Halfa Al-Jadeeda, they had to use tractors and harvesting machines. They also use certain machines to cut off the ripe wheat and crush it and pack the grain in big sachets. For the peanut, there was a special machine to pick the ripe peanuts from the ground. For the cotton, they had to pick the cotton flowers manually. During the cotton season, they gave the school students special permission to go and help in picking the cotton.

The other difficulty for the Halfaweyeen was the weather. In Wadi Halfa it was always dry, and it may rain every five or six years once. In Halfa Al-Jadeeda the rainy season was about four months every year. The rain was usually heavy in August and September. Some of the villages became almost isolated for a few days. Most of the cars were stuck in the mud because there were no paved roads.

Tractors were the only way of transportation.

All the cars, even the four-wheel-drive ones would be stuck in the muddy, unpaved streets.

I heard a joke about the Halfaweyeen. Immediately after they arrived in Halfa Al-Jadeeda, there was a thunderstorm. The lightning was making the sky very bright at night. One of the Halfaweyeen told his friend, "God looked for us in Wadi Halfa, and He was unable to find us, then God is now using his penlight to search for us here."

For the Arab nomads, the difficulty was to change their careers to be farmers. They also had to change their lifestyle.

Nomad village after the rain

Their old life as nomads was a constant movement from one place to another according to the availability of water and wildly grown grass. Now they have to settle and stay in their villages for all their life.

I remember that an American anthropologist came to New Halfa especially from New York to do research about the changes in the lifestyle of the Arabs in the Halfa Al-Jadeeda area.

I was astonished by the way the authorities distributed the people in Halfa Al-Jadeeda. They settled the people according to their ethnic origin, not only the Arabs and the Halfaweyeen but among the Halfaweyeen themselves. All the people from a certain ethnic group would be in the same village or in the same area in Halfa Al-Jadeeda. For example, there was an area of Halfa Al-Jadeeda for El-Basalwa.

Those were people who came a few generations ago from a small town in the southern part of Egypt called Besaleya. Their skin was not as dark as the others. Their hair was dark and smooth compared to the curly hair of the other Halfaweyeen. They speak Arabic.

Another ethnic group called Majarab was living in village 18. Those people were known as immigrants from Hungary, which was called Majar in Arabic. Those people had the same skin color as the other Halfaweyeen, but their eyes were green. I heard that some Hungarians came to Wadi Halfa tens of years ago and the Majarab were their descendants. They speak Halfawi like most of the Halfaweyeen. This is a spoken and not written language. It is not related to the Arabic language at all. Most of the older women could not speak Arabic. I learned some words during my period in Halfa Al-Jadeeda so I could communicate with them. It was nice when the patient recognized that you are trying to learn his language.

Some people of their origin was Aswan, which is the largest southern city in Egypt. They settled this group in a certain area in Halfa Al-Jadeeda. Our private clinic was in this area.

All the Copts were in another area, including the house of the priest of the Coptic Orthodox church.

I was not convinced at the beginning of these strict ethnic divisions. Later I discovered that most of the people were happy with this ethnic segregation.

The Arabs, this is the name that the Halfaweyeen call the nomads in the area before their immigration. Those are of the Shukreya tribe. Their original language is Arabic. They have the same skin color as the Halfaweyeen. All the Arabs are living in their villages around Halfa Al-Jadeeda, and not in the city. The Shukreya tribe is one of the high standard tribes in Sudan. It is a big tribe. They live mainly in the central-eastern part of Sudan. Many of their children get high standard education and are now living in different cities in Sudan. They are very famous for their poetry.

The good thing that no ethnic conflicts or wars happened between the Arabs and the Halfaweyeen.

All the government employees were living in the Haye El-Mowazafeen. There was an area for the high-ranking officials. This was where we lived. The middle-ranking employees had their area next to our area. Then the last area for the low-ranking employees.

Our house in New Halfa

When we arrived at Halfa Al-Jadeeda, they gave us a nice big house, the house for the ophthalmologist. It had two bedrooms, a dining room, and a sitting room. It had two big verandahs; both of them had mosquito nets. Mosquitoes were present in all parts of Sudan, but more in the agricultural areas such as Halfa Al-Jadeeda.

Surrounding the building area of the house, there was a huge yard, limited by the house walls. The walls were about two and a half meters high, built like the rest of the house by concrete blocks. The yard was huge.

We found a palm tree and one shade tree. During our seven and half years in Halfa, we planted four guava trees, a mango tree, three lemon trees, and a tree called gishtta. We used to put our two cars in a small part of the front yard.

Breakfast in our yard

There was also a room and a bathroom for the servants. We never used this room because the servants were girls, and they were afraid to sleep alone in the servants' room. They used to sleep with the children in one of the rooms inside the building or in the dining room. In addition to the servant girl, we had a male servant who was responsible for washing our clothes and ironing them. Once a week we had a gardener come to take care of the garden. One of the main jobs of the gardener was to bring male seeds from a male palm tree to fertilize our tree. When he did this at the right time, we could get dates from our tree. If he neglected this important step, the produced dates would be small and very bitter. We used to eat from our tree very tasty dates every year. We ate guavas from our trees for a few years. Also we ate gishtta from our garden.

The house had a big door. It was big enough to let our cars get inside the house. I made a special metal bar to keep the door closed and let anybody open the door from inside or outside. We usually lock the house door only when we leave for our annual vacation. In most cases when we return from our vacation, I lose the key for the lock of the house door. So I had to break the lock to be able to enter the house. Our other problem with the door was our neighbors' goats. They used to push our house door and squeeze their bodies into our house. The reason was the green plants they see in our garden. I remember once I made a metal skeleton to shade our cars. I then planted a creeping plant to create the needed shade. The creeping plant grew nicely and very rapidly. One day when we returned from work, we found that the goats came in and ate the stem of the creeping plant. The next day the rest of the plant died. Because the door was big and its design was not good, we dropped the idea of the car shade.

Immediately outside the main building of the house, there was an area of the yard elevated and covered by bricks. We called it *mastaba*. We used it to put our chairs in the afternoons to drink our tea. On hot days we sprinkled water over the bricks, the weather would be cool and nice. The weather in Sudan is always dry, so the humidity will give a cooling effect.

The sewage system in Halfa Al-Jadeeda was unique. The drainage tubes led to a septic tank, which drained to a special primitive well. This well was about three feet deep and was filled with bricks. Most of the wells remain functioning well for many years. Some needed to change the bricks after a few years. We were lucky because in our house this did not happen during our seven and half years of living there. The water in Halfa Al-Jadeeda was clean and without a bad taste. It was coming from the Atbara River. There was an electricity supply in Halfa Al-Jadeeda and all the Halfaweyeen villages, but no electricity in all the Arabs.

The streets in Halfa Al-Jadeeda were wide and straight, but not paved.

Halfa Al-Jadeeda was a limited-sized town. Most of the people know each other. When I went to the market to buy anything, all the merchants knew me and immediately addressed me as Dr. Victor. In Sudan and Egypt, we used the first name and not the last name. When I drove, I almost knew most of the passing cars. I knew, for example, that this was the car of the president of the agricultural scheme. I knew that he would take a left on the next crossing to go to his office, and I would drive accordingly.

Living in Halfa Al-Jadeeda was comfortable for us because all the people respected us very much. They gave us special treatment. For example, if there was a shortage of gas for cars, they gave us special permission for extra quantity. As you expect, I was the only eye doctor in the Halfa Al-Jadeeda area. Leila was the only skin doctor as well.

If I went for my annual vacation, all the patients would wait for me till I came back. Only the extreme emergencies were obliged to go to the nearest eye doctor in Kassala, which was about a three-hour drive.

Most of the patients were farmers, and many of them were illiterate, especially women. They appreciated the service that I gave them. I remember one of my patients. She was a sixty-five-year-old woman. I did a cataract operation for her in the hospital. There was no charge for all the treatments and surgeries in the government hospital. She was happy with the improvement in her vision after the surgery. To show me her appreciation, she gave me a gift of one and a half cents. I usually did not accept any money from the patients, so I refused. But she insisted, and I felt that she would be upset if I insisted on refusing. So I accepted her gift. Another similar patient gave me three eggs.

One of my patients saw me on the train when we were traveling to Port Sudan for our annual vacation. We were about seven hours away from Halfa Al-Jadeeda. She told me, "I lost my prescription that you gave me three months ago. Can you write it to me now?"

Building a new operating theater for the eye department

When I arrived at Halfa Al-Jadeeda, I found the eye department was in bad condition. On the first operating day and after the first operation, we had to cancel the rest of the operations. There was an emergency cesarean section. We were using the same operating theater as the surgery and obstetrics. On that day, I decided to build a new operating theater special for the eye department. I contacted the officials in the Ministry of Health and asked for that. Their simple answer was there were no funds. I immediately contacted the officials in the agricultural scheme. I explained to them the importance of having a separate operating theater. I also convinced them that I was treating their farmers. I asked them to purchase the operating theater instruments. I went to Khartoum and ordered all that I needed. Also, I raised funds from different places. A new building was erected. There were up-to-date instruments for the operating theater and refraction department a few weeks later. One of my patients had a workshop building chairs. I showed him a picture of the transport stretcher trolley. I asked him to make a similar simple one. He made two of them and donated them.

In a few weeks, I started the eye surgeries twice a week, five to seven operations each day.

For the wards, all the bedsheets were dirty and old. I contacted some merchants, and I persuaded them to donate new sheets for the eye wards.

There was no dermatology department in Halfa Al-Jadeeda Hospital. I arranged a room in the eye department, and we created a new dermatology clinic for Leila.

The dermatology department became very busy.

When we left New Halfa, the Ministry of Health was obliged to send a dermatologist to the New Halfa dermatology department.

The hospital of Halfa Al-Jadeeda was, as expected, a new hospital. It had a general outpatient department. There were specialists in medicine, surgery, obstetrics and gynecology, pediatrics, and I was the ophthalmologist, and Leila was the dermatologist. There were about six general-duty doctors, and they rotate between the different departments and the general outpatient. There was a hospital director, who was the oldest specialist. Most of the time, the director was the physician. There was also a *hakeem basha*. Hakeem means doctor, and basha means in the Turkish language the boss. The hakeem basha was the oldest general doctor. He was responsible for the nurses and the general-duty doctors. During our period in Halfa Al-Jadeeda, two doctors were doing their internship in the hospital. One of them did part of her internship in the eye department.

Chapter 36

Two Eye Conferences in the USA in 1980 with a Limited Budget

When I started to do my thesis in glaucoma, I discovered that I have to review the literature to get up-to-date information on this subject. I tried to read all the papers written about the surgical treatment of glaucoma. I went to Khartoum University Medical School Library. I discovered that they had a limited number of ophthalmology magazines. To my surprise, I found that the last four years were missing. When I asked them, they told me that because there was not enough money, they were obliged to stop their subscription to those magazines. I found that the only way to get those was to go to England or the USA. I found that there would be two conferences about glaucoma in the USA in April 1980. I decided to go. I tried to get some financial help from Khartoum University and the Ministry of Health in Sudan. Both of them refused because they had no funds. I booked for the two conferences, and we decided that Leila would join me on this journey.

We planned to visit first Egypt and to leave Tony, Sandra, and Jennie with Leila's parents in Assiut. We thought of visiting England on our way to America.

The two conferences, one was in Orlando, Florida, and the other in New Orleans, Louisiana. There was a difference of about one week in between.

In medicine, the medical book usually is five years old in its information. For scientific magazines, any paper is about two years older than the present state of the art. Any paper presented at a scientific conference is usually one year older than the up-to-date information.

I insisted on being up-to-date and attending those two conferences. I planned for this journey for a long time before the expected date of the conferences. This was difficult because we were living in Halfa Al-Jadeeda, which was away from the capital. The telephones were unusable. A call from Halfa Al-Jadeeda to Khartoum was usually difficult to do, and the lines were unclear. So the only way was the post office. To send a letter to America and receive the response usually took about a month in the best conditions. I contacted the Institute of Ophthalmology in London, where I studied for some time. I asked the dean of the institute if I could use their library to take photocopies of the papers I need. His answer was upsetting. He told me that I have to be a full-time student to do that. I contacted one of the ophthalmologists who was a teacher in the institute and was one of my good friends. He told me to forget about what the dean said and just come and go to the library and do whatever I wanted.

The good thing about Sudan was our vacations were forty-five days. So we drove to the capital by our own Land Rover car. We then took the flight to Cairo. From Cairo we took the train to Assiut where Leila's parents lived; it was a six-hour journey. We spent a few days in Assiut so the children were acquainted with their grandparents. Jennie was three months old at that time. This was the first time for us to leave the children. It was tough for the children and us. We left Assiut, Leila and me. This was a nice time that we could spend time together alone. We booked in Lillian Penson Hall for the time that we would spend in London. This student lodge was the place we lived in for the first six months when we were in London in 1973. It was nice to go back and live there. We found everything was more expensive than before. This was more evident with our limited budget. I went to the Institute of Ophthalmology in London, and I did what my friend told me to do. I went to the library and started to photocopy the articles that I needed.

I did some of them, but the photocopy in the library was 10 pence for each page. I did some of them, and I was unable to find others.

Leila started to get abdominal colics. I took her to St. Mary's Hospital. They diagnosed her with a gallbladder problem. We asked for the advice of our friend Dr. Zoser. He was a surgeon in Sudan and did his fellowship in London. He worked for many years as a senior registrar (resident) in surgery. He discovered that he would not get a job as a surgeon in a teaching hospital in London because he was not of English origin. He had citizenship, but he had to be of English origin to get such a job. So he changed his career to radiology. He started to be a registrar in radiology then a senior registrar. He was hoping to get a job as a radiologist in a teaching hospital in London. He lost about six years of his life to do this transition. Dr. Zoser advised us to postpone our travel to America for a few days. We did and stayed this extra time with my brother Nabeel and his wife Suzy and their son David. We celebrated our tenth wedding anniversary with them. From London, we bought a Greyhound bus ticket which was open for any travel in the USA and Canada for a whole month. The cost was forty English pounds—those tickets you could only buy from London and not from the USA.

We managed to fly from London to New York. In New York, Leila's sister Suad and her husband David were waiting for us at the airport. We stayed with them for a few days. We went with Suad to see the World Trade Center, the Statue of Liberty, and the United Nations Headquarters.

We had a good time with them. David was very generous to the extent that he became very angry when I tried to pay for some of what we bought together in the supermarket.

Leila in New York, Statue of Liberty

From New York, we took the Greyhound bus to Washington, DC. We locked out bags in the bus station. They had lockers for storing luggage. You pay a quarter for two hours. It was very convenient. We washed our faces and started to take a tour of the city and in the end, came back to take the next bus to our next destination.

The Greyhound buses were very convenient. They had a toilet inside the bus. The chair could be reclined. Every two hours there was a big stop that you could go and eat and come back to join the same bus. Most of the bus stations had freshly cooked food. In small stations, there was ready-made food and microwaves to heat it. This was the first time for us to use the microwave. Leila told me I was not going to gamble by putting the food in this thing. I remember in one of the stations there was a blood pressure machine that worked using coins. Most of the stations had small TV sets in every chair in the waiting area. I think now the bus stations were of much less quality than in 1980.

The journey from New York to Orlando, Florida, took more than twenty-four hours because we stopped in Washington, DC. We enjoyed the journey very much because this was our first time in such places. We were very impressed by the high technology and facilities in America. We were comparing our journeys from Halfa Al-Jadeeda to Khartoum where the stops had no toilets, to here where there was a toilet inside the bus.

I noticed that the buses were always half empty. Also, I noticed that most of the people were of low class. I had no idea that most of the people either fly or drive. I thought that with such high-quality service, all the people would use the Greyhound buses.

Chapter 37

Conference in Orlando, Florida, Staying in a Caravan

We reached Orlando in the morning. It was an exhausting, long journey, but we enjoyed it. In the Greyhound Bus Station, there was a list of hotels and different places to live in. For each listing, there was a telephone number to dial and contact them immediately. We contacted different places, and at last, we decided to choose the cheapest. It was a big caravan with a bed, a small kitchen, and a bath.

In Orlando, we stayed in a caravan

The owners were an old couple living in their house at the same place. They were very nice and friendly. The place was very comfortable for us. We used to go to the supermarket and buy fresh ingredients and Leila used to cook. This was the cheapest way to live at that time. At night when we came back, the old couple came and invited us to their house. They started to ask where we came from. When we told them from Sudan and Egypt, they had no clue where these countries were.

At last, they asked if this was near Turkey. We explained that it was in Africa. Then they asked again if Africa was near Turkey. They said that they knew some people who came from Turkey. We discovered that some Americans knew very little about the outside world. The next morning the old lady brought some honey to Leila as a present. The next night they invited us to their home and showed us the pictures of their children. On Sunday, we went to the nearby church. In the church, they gave us cards to fill and greet us. They were very friendly. When we returned to Sudan, we received a letter from this church.

On Monday we went to the ophthalmology conference. I discovered how they arranged those conferences in a very high-quality way. The fees for the conference were high, but for residents, they had a special, low price. I brought a special letter from Sudan, certifying that I was a resident. When I spoke to the registration desk about this, the secretary told me OK. So I started to look for the letter. She told me no need to do that, just pay the resident's fees. I was amazed because in Sudan and Egypt, we had to prove everything.

Victor in Kennedy Space Center

Orlando is one of the most famous places for tourists. First, there is Disney World, which is one of the greatest amusement places in America. Secondly, there is the Kennedy Space Center.

There are many other places to visit. We spent about a week in Orlando. It was great. In spite of our limited budget, we managed to visit all those places. Leila got a T-shirt with her name from Disney World. We took many pictures.

Leila visiting Disney, Florida

We visited Miami City and Miami Beach. The weather in Miami was very humid. In Miami, I remember we went to a place near the harbor. In that place, there were many ugly huge-shaped birds.

In Miami Beach, we went and Leila swam there. I just pulled my trousers up and went into the water. The water was very shallow from a long distance.

Leila in Miami Beach, Florida

Chapter 38

Another Conference in New Orleans, Living in YMCA

My next conference was in New Orleans, Louisiana. It was more than twelve hours from Orlando by the Greyhound bus. With our bus tickets, we had the choice to stop at any place and stay for as long as we wished and then take any bus to anywhere. We were not interested to do that because we had no interest in visiting those strange places in between Orlando and New Orleans. We studied the maps, and we were checking the schedules of the bus. This was important so as not to miss the bus and at the same time to enjoy all the time when we were at the bus stops. In some stations, the bus stopped for only ten minutes and in others half an hour. I think we had to change the bus once. The strange thing was those Greyhound buses go for very long distances. For example, the bus we took from New Orleans was going to Toronto, Canada. It usually stopped for gas, oil change, and every six hours, they changed the driver.

During our journey from Orlando to New Orleans, we passed through a very long bridge. This was actually two bridges, one of them for one way and the other in the opposite direction. The bridge as far as I remember was about twenty-four miles long. It crossed over Lake Pontchartrain Causeway. When the bus was in the middle of the bridge, we had the feeling as if we were in a boat. You'd feel that the whole bridge was moving with the motions of the waves. When we came out of the bridge, we entered Mobil City. We found most of the trees were knocked out, and all the big signs were broken. This was the first time for us to hear or even imagine the disaster that could happen from a hurricane.

Once we looked at the schedule and found that the next stop would be in a certain city after one hour, after one hour and thirty minutes, we found the bus was continuing to travel without stopping. We thought that this was a very bad service. The bus, at last, stopped after two hours. When we looked at the name of the town, we found the name of the town that we were supposed to reach one hour ago. We were very upset about the service and the timing. The confusion became more when we discovered that the clock inside the bus station was one hour earlier than our watches. When we asked, they told us that we were now in a different time zone. This was strange for us because we thought in the same country there was only one time zone. America is a huge country with three different time zones.

We reached New Orleans. We looked for a hotel to stay in for the next four or five days. We found that the least expensive was the YMCA. I think the room was $13.00 a day for both of us. The bathrooms were common. Our budget was very limited, and no luxury was permissible on this journey.

Living in YMCA, New Orleans

The YMCA was very convenient. It gave us the impression of being in a dorm. We took some information about the city and started to walk and see the nearby streets. We discovered that there were many beggars. They were very rude. They asked everybody, "Do you have a quarter?" The first time I heard that, I was unable to understand what he meant. After a few times, I recognized that he wanted me to give him a quarter. The way the beggars approach us was scary. We felt that they were ordering us and not begging. Somebody told us that it was not safe even to open our wallet and give them money. My impression was that all those beggars were drug addicts and thieves.

We went to the Superdome. This was one of the main characteristics of New Orleans. It was a huge stadium with a huge dome-like roof. It is considered the largest covered stadium in the USA at that time. Next to the Superdome was the hotel where my conference would be. There was a special passage between the hotel and the Superdome.

New Orleans is famous for its French Quarter. This is the old part of the city. It is an old quaint building with peculiar, well-decorated metal balconies.

One of its streets was famous for the nightclubs that were the original place of jazz music. We walked through this street in the morning, but we felt that it was not safe at all to be in such a place. This part of New Orleans was called the French Quarter because the whole area was under French rule for many years.

French Quarter, New Orleans

In New Orleans I went to the public library to check if I could get copies from the papers that I was unable to get from Khartoum and London. The librarian took me to the chief librarian. I explained my situation and what I wanted. He was very nice. He explained to me that all the state libraries were linked together by a computer system. Also all those libraries were linked to a central library in Washington, DC. If I wanted a paper about glaucoma in Africa in children, I would just write glaucoma then Africa then children. The computer would give me a list of all the papers published in any language about this subject during the last ten years. The computer would indicate if this library had the magazine containing this article.

If this state library did not have the paper, they had two options. The first one was to order it through the computer, and this would cost about fifteen cents. The other option was to ask the other library to send it by mail and this would cost nothing. I showed him a list of the papers I wanted to get. He then said, "This is a long list and since you are traveling, it is better if we send them to you in your country." He then told me the cost for each photocopy was ten cents. I told him that I had no money to pay. He said, "OK, when you go back home, you can send the money." I explained to him that in Sudan, it was impossible to send money outside the country. He immediately said, "No problem, we can pay for you all the cost of the photocopies." When we returned to Halfa Al-Jadeeda, I received all that I asked for in different packages. I felt that in America, life was easy, and the people were very helpful.

I was not impressed by New Orleans as a city. If I have the choice, I would not visit this city again. On the reverse, I'd love to go back to Orlando.

The eye conference in New Orleans was great. I saw at this conference most of the people working on glaucoma in the world. I saw Dr. Cairns who was the first surgeon who described the trabeculectomy operation for the treatment of glaucoma. I saw Dr. Richard Simmons who sponsored me to come to America in 1985 and all of us in 1990.

I was amazed when I saw the Coca-Cola Company participate in the conference by putting two machines to drink Coca-Cola from them for free. Those were just like water machines. You just put the empty cup and press, and the Coke machine would fill the cup.

Leila was invited with all the other wives on tour in New Orleans. A wife of one New Orleans' eye doctor took them on tour and ended up in her house. Leila was shocked when the lady pointed to a part of the house and told them, "This is the slave quarters."

On the last day of the conference, they made a big reception for all of the participants. They served a magnificent dinner. At the end of the dinner, a band started to play loud music and about five men dressed in very colorful costumes entered the place. Each one of those men carried a huge burning torch. They went to the center and started to pour certain wine and coffee in a big pot. In the end, they started to serve this drink to everybody. This was the famous New Orleans coffee. Of course, we refused to taste this. At night Leila got severe abdominal pains. Leila had a gallbladder problem, and the heavy meal initiated these pains. The next morning Leila went to the emergency department of the nearest hospital. They took X-rays and found gallbladder stones. We decided to start her treatment in Egypt or Sudan.

I learned a lot from this conference about the up-to-date diagnosis and treatment of glaucoma.

We left New Orleans and went on our way back to New York. This was a very long journey. It took, as I remember, more than thirty hours. The scenery was beautiful in the daytime but boring during nighttime.

Our first visit to America was very nice. I felt that America was a nice place to live in. The people were friendly and easy to communicate with. This may be the reason that I decided later to immigrate to America.

Chapter 39

The Church in Halfa Al-Jadeeda 1975–1983

When we arrived at Halfa Al-Jadeeda, we asked if there was a church? We found that there were two churches. One of them was a Catholic church, and the other was a Coptic Orthodox church. From the first week, we went to the Coptic Orthodox church. The church, like all other buildings in Halfa Al-Jadeeda, had a new building. The people attending the Sunday service were about thirty. Fifteen of them were children. Five of the attendants were Egyptian teachers. They teach in the Egyptian school in Halfa Al-Jadeeda. The others were the Copts who lived in Halfa Al-Jadeeda. The priest was a seventy-year-old monk. He was a very heavy smoker. As soon as he finished the service, he would go outside the church to smoke his cigarette. I remember once I persuaded him to quit smoking. He had a heart attack before. He told me, "If I stop smoking, I will be very nervous. I will quarrel with everybody in the church. My job obliges me to treat the people nicely." He continued to smoke till he moved to another town. I remember one day he had a big fight with his assistant Al Moalim. There was a lot of shouting, and even they tried to throw the chairs toward each other. This was during the mass. This priest died after another heart attack. The next priest was a young monk. He was about twenty-six years old. He was very active in his service. The people started to reject him because they thought that he wanted to enjoy his time with the young girls. Actually, he was good. But the people were very conservative. They consider any chat between two different sexes was questionable till proven otherwise. They kicked him out of Halfa Al-Jadeeda after a few months. During his period, it was the celebration of Mar-Girgis festivals or what is known here as St. George. All the people come to the church every night to attend a short church service. After the service, they sit in a big circle in the churchyard. They eat food and play games. I remember one of the games was tombola. I told them that I would not join because I consider it gambling. The priest told me that all the income would go to the church. I told him, no. I would not join this game. Those nights were nice because they were lovely social gatherings.

The last priest was a middle-aged married priest. He had five children, one boy and four girls. They continued to get more children with the hope of getting another boy. When we left Halfa Al-Jadeeda in 1983, they had seven girls and still one boy. The priest was very friendly and helpful to everybody. He was doing his best to give the best service. All the people loved him and his family. He made friends with the Catholic church priests.

He had a good relationship with his Muslim neighbors. I saw him several times praying for them. He was very generous. When we visited them in their house, he usually insisted on giving us many things. Sometimes he gives us figs from his tree. Other times we take freshly baked bread made by his wife. Also he insisted many times to give us chicken. When I think about him now, I am astonished. His income was minimal. He had a large family. But he was very generous to all the people, not just to us. The good thing was that we felt that he was doing this with all his heart. He usually becomes very angry if we insist on not accepting his gifts. To increase his income, he planted some vegetables and fruits in his house and in the churchyard. He usually donates most of the product to his friends.

I remember once he was visiting us, he noticed that we had a big shade tree. He said that they usually cut part of the branches so the tree would grow upward. He said that he could do that for us. He insisted on doing it by himself. The Coptic priest usually wears a long black gown. It looks like a thick dress of the Catholic monks. In a minute, he climbed the tree and cut the branches one by one. He asked if he could take the branches. They use the dry branches as fuel for baking their bread and the communion bread. Another visit was for the palm tree branches. This was to take the layer of fine fibers that grew around the leaves. They use those thread-like fibers, *leef*, for cleaning the dishes. He gave us a good amount of it and took some.

He was a good friend, and I felt that he was an honest, godly man.

Leila found that the children in the church knew nothing about God. So she started Sunday school.

We used to drive our Land Rover and pick up the children from their homes. We went to the church, and Leila taught them. She used to do this every Sunday afternoon. She used to teach them the Bible stories and the children's hymns. She brought the teaching books and the song taps from Assiut. The children and their parents became happy with what Leila was doing. The priest was happy as well. He encouraged Leila to continue.

Sunday School in New Halfa

One of the Egyptian teachers became upset. He felt that Leila was only teaching the Protestant way. Apparently, he was jealous. We invited him to come and share in the teaching. He refused but became one of our best friends. Another lady teacher came and helped Leila in teaching. She taught some of the Coptic Church songs. It was good. Leila did this for the seven and a half years that we spent in Halfa

Al-Jadeeda. It was a very successful service. Leila heard that one of her six-year-old Sunday school children would leave Halfa Al-Jadeeda. Her family was moving to a small town where there were no churches. I asked Leila to record the songs with her voice on a tape. She did and Tony and Sandra sang with her in parts of the tape. Tony was about six years old, and Sandra was four. On one side of the tape, there were songs for children and the other side were regular adult hymns. We made twenty-three copies of this tape. We gave almost every Christian family in Halfa Al-Jadeeda one copy. Also, we sent some to my family and Leila's family. Till now, I like to hear this tape. It had no music, but Leila's voice was better than all the music. In a part of the tape, the singing of the birds and chicken was clear. We recorded the tape in our house. There were always many birds in our garden.

We had some chicken as well. We used to collect eggs from the chicken. We had a few of them in a special large cage. At a certain time, the chicken sat on the eggs. It sat on the eggs for three weeks. After three weeks, the eggs hatched. It was a very nice thing to watch as the new chicks came from the egg. We were not successful in most cases. Most of the time the result of eight eggs would be only one or a maximum of two newly hatched chicken. Sometime after they hatched, they died. I remember we used to buy freshly hatched chicken. We usually buy about twenty at a time. The problem was how to keep them alive for the first two weeks.

On the first day or two, many would be killed from overcrowding. They would sleep near each other to keep warm. The result was suffocation because they stepped over each other. The newly hatched chicken was usually yellow. They were very beautiful. I liked to see them, but I hated to see them die without a logical cause. We managed on different occasions to raise ten or twelve at a time. They gave us after about three months a fair amount of eggs. Tony and Sandra used to go with us to collect the eggs. Sometimes they were afraid of the mother hen who liked to sit over the eggs. Those hens usually attacked anybody who dared to come near the eggs.

We had some pigeons. We used to put them in big tins. Every couple slept in one tin. The pigeons were good in their family life. The couple usually lived together all their life.

They usually produced two newly hatched pigeons every few months. To watch those birds was a nice thing. The parents of the birds fed them and taught them how to fly.

With the help of the Catholic priest, I went to their Khartoum center. From there, I brought sets of projector slides of the famous film *Jesus of Nazareth*. The slides were in six sets. In each set, there were 100 slides. There was an Arabic translation tape of the film accompanying the slides. We used to ask all the Christians of Halfa Al-Jadeeda to come to our house to see and hear the film. Leila used to make cookies and cakes for them in addition to the drinks. It was nice to give the adults and children a chance to see such a good film. It took us two nights to finish that film. For Sunday school, I remember Leila bought Bible stories with pictures that could be stuck on a flint cloth.

The Coptic Christians of Halfa Al-Jadeeda were very friendly people. We used to visit all of them. Most of them had low income. All of them, on the other hand, were very generous. One family, the husband, was working as a salesman in a beverage store. The wife, like all the other families, did not work. They had one son in high school. In one of our visits to their house, the lady insisted on giving Tony a five-day-old chicken. Tony held the chicken from her neck and tightened his grip. He was afraid. He was about two years old. We tried to tell Tony to let her go. But the more we told him, the more he tightened his grip.

I could not remember the fate of that poor chicken. This same lady took care of a Canadian man who came to visit Halfa Al-Jadeeda and became sick. She, as her habit, gave him shelter and food daily during his five-day visit. After a few years, the Canadian Embassy representative in Khartoum came to Halfa Al-Jadeeda and asked about this lady. The story was strange. The Canadian visitor died in Canada. In his will, he gave a few hundred thousand dollars to this lady's son. The Sudanese government claimed a good portion of it. The son was in college at that time. He went to Canada to collect his unexpected money.

Another family in Halfa Al-Jadeeda was living in Al-Mahlagg. This was a place where they packed cotton into huge bags after taking out the seeds. The father was working as an accountant. He had three boys and three girls. Their older daughter graduated as a medical doctor and worked in Halfa Al-Jadeeda Hospital. Another man was an accountant in the electric company. He and his wife were very good friends. They had no children. Leila used to go to their house after the clinic. I usually went later to join her there. I used to stay in my clinic until a later hour at night. During our period in Halfa Al-Jadeeda, the man retired. They decided to settle in Egypt in Aswan. They had some relatives there. It was difficult for us to say goodbye to them when they moved. We saw them a few years later in Khartoum when they came for a visit.

Another family was the family of Haleem and Samia. They had a son and a daughter. His father, mother, brother, and sister were living with them. They were a nice family. We used to visit them a lot. He was working as a clerk in the agricultural scheme. They moved from Wadi Halfa during the massive immigration. We used to spend happy times with them. The husband and his wife liked to tell jokes about anything. We usually laughed all the time when we visited them.

Haleem's sister Mary was just going to college. She finished college in Khartoum and got married. We met her in London recently. She mentioned that she had four married daughters.

We used to visit some of the Egyptian Christian teachers in Halfa Al-Jadeeda. Some of them came from Assiut. So they were friends and colleagues to Rafaat, Leila's brother. We continued to visit some of them even when we visited Assiut. One of the teachers, Basim and his wife Magdoline, came from a town in the northern part of Egypt. We became good friends. We used to visit them frequently. They had a son and a daughter, older than Tony. They usually served tea to drink. Their tea was usually very strong, I mean heavy. Apparently they boil the tea for a long time. After drinking their tea, both Liela and I usually became very dizzy. In the beginning, we did not relate this dizziness to their tea. Later on, we recognized the relationship. After that, we asked them to make our tea very light. All Egyptian teachers stay for three years or less. This was the reason that we knew many of them.

For a short period, we had one Egyptian teacher who was very good at preaching. He belonged to the Plymouth brothers. He used to preach in the church every Sunday evening. Those Plymouth brothers were very good at studying the Bible. When he left Halfa Al-Jadeeda, they stopped the Sunday evening meetings.

We enjoyed our time in New Halfa.

We felt that it was part of our joyful period of our life.

Chapter 40

Our Journey to Port Sudan 1977

We thought of visiting my brother Baheeg and his family in Port Sudan. They settled in Port Sudan about ten years ago. Port Sudan is on the Red Sea and the only port in Sudan. In summer the weather is very hot and humid. In all the cities in Sudan, the weather is very dry, except Port Sudan because of the presence of the sea. I visited Port Sudan with my schoolmates in 1958. I was in junior high school. It was a school trip, and I was only thirteen years old. We spent two weeks there. I remember a few things vaguely from that visit.

For Leila, this was the first time to see Port Sudan. For Tony he was very young. I think he was only two years old and Sandra was a few months old.

We took the train to Khashm El-Girba. From there, we changed trains to a bigger one. This train was faster and had a restaurant. The train stations in between were very poor. Very few things were sold in those stations. They sold only peanuts and *dome.* Dome was a hard fruit the size of an orange. It has a very hard seed that was almost the size of the fruit. There was a very thin layer of crusty, dry, eatable brown material covering the huge seed. In order to take this thin brown layer, we had to hit the dome with a hard thing like a hammer. Some children could eat it without hitting it first. I never was fond of eating dome.

All the eastern part of Sudan is famous as well for the way they cook the meat. They chose some big marbles and put them over the hot lit coal. Over those hot marbles, they put the meat to be cooked with the heat coming from those marbles. The meat gets a special taste. I ate this sallatt once only. I think in only one railway station they were selling the sallatt, which was the name of this specially cooked meat. This was the largest station on the journey. When the train stops in a large station, it might stay for half an hour or more. In such stops, most of the people go down and pray. Most of the people were Muslims. They had to pray five times a day. If they missed the time of a particular prayer, they could do it later on, especially if they were traveling. Sometimes they prayed three or more postponed prayers together. Muslims usually prefer to pray together. The older person leads them. They have to wash their hands, feet, and face with water before they pray. Most of the people carry *ibreeg* and *muslaya* with their luggage. Ibreeg is a metal container that looks like a teapot. They fill it with water and wash their hands, feet, and face before each prayer. Ibreeg is usually locally made in Sudan by any blacksmith. Muslaya is a small piece of rug about one and a half foot by four feet. Some people use a similar piece made of palm leaves called birrish. The big version of birrish of about four feet by twenty feet is usually used for the prayer of many people together. Most of the mosques use them. Even in Halfa Al-Jadeeda's cinemas, they use them. In the intermission (interval) of the film, many of the film viewers pray together inside the movie theater.

We arrived at Port Sudan and found Baheeg and his family waiting for us. Hakeema, Baheeg's wife, and his two daughters, Suzy and Caroline were happy to see us. It had been a long time since we saw them. They live in Port Sudan and go to Khartoum once a year, and we live in Halfa Al-Jadeeda and go to Khartoum once or twice a year. So we rarely see them in Khartoum. Baheeg was working at that time in a company specializing in export and import. Baheeg was an accountant. He was responsible for releasing the goods from the port. We had a lovely time with them in Port Sudan.

We went to the seashore. In Port Sudan, there were no beaches as far as I remember. The land was rocky and not sandy. They took us to visit Sawakin. It was an old deserted city. It was the only port in Sudan. Then the British government built Port Sudan about forty miles to the north of Sawakin. I had no idea why they deserted Sawakin. The whole city was intact. All the houses were two or three floors high. All the windows and doors were missing. Many of the buildings lost one or two of their walls. Nobody gave me a logical reason for the presence of this deserted city. In the 1970s in all the cities of Sudan, the houses were just one floor. Even in the capital Khartoum, there were only a few new buildings with two floors or more. Sawakin showed that it was a very prosperous, well-developed city in the 1800s.

When we saw Sawakin, we found it was empty as if suddenly everybody left. There was no electricity or water supply, and there were no people in the city. The only inhabitants were huge cats. I heard that they ate fish from the sea. Apparently, the old buildings were good shelters for the cats.

I liked the water of the Red Sea. It was always very clear. You could see the colored fish swimming through the water.

Tony, Victor, Leila and Sandra, Port Sudan, Mav 1977

Port Sudan visit in 1977

I think we spent about a week or two in Port Sudan. Then we took the train back to Halfa Al-Jadeeda.

Chapter 41

We Lost Our Way in the Desert in 1978

Kassala was about a three-and-a-half-hour drive from Halfa Al-Jadeeda. I worked in Kassala in 1970, and Leila spent her first month after our wedding in Kassala. We thought of visiting Kassala to spend some time with my cousin Loweed and his family. Loweed was a dentist. His wife was Mary and his daughter was Dalia who was one year older than Tony. They had two sons younger than Dalia, Amgad, and Rami. Loweed and his family were loving and very friendly people. He, like all other doctors, worked for the Sudan Ministry of Health between 7:00 AM–2:00 PM. In the evening, he worked in his private clinic. They were living in one of the government houses. We stayed with them and spent a long weekend with them. We drove our car from Halfa Al-Jadeeda to Kassala. We had to take all the gas that the car needed back and forth The reason was the ration of gas to the public. The road between Halfa Al-Jadeeda and Kassala was not paved. We had to follow the track of the other cars. We had no problem till we reached Sassarabe. This was part of the Atbara River, about one hour from Halfa Al-Jadeeda. In this area, the river level was about one meter only most of the year. When we arrived at that point, we found a small police station. The police in this station were collecting twenty-five cents from every car passing. They called it service fees. Actually, there were no services at all done in this area. The road was unpaved. There was no bridge to cross the river. We paid the money and passed the police station. We reached the riverside. The water level was about one meter high in the lowest part. Many teenagers of about sixteen and seventeen years old offered to assist us in the crossing of the river. I learned that we had to cross the river with our Land Rover at the lowest level. I noticed that there were many huge holes in the passage under the water. We could not see those holes because they were covered by water and mud. I saw a big lorry stuck in one of those huge holes. A tractor was trying to pull the lorry out. The teenager's job was to walk in the water in front of the car. When they walked, they would show the car that there were no holes in that particular area. I was astonished by this primitive way of crossing the river. I paid the teenagers the amount that they asked for. It was a scary thing to do and drive your car across the river. We safely crossed Sassarabe. After less than half an hour, we saw the two huge mountains of Kassala, Taka Mountains. They were very scenic and beautiful. They had rounded tops and went very steep on the edges. After we saw the mountains, it took us the full speed of the car one and a half hour to reach Kassala. It was a good guide to the direction of Kassala.

Loweed and his wife Mary were very generous. Every day that we spent with them, they had ten to fifteen visitors invited to dinner with them. We had a nice time with them.

We left Kassala on our way to Halfa Al-Jadeeda at noontime. I drove confidently along the track of the other cars. It was rare to see any car passing. At a certain point, I felt that we lost our way. The path of the cars became very difficult to recognize. After some time, we found that we lost track completely. When I looked at the gas indicator; it was almost at the endpoint. I knew that the gas was not enough to go back to Kassala. At the same time, we had no idea where we were. We stopped and tried to look to see if there were any signs of any village or people. There was nothing seen in all the directions other than the tiny bushes. Those were less than one foot in height. Even those bushes were few in the whole area, about one in every one hundred meters. Leila became very worried and prayed a lot. Suddenly she told me that a man was coming toward us. I saw him. He was a simple person that looked like a shepherd. We asked him the directions to Halfa Al-Jadeeda. He told us to go back and follow our car track till we see the ground change its color to red. Then we stop there and wait till we see the public bus that went from Kassala to Halfa Al-Jadeeda. When the bus comes, we have to follow it till we reach Halfa Al-Jadeeda. We followed this unknown man's instructions. When we passed about half an hour, we recognized that the color of the sand changed to red. We stopped there. In less than five minutes, the bus came. We followed the bus until we reached Halfa Al-Jadeeda. The gas gauge was on the empty mark for more than an hour. When we thought about it, we were very surprised. First, about the man who suddenly appeared, we looked carefully at the whole area and in all the directions, there was nobody and nowhere could a person hide. The land was flat and bare at that place as in most of Sudan. We saw the man near us suddenly. The other thing was the precise instructions that he gave us. The herdsmen, especially in Sudan, were known for their lack of accuracy. The third thing was the public bus that passed only twice a day, how did we find the bus passing immediately after less than five minutes after we reached the red sand? The last thing was the gas, how was there gas when the gauge indicated the empty mark for a while? There was nothing wrong with the gas gauge, before and after this journey. So the gauge was correct. Our only explanation as Leila said that this was God's strong hand that was with us. Leila felt, and I agreed with her, that the person who suddenly appeared and disappeared was not a human being but God's messenger.

Psalm 34:7 states, "7 The angel of the Lord encamps all around those who fear Him, And delivers them."

Chapter 42

Some Stories of Our friends in Halfa Al-Jadeeda 1975–1983

We lived in Halfa Al-Jadeeda for seven and a half years. We went to Halfa Al-Jadeeda with Tony, who was only a few months and went out from Halfa with Tony eight years old, Sandra six years old, and Jennie three years old. We felt that Halfa Al-Jadeeda was our home city.

We had many friends from different origins, Halfaweyeen, Copts, Egyptians, Indians, and even English, Americans, Belgium, French, Russians, and Germans. They were Muslims, Christians, Hindus, and atheists. We were able to have a good relationship with all those people, visit them, and invite them to our house.

I remember one of the English friends was an old lady. Her husband was working for the World Bank. Leila told me that we had to visit her because her dog had a certain disease that was incurable. She decided to give him an injection to kill him because the dog was suffering. So Leila visited them. The lady was crying and sitting at the place in their yard where they buried the dog. It was difficult for Leila to comfort the lady. This was the first time for Leila to attend a funeral for a dog. The lady told Leila that she was reading some stories to the dead dog.

***

Another World Bank official told me about his story in Bangladesh. He said that the Bangladeshi milkmen used to cheat by mixing milk with water. To avoid this, he asked the milkman to bring the cow with him and milk it in front of him. The first few days, the milk was good, but after a few days, the milk was clearly mixed with water. He said I was very keen to know how this milkman did that. He finally discovered after a very good observation that the milkman carried a bottle of water and hid it in his shirt sleeves. When he milked the cow, he let the water come from the bottle under his sleeves.

***

Another couple was from West Germany. He was doing a thesis on the way the Shukreya spoke Arabic. His wife was a medical doctor. She was not licensed to practice in Sudan. She used to come to the hospital a few times to watch. She used to ride a bike in Halfa Al-Jadeeda. This was strangely seen in Halfa. I remember once she came to the hospital and found the gate was closed. The porter was away. She immediately jumped over the one-and-a-half-meter wall and went into the hospital. She had a two-year-old boy.

***

Once I visited one of the Shukreya villages to do some research about glaucoma. I found her with her son, who was not wearing Pampers or even underwear. This was the habit of the very-low-standard Shukreya villagers. Her husband used to come to our house in flip-flops. In Halfa Al-Jadeeda where there were no paved roads and sidewalks, walking in slippers means that the feet would be very dirty. He also used to wear Sirwal, which was long wide pants and Arraggi which was like a middy dress. This was the traditional Shukreya dress.

***

I used to play tennis twice a week. One of my friends was Mohamed. He used to play with me regularly. He was fifty years old, halfway in origin. He was married to two wives. Leila used to visit one of them.

He usually brought both of them with him to the cinema. He had two houses, one for each wife. Both houses were facing each other.

***

The owner of our private clinic was Hussein. He was sixty-two years old. Leila used to go and chat with his wife. She was about sixty years old. She was a heavyweight and could hardly walk. They had four sons and daughters; all of them were married. Once Leila found the old lady crying. The story was her husband went to Aswan in Egypt for his vacation. Aswan was the town of their origin. She heard that he got remarried to a forty-year-old lady. A few days later, Hussein came back with his new wife. Of course, he decided to keep her in the same house. After two weeks, Hussein told me that he divorced the new wife because she did not know the proper technique to present the food on the table.

***

One of my close friends was Dr. Ali. He is a medical doctor and at a certain time, was the head of the public health department. He graduated from a medical school in Russia. He married his wife Mira while he was a student in Russia. Mira was Russian. She usually wore regular European dresses, just like Leila. This was the reason that they were very close friends. We used to visit them, and they came to us very frequently. Ali and Mira had one son Omar and two daughters, Salwa and Randa. Their youngest daughter Randa was about three years older than our son Tony. The children were always together with our children. Dr. Ali was a Muslim, but his wife Mira was an atheist. She told me that her parents were baptized when they were young. For her generation, no one was baptized. She told me that they had an experiment in school in Russia to prove that life could be created from nothing, which was proof that there was no God. She said that they put a small piece of jam in a closed container. After a few days, there were small worms in the jam. I explained to her that this was scientifically wrong. If they sterilized and killed all the bacteria and the small eggs of those worms, the jam would be clear of any worms. This was simply the way of sterilization.

The communist regime in the Soviet Union wanted to prove that there was no God even by using the wrong science experiment.

Leila used to go with Mira to visit other ladies. The tradition in Halfa Al-Jadeeda and in most of Sudan that the ladies go to visit each other without the men. Mira was not working. She showed Leila many delicious recipes. One of them was how to make simple cheese. Our children liked this cheese and called it Mira's cheese. Leila was working in the hospital in the daytime and at her private clinic at night. Leila was still able to join the other nonworking ladies in their activities. Leila was the only lady among the government's employees' wives that was working.

***

Once the daughter of the surgeon of the hospital was ill. So the pediatrician's wife and other doctor's wives took her to a local lay doctor. This was an uneducated person who usually gave the patient some written paper to put under his pillow. To treat jaundice, the lay doctor burnt the patient's arm with a hot metal rod. The funny thing was those ladies went to this lay doctor by the hospital car, the ambulance.

***

I remember I saw one patient who came to me complaining of irritation in his eyes. He said that he went to a lady lay doctor. This quack doctor told the patient that he had two of the lemon seeds in his eye. She licked his eye with her tongue and gave him those two lemon seeds that were in his eyes. He showed me the two lemon seeds. He asked me to see if there were more seeds in his eye. It took me a long time to convince this patient that there were no lemon seeds in his eyes.

***

Another patient came to me with a severely red eye. He told me that he went to a lay doctor because he was unable to close his eyes. The lay doctor poured ox bile into his eye. When the eye became very red and painful, the doctor told him that this was because the blood started to circulate into his dead eye. The patient had paralysis of the muscles that were responsible for the closure of the eye. I treated this patient for two weeks for the severe inflammation from the ox bile, and then I gave him treatment for his paralysis.

Some of those lay doctors do cataract surgeries. Yes, this is true; they do *tashleeg*. This was a well-known operation for many centuries all over the world called couching. It was common in Europe in the 1700 and 1800. I saw many patients who had this operation in Halfa Al-Jadeeda. The lay doctor was usually of Nigerian origin. We call them in Sudan Falatta. He usually came to a village and announced his arrival. He asked the villagers to bring their blind patients to him. He took his fee first. He laid the patient on the bed and held the patient's head with one hand, and with the other hand, he carried a small metal probe. He suddenly gave a strong hit to the eye between the white area and the colored one. In this way, he was trying to dislocate the lens, the cataract, away from its place. The aim was to drop the lens into the back of the eye. You may be astonished if I tell you that some of those patients get 20/20 vision after giving them the appropriate glasses. About 90 percent of the patients, unfortunately, get internal bleeding or severe inflammation that led usually to blindness. Those lay doctors usually cover the patient's eye for twenty-four hours. They also asked the patient not to sleep until the next morning. They warned the patient that the operation would fail if the patient slept. Of course, no one could stay awake all night. So if the patient did not improve, the doctor would tell him that the reason was the short nap he took at night. There were no medico-legal suits in Sudan. Even if there were such suits, nobody could sue such lay doctors because they left the village within a few days, and nobody would know where they went or their email!

***

One of our neighbors moved from Halfa Al-Jadeeda. The lady was a very good friend to Leila. She brought about twelve pairs of pigeons. They bred the pigeons to eat their offspring. The lady cut the pigeons' wings so they would not fly away. The next morning we found all the pigeons had managed to walk away from our house. The pigeons were very loyal to their place. (In Sudan and Egypt, we eat pigeons.)

***

At the end of every year, we pay income taxes on our income from the clinics. I usually register my income very accurately. One year I received a bill from the tax department that I had to pay. I found that it did not match my numbers. If for example, I wrote my income was five thousand, they estimated my income as ten thousand. I went to the director of the tax department in Halfa Al-Jadeeda. He told me, "We do this with all other doctors because all doctors lower their actual income." I told him, "OK, but I put exactly my income, and I will not pay taxes for income that I did not gain." I left the office. After a few days, I received a letter warning me if I did not pay the money, they would sell my car and other belongings. At that point, my colleagues interfered and convinced the man that what I said was true. This tax director later came to my clinic in Khartoum several times, bringing his mother and other relatives for eye exams and operations.

***

There was no operating microscope in the operating theater in Halfa Al-Jadeeda. I used to operate using my own private binocular operating glasses. It was specially made for me with my own glasses prescription. It had a special case of wood. Once I went to the hospital to do five scheduled operations. When I reached the hospital, I found that I did not have the operating glasses. I usually took the glasses with me to my home and bring it on the operating days only. I was sure that I took the glasses from the house. The story was like this, I put the glasses on the top of the car to open the door. Then I forgot to put it inside the car. When I drove the car, the glasses fell down on one of the main roads. The glasses box opened and the glasses went out of the box in the middle of the road. A big truck with a trailer was passing. The driver of the truck noticed the glasses just in front of him. He was unable to avoid them so he turned and stopped to see what was there. He found that the truck destroyed the case, but the glasses were intact. He stopped in a garage. God arranged that the owner of the garage was one of my friends. The truck driver gave the glasses to my friend. My friend, after looking at the glasses, said those special glasses most probably were Victor's. So he phoned me in the hospital and asked me if I lost special glasses. I went to him immediately and took the glasses and returned to the hospital to do my operations. I did all the operations without any delay. If by chance, I lost those glasses, I had to wait at least a few months to get a new pair of glasses from England. Those special glasses were not available in Sudan.

***

A few weeks after my arrival at Halfa Al-Jadeeda, I got an invitation to my friend Abd Al-Salam's wedding celebration. We worked together in many places. Dr. Abd Al-Salam's wedding was in a village near Halfa Al-Jadeeda. I was still not comfortable with the directions to that village. I chose to go with some of my colleagues who would go to the celebrations. We went to the village, and I enjoyed the beautiful dancing of the Halfaweyeen. In the dance, the men stood in a line facing the women's line. They did regular steps and went gradually till they reached the other group, then they went away from them. Usually in each line, there were at least ten. The Halfaweyeen ladies wore long black dresses. The dress was always made of light material and widened as it went down. They put a dark-colored scarf over their heads. They did not use the toub as other Sudanese women.

After the celebrations, I went to the car of my colleagues to go back to Halfa Al-Jadeeda. I discovered that the driver, Dr. Abdel-Mutaal was drunk. He started to drive very fast and turned suddenly in the crossings. The problem was the streets were unpaved and there were narrow bridges over deep, uncovered irrigation canals. Sitting next to

Dr. Abdel-Mutaal was another doctor; he was drunk as well. He started to move his hand and told Dr. Abdel-Mutaal, "Slow down. Slow down," and then he took a nap and then repeated "Slow down. Slow down." It was very scary. Both of them were drunk. I was the only one who was awake. Dr. Abdel-Mutaal was driving very fast and then suddenly turned 360 degrees and stopped. I asked him what happened. He told me, "I want to pass water." He got out of the car and passed water on the ground and resumed driving. We finally reached Halfa Al-Jadeeda safely.

***

Most of the doctors at that time drank alcohol regularly. I was the only one who did not drink. There was another doctor who did not drink. He was a fanatic Muslim.

I remember now Dr. Saad. He was the physician and the director of the hospital. He was about fifty years old. He was Halfaweeyeen. He was very intelligent. He got his degree from England, and he passed the American equivalent exams. He used to drink alcohol heavily and smoke cigarettes as well. One night after drinking heavily, he drove the hospital's new car and hit the wall of a house. The car went into the house and stopped by a tree inside the house. The family of that house was sleeping in the yard just a few meters from that tree. Dr. Saad simply got out of the totally lost car and walked to his house. On another occasion, he came home totally drunk as usual. He tried to open the door but was unable to do that because the door was locked. He finally started to climb the wall to get in. He suddenly found a man coming from inside the house with a gun pointed at him. Dr. Saad went by mistake to his neighbor's house. His neighbor was the head of the wildlife guards and owned a gun. The man thought that Dr. Saad was a thief. Luckily enough the man recognized Dr. Saad. He told Dr. Saad, "This is not your house. Your house is the next house."

Dr. Saad got married to his cousin during our period in Halfa Al-Jadeeda. He never stopped drinking. He once went to Khartoum for a short visit. He was planning to fly to Halfa Al-Jadeeda on a certain day, but he missed the plane. He returned from the airport to a restaurant, and he drank heavily. On his way out, he fell down and died. Nobody recognized him because he was not carrying ID cards. They took him to the hospital and stored his body for three days. His wife did not ask about him, thinking that he was still with his relatives in Khartoum. His relatives in Khartoum thought that he left for Halfa Al-Jadeeda. His wife on the third day reported his absence. It is strange that Saad was an intelligent doctor and knew exactly the sequences of drinking and still continued drinking.

Addiction is bad, and we have to teach our children not to start drinking alcohol or any addictive substances.

***

I remember as well Dr. Hussein. He was the chief medical officer in the hospital. He used to smoke heavily. I tried to persuade him to quit smoking. He told me, "Look, Victor, if in heaven they told me that there is no smoking, I will not go there."

***

Dr. Gadir was a pediatrician. He was fifty years old. He was married and had three young daughters. He used to drink, smoke, and gamble regularly. At that time, he had two heart attacks. They advised him to stop drinking and smoking, but he continued. He left Halfa Al-Jadeeda and worked in El-Gedaref. We heard that he died one year after leaving New Halfa.

***

Merghani was my surgical assistant, he was a very good, godly man.

On one of the Ramadan days, he invited me to come and have Fatour Ramadan with them.

He said we usually came together on the street for all our neighbors to eat together.

I promised him to come. I went at the right time. I found a group of about ten sitting on the floor and eating together. As soon as I came, all of them greeted me, "Dr. Victor" and invited me to join them. I sat down and ate, but I noticed that Merghani was not there.

The next morning I asked Merghani, "Why were you not in Fatour Ramadan yesterday?" He assured me that he was there, but apparently, I went to another street. In New Halfa, every street, they gather together to eat their Fatour Ramadan together. It was a good habit.

Chapter 43

My Research Studies in Ophthalmology 1975–2017

When I became an ophthalmologist in 1974, I became interested in research. I started in 1976 by choosing glaucoma as my research subject. I thought of writing a thesis with the title "Trabeculectomy in the Treatment of Glaucoma in New Halfa District, Sudan." I went to Khartoum and I asked for the advice of Dr. Abdel-Gadir. He was the chief ophthalmologist in Sudan. He showed a great interest in the idea. He took me to Khartoum University, department of higher education. He knew the head of the department. He introduced me as the best of his students. His introduction facilitated the whole process. I filled the papers, and I applied for the degree, master of surgery. In Khartoum University medical school, the thesis degrees were divided into two main categories. Any subject that was preclinical, anatomy, physiology, biochemistry, pathology, histology, and microbiology, the degree would be PhD or doctor of philosophy. The clinical subjects were further divided into medical subjects and surgical subjects. The medical subjects like medicine, pediatrics, psychiatric, the degree would be MD or doctor of medicine. For surgical subjects like surgery; ophthalmology; ear, nose, and throat, the degree would be master of surgery. So you could not apply for a PhD in ophthalmology from Khartoum University. I chose to research because I loved to do research.

The other reason was to get a higher degree in ophthalmology to have the advantage over my colleagues and have the opportunity to work in Khartoum. As a medical doctor in the Ministry of Health in Sudan, you had to work in different parts of Sudan. You cannot say no. Most of the doctors work in different cities in Sudan, and the lucky ones would end up working in the capital Khartoum at the end of their career because private clinics in Khartoum could bring a lot of income.

For any thesis, there must be supervisors appointed by Khartoum University. The job of the supervisor was to help the candidate to write the thesis the right way. I chose Dr. Abdel-Gadir to be one of my supervisors. I also chose Dr. El-Hadi, who was the head of the ophthalmology department at Khartoum University as the second supervisor. Dr. El-Hadi suggested that we put the name of the head of the surgery department at Khartoum University as the third supervisor. I told him that this person had no idea about glaucoma because he was not an ophthalmologist.

Dr. El-Hadi mentioned that ophthalmology was part of the surgery department at Khartoum University. He said that this would be just in paper and get his approval as the head of the department. Dr. El-Hadi said that he was not expecting him to do any supervision because he was ignorant of this subject. The head of the surgery department was a plastic surgeon. I met with all the supervisors and explained to them my expected thesis. The three of them had no objection, and all agreed with my plan and signed the papers.

I decided to do a prospective study of the surgical treatment of glaucoma. This meant that I examine new patients with glaucoma and record all the data and then do the surgery. Then follow up with the patient every month to see the effect of the surgery on the vision, visual fields, and the pressure of the eye.

Glaucoma is characterized by high pressure that restricts the visual fields and in the end, causes blindness.

I discovered that most of my patients were not living in Halfa Al-Jadeeda. Many patients came from other cities in Sudan. They come to Halfa Al-Jadeeda to their relatives and to have their eyes examined. Most eye doctors in Sudan and other parts of the world treat glaucoma with eye drops only. I found that our patients in Sudan usually did not continue to use the drops for more than a month. They usually stop after that. The reason was that in glaucoma, the drops lower the pressure of the eye, so it would prevent further deterioration of vision. There would be no improvement in vision. Most of the glaucoma drops have some side effects. Some drops constrict the pupils, so it would deteriorate the vision temporarily, especially at night. Other drops could initiate or aggravate bronchial asthma. One of the glaucoma drops could lead to heart problems in some patients. So the patient on the glaucoma drops or tablets would not get better vision and in many cases would have some side effects from the treatment. This was the reason that I found most of the patients stop the glaucoma treatment or at least use half of the recommended dose. This would lead to a gradual loss of vision and in the end will result in total blindness. In addition, the glaucoma treatment was an expensive one, and in Sudan it was not available most of the year.

I found in Sudan, the best treatment of glaucoma was surgery. I felt that if I did the surgery, I would save the patient's vision. If I prescribed drops, the patient would lose his vision gradually and become blind later on. The other problem in Sudan was the lack of follow-ups. It was practically very difficult for the patients to come for follow-ups, financially and socially.

When I started to discover those facts, I decided to do surgery as early as possible. I found that the patients after surgery maintained their vision and lost nothing. Actually, many patients got a slight improvement in vision after surgery.

I became known as the doctor who did surgery for glaucoma. Many patients not living in Halfa Al-Jadeeda came to Halfa Al-Jadeeda just to see me and get the surgery. I guess I did glaucoma surgeries five times more than all other ophthalmologists in Sudan together. Most ophthalmologists try to avoid glaucoma surgery, because the patient's vision would not improve, and if any complication happens, the vision will deteriorate. So the ophthalmologist will be happier to do cataract surgery, which in all cases will improve the patient's vision dramatically. I do the glaucoma surgeries because I felt that if I put the patient on drops, the patient would be blind, and if I do the surgery, I would save the patient's vision.

I did many surgeries for glaucoma and combined cataract removal and at the same time glaucoma surgery. I did more than five hundred for a period of five years. I tried to follow all of them for as long as I could. I selected for the thesis only patients who came regularly every three months and for at least one year.

The selected eyes were 201, who had glaucoma surgeries and 41 who had combined glaucoma and cataract surgeries.

I discovered when I came to the USA that this number was huge when I compared it to the number of glaucoma specialists did in the USA.

I paid for all the expenses of my research by myself. I did many journeys from Halfa Al-Jadeeda and Khartoum to meet my supervisors.

I traveled to the USA to attend two glaucoma conferences at my own expense.

I wrote each chapter at least five or six times. Leila helped me a lot in checking and reading each chapter.

My father-in-law, Hezkial Bestourous, suggested some changes to correct the grammar, and I changed them. He did this many times either in his visits to Khartoum or on my visits to Assiut.

All the histograms, I had to draw them manually.

Even the map of New Halfa and the villages, I had to create them.

When I started writing my thesis, computer printers were not available yet. So we had to use the manual typewriter.

My sister Thuraya did the typing of the thesis in stencil paper. This type of paper was a special paper covered by a layer of wax. When we type over it, the letters would be engraved on the layer of wax. The engraved paper would be passed between a roller soaked with black ink and a white paper. The black ink would pass through the waxy paper to be printed on the white paper. Typing on stencil paper was very difficult. If any mistake happened, you had to change the paper. The final version was printed and made into seven books. This was the regulations of Khartoum University, the thesis must be presented in hardcover books and at least five copies must be prepared. This was difficult because there were many pictures.

Before I printed the final version, I checked with two of my three supervisors. They were happy with it. I asked Dr. Al-Hadi about my third supervisor, the plastic surgeon. He told me that he was working in his new post as the dean of Juba University. This university was in the southern part of Sudan. Dr. Al-Hadi told me that the plastic surgeon would have no objection especially because his knowledge in glaucoma was very minimal.

The university fixed a date for the discussion of the thesis. The examiners were three. An external examiner was Professor Gorra. He was the head of the eye department at Alexandria University Medical School. He came specially for the discussion of my thesis from Egypt. There were two other examiners from Khartoum University. One of them was an ophthalmologist from Khartoum University. The other examiner was a professor of general surgery at Khartoum University.

When I entered the examination room, I found all the examiners and my three supervisors waiting for me. After I greeted them, I sat down and waited for the discussion. The usual protocol was to let the external examiner start the questions. I found the first one to start was my supervisor, the plastic surgeon. Usually, the supervisors help the student if the examiners push hard. They usually give excuses and try to convince the examiners that what the student did was acceptable.

To my astonishment the plastic surgeon started by telling me that the whole thesis must be written from the beginning. He said, "You wrote only about the surgical treatment of glaucoma." He continued, "You have to select two groups of patients. In one group you do surgery, and in the other, you give them only medical treatment. After a certain period, you compare the vision of the two groups." This means I had to start a new thesis and spend at least another four or five years. I answered him immediately that I had two reasons not to do this. First, the drops and tablets for the treatment of glaucoma in most of the year were not available in the hospital and even in the private pharmacies. The plastic surgeon answered that Khartoum University could export them for me. This was a big lie because I paid for everything in this research. I also knew that Khartoum University's budget was always very limited to the extent that at that time, they stopped most of the medical journal subscriptions because of a lack of funds. I told him, "Secondly, in my experience in Sudan, the patients usually do not continue using their medication. This is seen more in cases of glaucoma because they feel no improvement in vision with the drops, but there may be some deterioration. The end result will be the loss of the patient's vision." I told him, "I feel that this is against medical ethics. I cannot do that and will never do it. Can I lead the patient to blindness just to get my master's degree? If you insist on this request, I will not do this thesis."

The exam room was tense. They asked me to go out for some time, so they could discuss the situation together. After a few minutes, Dr. Abd-El Gadir, the third supervisor, came out of the room and left. I noticed that he was outraged. I knew he was very upset by the plastic surgeon's request. After about half an hour, they asked me to come in. The external examiner Dr. Gorra asked me a few questions and also the internal examiner did. Then they asked me to go out and wait. Dr. El-Hadi came out and talked with me alone. He told me that the plastic surgeon insisted that I do the thesis again his way. The external examiner, Professor Gorra, told him, "Since you signed the title of the thesis, and it was only surgical, you have no right to ask for medical treatment now." Then the rest of the examiners and the supervisors intervened and reached a compromise. They suggested that I can add a paragraph on the medical treatment of glaucoma. Since I insisted not to put any patient on medical treatment, they asked me to pick the data from the records of the glaucoma clinic of Khartoum Eye Hospital.

I told them I agree, but I was working in Halfa Al-Jadeeda. They told me that they would ask the Ministry of Health to transfer me to work in Khartoum.

I was not happy at all. I asked God why he did not help me; do I have to go through all this thesis writing again?

Dr. El-Hadi told me after a few days that Professor Ahmed Gorra the Egyptian external examiner told him that the thesis was great. He asked him, "Do you have religious discrimination in Sudan. Why did the plastic surgeon do that with Victor?"

After one week, the Ministry of Health declared new regulations. They decided that the capital, Khartoum, was saturated with doctors and not a single doctor would be transferred to Khartoum. I discovered that I was the only ophthalmologist that was transferred to Khartoum. The only colleague that got a master's degree applied to be transferred to Khartoum but was denied. At this point, I thanked God and felt His good care of me. If I passed my master's, I would never be able to work in Khartoum.

I went back to Halfa Al-Jadeeda and packed our luggage, and we moved to Khartoum.

In Khartoum, I picked the records of patients who came to the glaucoma clinic and were diagnosed with glaucoma five years ago. I chose only patients who came for follow-up for at least five years. I divided those patients into two categories. The first group was the patients who did surgeries. The second group was for patients who used medical treatment. I found the loss of vision in patients who used only medical treatment was twice the blindness in patients who had surgery. I was quite sure that many patients who had medical treatment lost their vision and never came back for follow-up. The glaucoma patient in Sudan who came for regular follow-up was a rarity. In addition, glaucoma surgery was much safer than many ophthalmologists thought.

I prepared the new paragraph and added it to my thesis. I had a vacation, and I decided to print the thesis in Assiut because it was cheaper than in Sudan. It was a terrible experience. I went to a professional typist office in Assiut. I sat with the typist all the time to spell every word to him while he was writing. After he typed each paper, Leila had to recheck it. Unfortunately, on each page, there were about fifteen to twenty wrong spellings.

I managed to finish the second version of the thesis after one year of the unsuccessful exam. In the second exam, there were no problems. I passed this exam and got my master of surgery degree at Khartoum University (1985).

I am receiving my master's degree from the president of Sudan and the president of Khartoum University in 1985

I wrote five papers in ophthalmology. I will mention them in a few words.

My first paper was a paper with the title "Blindness in New Halfa, Sudan." I thought of checking the different causes of blindness in Halfa Al-Jadeeda. I took all the records in the Halfa Al-Jadeeda eye department. I found that my previous colleagues were not accurate in their recording of the patient's data. I checked the records of the patients seen by me only. I took all the patients with blindness in one or two eyes. I looked at the different causes of blindness in each case. This was my first paper. I presented this paper at the Sudanese Ophthalmological Society meeting in Khartoum in 1978.

My second paper was presented in the VII Congress of the Sudanese Ophthalmological Society in 1983. The title of this paper was "Color Blindness in Khartoum, Sudan." I wrote this paper with two of my residents. I found that the incidence of color blindness in males was 6.9 percent, which was about the average as in other parts of the world.

Victor during a research in a village, Sudan 1977

I am doing research in a Nomad village.

I did a small survey in this village, and in other villages, I checked the eye pressure of everyone in the village over the age of eighteen years old. All the people with the possibility of glaucoma, I asked them to come to the hospital for further exams and possible treatment.

My third paper was "My Experience with Intraocular Lens Implantation in Sudan." I was the first one to do intraocular lens implantation in Sudan. I wrote in this paper the results of my operations. I addressed the advantages of doing this operation compared to the traditional cataract extraction without implantation. I presented this paper in the VII Congress of the Sudanese Ophthalmological Society.

My fourth paper was "Trachoma Causes Angle-Closure Glaucoma." This paper was presented to the XVI Pan-American Congress of Ophthalmology. This meeting was held in the Dominican Republic. The conference was for all the ophthalmologists of America from Canada to the USA and all Central America and South America. The story of this paper started with a letter from Dr. Simmons, whom I did four months of fellowship in Boston in 1985. In his letter, he mentioned that the following Pan-American Congress of Ophthalmology would be held in 1987. He suggested that I present a paper at this conference. He asked me to send the abstract of the paper to Dr. Armaly in Washington, DC. Dr. Armaly was one of the top ten glaucoma specialists in the USA. He at that time was the president of the glaucoma congress. I chose a paper and sent the abstract to Dr. Armaly. The committee accepted my paper. I traveled to New York and from there to Santo Domingo in the Dominican Republic, the place of the conference.

The XVI Pan-American Congress of Ophthalmology conference entrance

When I entered the conference's main hall where I was going to present my paper, I was shocked. More than two thousand ophthalmologists were attending the first session. My paper was on the first day. The hall was on two levels, and there was instantaneous translation to Spanish and Portuguese languages. Some papers were presented in Spanish and some in Portuguese because the conference included all the ophthalmologists from Canada to Brazil.

I am proud that I presented this paper at such a large and prestigious conference.

My fifth paper was in 2017, I published a paper with the title, *A non-surgical approach to the management of exposure keratitis due to facial palsy by using mini-scleral lenses.*

Medicine (Baltimore). 2017 Feb; 96(6): e6020.

Published online 2017 Feb 10. doi:

Victor Zaki, MB, BCh, OD*

Reviewer of a paper. In March 2017 the Ophthalmic Plastic and Reconstructive Surgery journal (OPRS) asked me to review a paper before they accepted it for publication.

They wanted to see my opinion if the paper was good enough for publication or not, and I did.

Chapter 44

Moving to the Capital Khartoum in 1983 and Starting My Clinic in Khartoum 2

We packed our furniture and the clinic's furniture and moved from Halfa Al-Jadeeda to Khartoum. God arranged that one of the apartments of my parent's house became vacant at that time. So we moved to that apartment. It had two rooms and a verandah. My mother was living alone in the other apartment of the same house. She suggested that we add a hall that was part of her apartment to our apartment, so we had four rooms. We used one of the rooms as a clinic for me and the rest as a living area for us. Having the clinic and living in the same place was a new experience. It was not always convenient, especially when friends come after working hours. After their visit, they asked for an exam. Leila was very wise to keep the children in the back part of the apartment away from the clinic and the patients. Many of the patients who used to come from Halfa Al-Jadeeda and know Leila went inside the apartment to say hi to Leila. They were innocent and loving. They felt that this was a duty to come and meet Leila. Some of them were her patients in Halfa Al-Jadeeda, so they asked her to see them or their children inside our living space. If you imagine that Leila was a dermatologist, you can feel how Leila felt in such cases.

The transition was sudden for our children. To come from a small city like Halfa Al-Jadeeda to the capital Khartoum was a big culture shock. In Halfa Al-Jadeeda there was no television transmission. We had a video we bought from an American couple with few films. Khartoum had a TV transmission, but it was only from 6:00 PM to 10:00 PM. In Khartoum, the number of cars was about at least fifty times more than in Halfa Al-Jadeeda. In Khartoum, there were paved streets and high buildings. In downtown Khartoum, there were many fancy big stores. The River Nile with its two tributaries, the White Nile and the Blue Nile passed in the middle of the capital. There were big, modern hotels in Khartoum like the Meridian, Hilton, and the old Grand Hotel.

At night many of the Coptic families go to the Coptic club. This was a social club that had a big space of green grass. There was a huge hall for indoor parties to be used on cold nights in winter. Most of the year, the people sit in chairs around small tables over the grass. Most of the families sit together and join a few tables together. The club usually opens each evening and closes late at night at 1:00 AM or 2:00 AM. In the club, they used to serve dinner and soft drinks. Some of the people bring their alcoholic drinks with them. I do not drink alcohol. Many families celebrate their children's birthday parties in the club. All the members use the club for the wedding reception. In these receptions, most of the club would be occupied by the people attending the occasion. A few people may be sitting aside who were the regular club attendants. Most of the people attending the club regularly were relatives or good friends. On an ordinary weekend evening, there would be at least fifty to sixty families. There were ping-pong tables and basketball courts. All the children play with each other in different age groups. In many cases, the mother and children go to the club early; the husband joins them after work. We used to ask the children to go to the club after the Thursday afternoon mission class. Leila and I join them after we finish work in our clinics.

The director of the club for a long time was my cousin Adeeb. I think he was the founder of the club. He was doing this as a volunteer. As soon as we moved to Khartoum, he asked me to join the club, and I did.

In Khartoum, we used our two cars, the Land Rover 1950s model and the Volkswagen Beetle 1964. In Sudan, the cars can be used for many years because they do not rust. The weather is usually dry, except for a few days in July and August. In those days there may be some rain for a few hours or even a few minutes. The problem with cars in Sudan was the availability of spare parts. When we buy cars the first question was the availability of spare parts. In the 1950s and 1960s, the most common cars were English cars like Austin, Land Rover, Morris Minor, Hillman. Some of the German cars like Mercedes and Volkswagen were also available. I remember only one car was a Chevrolet which was a large and luxurious car. Another American car was the car of the American missionary that used to take us to their Sunday school. That car was a Ford station wagon. Most of the cars used as taxis were Hillman. In the 1970s the Japanese cars invaded the market due to the traffic change from the left side to the right side of the road. The Sudanese government made it in 1974. By the 1980s there were almost no English cars except the old ones that survived from the 1950s and 1960s.

Our cars were old. Our Volkswagen was about twenty years old when we arrived in Khartoum in 1983. We already did more than one massive repair to the engine. We changed many other parts, as well. I remember the mechanic who used to repair it in Halfa Al-Jadeeda was a very muscular one. He used to lie under the car, lose the engine of the car, and let it drop on his chest. Then he moved away from the car with the car engine on his chest.

In 1985 the Volkswagen car was always in need of repair. We decided to get a new car. We bought a new car Subaru 700. This was a four-door car but with a two-cylinder engine. If you are not familiar with this term, it means that the engine has only half of the parts of the regular cars. It's the engine that is almost like a motorcycle engine. It was very economical in gas consumption. This was a big advantage in countries like Sudan where there is a gas shortage. We gave our old Volkswagen to the person who was doing the repairs. We offered him the car for free. With the arrival of a new small car, the Subaru, I thought Leila would use it all the time and leave the tough riding Land Rover. Leila, to my astonishment, refused to use the new car for some time. She said that she was more comfortable with the Land Rover.

After a few months and due to the severe shortage of gas, Leila was forced to drive the Subaru.

For Leila and myself, our lifestyle changed. In Halfa Al-Jadeeda we used to go back to our house during the breakfast hour which was between 9:00 AM and 10:00 AM. Leila used to check out the children and prepare dinner. In Khartoum due to the long distances between work and home, the luxury of going back home for breakfast was not applicable. We used to have breakfast in our workplaces, which were the hospitals.

Leila worked in Khartoum Hospital, dermatology department. She used to work there before and after our period in London. Leila as usual loved her work and her patients.

In Khartoum 2, I opened my private clinic in my parents' house. Most of my patients were coming from New Halfa; some were relatives and friends.

In a few months, the clinic was very busy. When we moved to live in Imtidad Al-Jadeed, I added an operating theater and a room for the patient to stay overnight. A clinic for Leila was the last to be added.

Chapter 45

Living in Al-Imtidad Al-Jadeed, Khartoum 1985–1988

We settled in Khartoum nicely after I returned from the USA. The income of my clinic was fairly good and was increasing every year. This was mainly because of the presence of the operating theater in the clinic. Also now, many patients knew me in Khartoum. I was well-known for my glaucoma experience. I never remembered receiving any patient referred to me from any colleague. All my patients were referred to me by other glaucoma patients. I did glaucoma operations about five times more than all the Sudan ophthalmologists combined did in the same period. I was the only eye surgeon in Sudan who did all the glaucoma operations by the operating microscope. Leila was working in Khartoum Hospital, dermatology department. She was active in teaching the residents and the newly graduated specialists. Leila did some research in dermatology, mainly in leishmaniasis. She described a very unique phenomenon that nobody found before. It was called the IDE reaction. Leila was the only doctor who found this reaction in patients with leishmaniasis. Leila wrote three papers and presented two of them in the Sudanese Dermatology conferences, and one in the Arab Dermatology conference. Leila was very good as a dermatologist. She was very observant, and this was very important for dermatology. Many times when we were together, Leila would tell me to look at that man passing by, who had one leg shorter than the other. I usually could not detect such things easily. Leila was doing private practice in a clinic next to mine. We shared the same secretary and the patients' waiting area. She used to finish early with her patients' consultation and wait for me, so we could go home together. In the last few years, she started to come and help me in my clinic by writing the patient's data and the prescriptions. I always have a problem with writing. I am very slow. Leila writes very quickly, so she was very helpful to me. She used to do that after the end of her clinic.

Our children were doing fine. They get used to living in Khartoum. They had their own friends from school, church, and family. All of them used to go to Catholic schools in Khartoum. The boys' school was Camboni school, and the girls' school was Sister's school. For primary school, the girls attended the same school as the boys, and it was called St. Francis school. They studied all the subjects in English and studied the Arabic language as a separate subject. All of our children used to go with us to the Coptic Orthodox church on Sunday mornings and the Evangelical Sunday school on Sunday evenings. On Thursday evenings, they used to go to the American missionary. This was a Sunday school but held on Thursday, so it did not have any conflict with the other churches' regular Sunday schools. After they finished with the missionary school, they usually go to the Coptic club. Later on Leila and I join them in the Coptic club.

In Al-Imtidad we lived in Amin's house.

They live on the ground floor, and we lived on the upper floor. Amin was a high school teacher. I think he was a science teacher. When we lived in his house, he was retired. Amin had a quiet personality. I never heard him shout or get angry. He was very handy; he usually fixed anything by himself. He used to spend a lot of his time taking care of his garden. Apparently, his scientific background helped him a lot in getting a well-organized and healthy garden. In Khartoum, the weather was very dry and hot, so most of the grass was always dry. Amin's grass was always green and healthy. He always watered the grass. This was an expensive thing in Sudan. He usually had many flowers and roses. For us, it was nice to have a nice-looking garden in our house without spending time to care for it. During this time and while living in Amin's house, a bad thing happened.

Amin was climbing a ladder to fix something on the wall; unfortunately, he lost his balance. He fell on the floor and broke his hip. Amin had diabetes, but his diabetes was well controlled. They took him to a private hospital. They decided to proceed with surgery to fix the fracture. I remember his youngest daughter Salma came to Leila and told her that she had a bad dream. She saw in her dream a big tree in their house, and the main stem broke. She said she was not happy with this dream and was worried about her father's health. She said her dreams were always predicting what would happen. The surgeon proceeded with the surgery, unfortunately, Amin died ten days later. Is it true that sometimes we can see the future in our dreams? We missed Amin; he was a lovely person to know.

Amin's wife was Magdoline. She was the daughter of a Coptic Orthodox priest in Om-Durman, who died many years ago. I remember when I was young and living in Om-Durman, we used to attend the service in his church. He was very strict during the service. If any of the babies started to cry inside the church, he used to stop the service until the mother took the child out of the church. Now I feel that he was a very wise man. In this church, most people were not that good at restraining their children in the church. Magdoline was a very social and loving lady. She was a very good friend to Leila. She considered us as her own family. We used to leave the children with their babysitter alone. We relied mainly on Magdoline on supervising the children.

Many times Leila left the oven on and called Magdoline from work to turn off the stove. Leila used to go down and eat or drink tea with Magdoline and have a long chat with her. We never considered Amin's family as owners of the flat, but we considered them our family. About 1993, Magdoline and her son and three daughters and their families immigrated to Canada. When we visited Canada in 1997, we visited them and had a nice time with them. In 1999 they visited us in Boston on their way to Florida. In September 2000, Leila visited Toronto, Canada, and visited them as well.

Amin's older daughter was Mervat. She got married to Adel, who was my friend in high school and university.

They got married three months before us. Their older son was twenty-five days older than our son Tony. They were our best friends as a family. We used to go together on picnics. Adel and his family moved to the Arab Gulf countries in about 1976. In about 1988 they immigrated to Australia. Now because of the distances, we only contact them every year once or twice with Christmas cards and Easter cards. Now Adel and Mervat have four boys. My friend Adel became a Coptic Orthodox priest in Australia.

The second daughter of Amin got married to and moved to the Arab Gulf countries many years ago. They still live there, but their older children are studying in Canada. I think they plan to settle in Canada later on.

The third daughter is Mercy. She is married to Nabeel an engineer, who had a high post in the Sudanese government. He is a nephew of Anba Danial, who is the archbishop of Khartoum Coptic Orthodox church. This family, Beh family, owned some houses and lands in downtown Khartoum. Their grandfather was a high-ranking official in the Sudanese government in the 1880s. This was the reason that he got this name Beh, which was one of the honorary posts for high-ranking people. Nabeel and his siblings built a four-story building in their properties in downtown Khartoum. He lived with Mercy and their three children in one of those apartments for some years until they immigrated to Canada with his mother-in-law. Nabeel had a perfect relationship with his in-laws. A few years ago, he died in Toronto. Leila is still in contact with Mercy almost every week or two.

The third daughter is Salma. We know Salma from when she was in junior high school. After they immigrated to Canada, she got married to a Sudanese Coptic man. Salma has two daughters and a son. In 2020 Salma, without any previous disease, died suddenly.

Amin's only son finished his education in Sudan as a communication engineer. He immigrated with the rest of the family to Canada. He got married in Canada after they immigrated.

Amin's family was financially well off, good income, luxury houses, and a good social life. Why did they move to Canada and start a new life in Canada?

The answer is living in Sudan under Omar Al Basheer Islamic military rule was not safe for Sudanese Copts. The regime could accuse anyone of false crime and with Islamic judge, go to prison or be tortured.

We had other neighbors in the house just in front of our flat in Al-Imtidad. This was the family of Azer. He was a teacher in Comboni schools. He was old when we lived near them. His wife was Mona, and they had three sons. The older son was Edward. He was about twenty-seven years old at that time, but he was mentally retarded. He was unable to finish school. I think he was able to read a bit. His mother was giving him a lot of attention. All the time, she was observing him. He used to spend most of his time standing on the door of their house. Almost every five minutes, she would go out to check that he was OK. He was always well dressed. He used to go to Sunday school with our children. He was twenty-seven and the other children were five to ten years old. He used to enjoy riding the bus with the children and even play with them. In spite of that the older children tried to avoid him and the younger ones were always afraid of him. Edward was not mongoloid, and he looked completely normal. He could speak well and comprehend many things easily. I felt that it was a blessing from God that we had normal kids. At the same time, I admire how this family handled this problem in a perfect way. I never saw them complaining about having a mentally retarded child. Azer's family had no car. The father usually took public transportation. Their other two sons were studying, one in England and the other one in Cairo, Egypt. Their son in England got married to an English girl. After we left Sudan, Azer died, and the rest of the family moved to Egypt. We used to visit Adly and his family at Christmas, Easter, and on a few other occasions.

Our children used to attend Sunday school in the Coptic Orthodox Church. At a certain point, Tony's Sunday teacher persuaded him to be a *shammas*. Those usually dress in a special uniform and help the priest in the service by singing and doing other chores. Tony's teacher told him that the bishop would anoint him by praying over his head and make a cross-like cut in his hair. Tony was terrified by this idea. He insisted not to go to the Coptic Orthodox Sunday school again. Sandra had another problem. The church had a special bus to pass and collect all the children from their homes and bring them to Sunday school. The bus of the Coptic Orthodox Church was, as most of the other buses in Sudan were. locally made. There was a sharp edge of steel pointing out of the seat. Sandra, when she walked inside the bus, had a scratch on her leg with this sharp steel. She decided not to go to this Sunday school again. We decided to send them to the evangelical church Sunday school. All the Sunday schools in Sudan were held separately from the Sunday morning church service. So the Sunday schools were held on Sunday afternoons. The evangelical church had a smaller bus, which was new and was foreign made. Sandra was very happy with the new bus. Tony, Sandra, and Jennie found themselves to have special attention in this Evangelical Sunday school. The number of students in the Evangelical Sunday school was about one-tenth of the students in the Coptic Orthodox Sunday school. Our children continued in this Evangelical Sunday school till we left Sudan in 1990. They used to go with us to the Coptic Orthodox Church service on Sunday morning.

Jennie, one evening after coming from the Sunday school bus, fell inside the public gutter in front of our house. The drainage of rainwater in Sudan was through a system of gutters or small canals on the side of the streets. Some of those canals were deep and others were shallow. Most of those canals were not covered, so anyone could fall inside those canals easily. The one that was in front of our house was about three feet deep and had built sides. Actually, most of it was covered, but a few covers were missing. Jennie scraped her leg. Tony and Sandra managed to pull her out. In Sudan, safety issues were not greatly stressed.

Chapter 46

My First Visit to Boston, Fellowship in Glaucoma, 1985

After I got my master's degree in glaucoma, I felt that I had to gain foreign clinical experience in glaucoma. I wanted to see practically what the glaucoma specialists in developed countries did. I wrote fifty-one letters to different glaucoma specialists in the USA, England, Germany, Sweden, and Holland. I gave them an abstract of my thesis and asked them if there was any chance to work with them for a short period. There were only two positive responses. One of them was from Dr. George Spaeth, one of the top five glaucoma specialists in the USA. He told me that there were no funds in his university to support such a visit. He suggested that I come and spend the time I want with him and I could stay all this period in his house as a guest. He mentioned that we could exchange our knowledge during this period. It was very encouraging for me to hear this from one of the top glaucoma specialists in the world.

The other positive response was from Dr. Richard Simmons. He was one of the top five glaucoma specialists in the USA. He was a professor at Harvard Medical University in Boston. He offered me the position of a special fellow in glaucoma. No salary was offered, but he promised to provide residency free for me alone (not my family). The fellowship program was for twelve months. I thought that this was a good opportunity for me. So I immediately sent my acceptance letter. In August 1985, I landed in Boston for the first time. As soon as I reached the exit, I found someone lifting cardboard with my name on it. I introduced myself to him. He spoke with me in Arabic. He said, "I am Mustafa, an Egyptian eye doctor." He told me that he was a special fellow as well with the New England Research Foundation. This was the name of the research body that Dr. Richard Simmons directed. It was very nice to see Mustafa and especially when he mentioned that we would live in the same apartment. We took the taxi to the apartment. It was in downtown Boston on Cambridge Street. He pointed to an eight-story building just in front of the apartment and told me that the office was located in this building. When we reached the flat, he introduced me to the third special glaucoma fellow. He was George, an ophthalmologist from Venezuela. George told me that he was married and had two children. His father was an orthopedic surgeon, and his mother was an ophthalmologist. His older brother was an ophthalmologist as well, specializing in the retina. I found George an adorable, sociable person. He was always telling jokes and was very flexible. Mustafa was not married but had a strong attachment to his family. He used to call Egypt at midnight; it would be about 7:00 AM in Cairo. His telephone bill was always very high. He used to complain about the amount he was paying every month for the telephone, but he was unable to reduce it. The flat was very convenient and equipped with a full kitchen, microwave, and TV. Mustafa was fond of watching movies and cartoon films. He usually spent all Saturday and Sunday mornings on those cartoon films. It was good that no one was an alcoholic. Both George and Mustafa drank on social occasions only.

The next morning I met Dr. Simmons for the first time. I saw him before lecturing in one of the eye conferences in Orlando, Florida, in 1980. He was about fifty years old and was always well dressed. When I spoke to him, I found him very polite. He asked about my wife and family and if they were safe in Sudan. He introduced me to all the people in the office. The office had an outpatient clinic on the sixth floor, and the New England Glaucoma Foundation was on the fourth floor. There were eight glaucoma specialists working in the office and four regular fellows, Americans, and we were four special fellows. The fourth special fellow was a girl from Iran called Faeza. Her husband was in Iran, working as an orthopedic surgeon. She had two daughters living with her in Boston.

Dr. Simmons introduced me to his wife Anne. She was working as the director of the New England Glaucoma Foundation. She was a very sociable lady and was always smiling. She was very active and worked hard.

Life for me in Boston was a lot of fun. There was no real responsibility. My time was between watching all Dr. Simmon's operations and watching him examine almost all the patients. For me seeing the way he dealt with patients was a bit strange at the beginning. I found him very polite to his patients. He usually took a lot of time to explain the problem to the patient. Also, I noticed that before he saw the patient, he usually studied the patient chart very carefully. I was very impressed by him as a doctor and as a person. He was an honest and very gentle person.

Watching the operations was an excellent experience for me. I noticed that Dr. Simmons was using the operating microscope in all his operations. There was also a video camera attached to the microscope. So all the operations were videotaped. There was a TV screen in the operating theater to watch the operation with the same magnification as the surgeon. So I used to watch his hands working directly and at the same time watch the TV screen. I must say that he was a good surgeon; he was a perfectionist. He never rushed to finish the operation. I learned a lot from him as a surgeon.

After the first week, Dr. Simmons started to trust me more and asked me to see the patients and discuss with him the results as the regular fellows. He then saw the patients and treated them. This was also a very good experience for me. I learned all his techniques for treating glaucoma patients.

I started to go around the clinic and watch the technicians using different instruments. I learned for the first time how the automated visual field machines worked. They had Octopus and Humphrey automated visual field machines. At the beginning, this was difficult, but I took all the manuals and read all of them. I also studied all the related books which were in the New England Glaucoma Foundation Library. I also watched other tests like ultrasound machines and photography machines. I must say that it was a cultural shock for me the first month. Quickly, I managed to master all the visual field machines and did the tests by myself.

I used to attend all the lectures that the regular fellows attend in Mass Eye Ear Infirmary. This was the Ophthalmology Department of Harvard Medical School. It occupied a thirteen-floor building and was considered the most advanced eye institute in Boston, and maybe the USA and the world. I discovered that my clinical experience was very good in relation to American fellows. I learned more in some very specific specialized subjects, mostly about research.

During one of the lectures, I spoke with the chief ophthalmologist of the retinitis pigmentosa department. He showed me his department. I saw all the advanced instruments he was using in this department. He then offered me a permanent job to work with him (a paid job). I contacted Leila in Sudan and mentioned the chance of getting a permanent position in America. In this case, Leila and the children would come and settle with me. Leila refused the idea completely. So I apologized to the retinitis pigmentosa doctor.

After four months in Boston, I started to be more worried about Leila and the children. The political situation was not that stable. At the same time, I found myself learning all that I could learn. So I felt that staying more in Boston would not benefit me.

I spoke with Dr. Simmons about going back to Sudan. He was very understanding. He told me, "OK, you go now, and at any time, when you feel the situation in Sudan is better, you can come again."

I decided to incorporate all the modern methods in the operations in my clinic in Khartoum. I bought an operating microscope and a set of the most advanced instruments for the operating theater. Actually I took the list from Dr. Simmon's operating assistant. Also, I bought all the instruments for cataract extraction and intraocular lens implantation. I got the lenses that I would put in the patient's eyes and the special solution they used to insert these lenses in. It was an expensive project.

I felt if I wanted to start the lens implantation in Sudan, I must have the right instruments.

During my stay in Boston, I learned the technique of lens implantation from Dr. Simmons, and I bought the same instruments he was using. This was the first step to start lens implantation in Sudan for the first time. I was the first eye doctor in Sudan to do lens implantation. Also, I was the first eye doctor in Sudan who did all his surgeries with the operating microscope.

Chapter 47

The Park Street Church in Boston

The first Sunday for me in Boston, I walked in the street around the apartment where I was living, looking for a church. I found a church. I could not remember the name of that church. The preacher spoke about racial discrimination in South Africa. I felt that this was not what I went to the church to hear. I decided to go to another church the following week. The following week I went to Park Street Church. At the door, there were some people greeting the people who came to the service. The person who greeted me asked me from where I came and which language I speak. I told him I came from Sudan, and I spoke Arabic. He told me that there was an after-church service, a special meeting for people coming from other countries. He also mentioned that the pastor who was responsible for that meeting spoke Arabic. I attended the main church service, and it was very good. The preacher was an old guy who was preaching about the sermon on the mountain. Actually, the preacher continued with the sermon on the mountain every week for all the four months that I was in Boston. He was a very good preacher. After the main service, I went to a special meeting for the foreign students. They call this meeting FOCUS, which stood for Friendship of Overseas College and University Students. The pastor who was responsible for that meeting was of Syrian origin called Joseph Sabounji. He was able to speak Arabic, but he usually preferred to speak

English. Apparently he wanted everyone to understand what he was saying. I found the meeting was very nice. There were about twenty at that meeting. Most of them were of Chinese origin. There were also people from Japan, Korea, Iran, different countries from Africa, and a few volunteers from the USA.

FOCUS, Park Street Church

They first pray then sing simple English songs. Usually, Joe, as everybody calls Joseph Sabounji, gives a short talk. Some give their testimonies, and the newcomers introduce themselves. In the end, they put some snacks to eat. Usually, there is food from different countries. There was a Swedish lady who used to put the food on the table and clean at the end. I discovered later that she was a professor in one of the universities in Boston. Another lady called Sandra originally came from Brazil and married an American. Sandra and her husband were old, but many times they invited us to their home. She used to bring food with her to the FOCUS meeting. I found FOCUS a very simple, nice meeting. Joe gave me the schedule for the next month. Every Saturday, they have a trip to some of the places around Boston. Once we went to the Kennedy Memorial Library, another time to the science museum. I will never forget the time we went to watch an American football game. It was raining very hard, but the game continued and we stayed till the end. Each Thursday evening and on another morning, there were English classes.

Some American volunteers used to come and teach. Those English classes were free and for any person, even non-Christians. I attended the Thursday class during my four months stay in Boston. I had a very good relationship with those volunteers. One of them was studying to be a missionary; his name was Paul. Later on, he got married to an Ethiopian girl. He sent me his wedding pictures when I was in Sudan. When I visited Boston in 1987 for one week, he invited me to his house. I went and had dinner with him and his Ethiopian wife. He lived in Dorchester, and this was a big town east of Boston with a very high African-American population. He mentioned to me that he chose this town, so his wife would feel that she was living among people who looked just like her. He told me from the first day he had problems with his car. One day the side mirror was stolen, the other day, they scratched the whole car with an iron nail. The kids of this community did not like a white person to live among them!

In FOCUS many Chinese and other nationalities came to know Christianity and became true believers. In FOCUS we were invited to many American houses for dinner. I remember we were invited once to the American family on Saturday morning, and we stayed there all day long. The family had five adopted children. The children were originally from different countries. We felt that this family was one of the real, good Christian families. They welcomed all members of our group, who were about twenty. They prepared a very delicious meal for us and served plenty of soft drinks. Their attitude was amazing, and they were very friendly as if we were their relatives who came after being away for a long time. I felt in FOCUS as if they were my second family. You feel only pure Christian love. You do not see in FOCUS the competition to be the leader. This attitude is the main problem that destroys all other churches.

On Thanksgiving day, FOCUS did a big dinner banquet. They serve many turkeys and high-quality food. Many of the volunteers from the main church did the cooking and served the food. At least three hundred people came to this dinner.

When I was ready to leave Boston for Khartoum, FOCUS did a small celebration for me. They gave me a T-shirt with FOCUS printed on it. Park Street Church was one of the main reasons that I decided to come back to Boston.

In 1990 when we came as a family to Boston to live for good, we used to go to Park Street and FOCUS regularly for the first six months. After the first six months, we found the Arabic Evangelical Baptist church through one of the FOCUS pamphlets. The children were, to some extent, homesick and needed to be with Arabs, so we started to come regularly to the Arabic church.

Till now, our relationship with Park Street Church is very good. All our children will not hesitate to go to Park Street Church if there is any chance.

Chapter 48

Back to Sudan with the First Operating Microscope 1985

I decided to go back to Sudan and cut short my fellowship in glaucoma in Boston. I felt that I gained enough knowledge and staying more would not help a lot. The other hidden factor was that I was keen to be back with my wife and children. I returned to Khartoum a few days before Christmas. It was December 21, 1985. It was a nice sensation when you see your wife and children after four months. Leila was willing to make any sacrifices to keep me happy. She stayed in Sudan, where she had no relatives. She was responsible for all our four children. She was taking care of my clinic and her clinic. Dr. Nabeela worked in my clinic during my study in the USA. During this period, my son Tony got his first glasses. Diana, at that time, was about two years old. I felt that I was away for years. Everything changed; my children were older.

I decided to start working full time in my private practice. As I mentioned before, I took an unpaid vacation for eighteen months to go to the USA. So I simply continued with my unpaid vacation and worked in my private clinic full time.

I brought instruments for eye operations from the USA. I could continue doing the operations in private hospitals, but I decided to have my own operating theater in my clinic. To accomplish that, first we moved to live in a new apartment away from the clinic. God arranged that at that time the apartment of Amin in the New Extension was vacant. This was the same apartment we were living in, in 1974–1975. Amin and his family were very good friends. His daughter Mervat and her husband Adel were our best friends. Adel was my schoolmatein high school and went to study at Assiut University at the same time. So we moved to the new apartment. It had four rooms and a huge living room in the middle. In addition, there was a huge balcony for sleeping at night and staying in all day long except if it was sunny. In Sudan, the sun is really hot. I remember many times, I bought a thermometer for my clinic, and when I reached my house, the thermometer burst. In my car, there was no air conditioning, and the sun usually was very hot. This is the reason that the temperature usually goes very high. The space in the glass of the thermometer was usually not enough for the mercury to expand.

The clinic now had two extra rooms. I converted one of them to be the operating theater, and the other one was the patient's room to sleep in till the next morning. It was the tradition at that time to keep the patient after the eye operation till the next morning. This tradition was even in the USA. In the patient's room, I put two beds. One of the beds was for the patient and the other for his relative. In Sudan, family bonds are very strong. I had a nurse that stayed with the patient all night, just in case! I now remember that all patients who came for eye surgeries had a relative with them except one patient. This patient was working as a guard for a nearby elementary school. He was very poor. He was living in the school. The teachers in the school brought him because he was completely blind from cataracts in both eyes. They told me that he had no money or relatives. I did his operation for free. The next morning, I took off his eye patch, and he was able to see. He took his small bag of clothes and walked to his school. I felt that God rewarded me a lot by simply taking care of this patient. I felt how God takes care of all of us even if we have no relatives or money. Another special patient was a very poor Eritrean priest. He fled from his country because of the civil war. I did a combined cataract and glaucoma operation on him. Actually, this priest paid me. He used to stop me from starting the exam and asked me to bow, and then he prayed for me. He used to come for follow-ups regularly to monitor his glaucoma. He never let any exam start without his nice, short prayer. I am not sure what happened to this priest after I left Sudan, but I am sure that God will find someone to take care of his eyes.

Once, I told this Eritrean priest about the story of one of my friends in Boston. This friend was an Eritrean student who came to study in the USA. In his first few months in the USA, he went into a bad car accident and had paralysis of both legs. So he was using a wheelchair permanently. During his illness, he got to know God more. He changed his studies and went to be a priest. My poor priest patient's comment was funny but very true. He said, "Sometimes God has to break our legs to get our attention, but this is better for us."

To furnish my operating theater, I asked someone to build a special operating table for me.

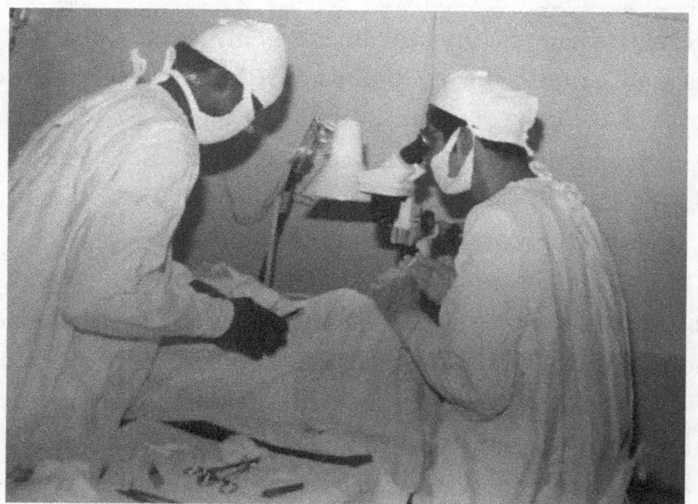

First operating microscope in Sudan

This was special because I have to fix my operating microscope on it. Actually, it was great. It had the right height, and much better than the ready-made ones. I bought an autoclave to sterilize the towels and the operating gowns. Also, I bought a hot-air oven. It is a special oven to sterilize the fine-eye instruments. The autoclave usually destroys the sharpness of the instruments. My brother Joseph helped me to buy those two instruments. Leila tailored some gowns and towels. The rest of the gowns were done by one of the surgical assistants, who was a tailor by chance.

In Sudan the electricity cuts were widespread. I could not tolerate this during an eye operation, so I bought a generator for such emergencies. At a certain period, there was also a gas shortage. At that time there was no gas to put in the generator. So I invented another alternative. I put connecting wires from the operating theater to outside the clinic. In case of an electricity cut, I ask my assistant to connect those wires to my car battery. In the operating theater, I connected the other end of wires to a car lamp. Actually, I used this method a few times. I usually did not start an operation like this, but I could finish any operation without a problem like this.

Speaking about the electricity cuts, I bought from Boston some rechargeable batteries for my instruments in my clinic. There was always a shortage of batteries for penlights and the other bigger batteries. I bought a voltage changer from 220V as in Sudan to 120V as of the battery charger. Unfortunately, at a certain period, there were electricity cuts continuously to the extent that the time I charged them was not enough and they were useless after a few months.

I had up-to-date surgical instruments. Most of the instruments, I was the only one to have them in Sudan. One of those instruments was a diamond knife. The blade of this knife was made of real diamond. The price of this knife was about one thousand dollars. The advantage of this knife was its sharpness. You can do very precise cutting in any tissue with this knife. Of course, it needed very special care otherwise, it could be destroyed easily.

So my clinic in Khartoum had high-quality instruments but at the same time, adapted to the most primitive life.

As soon as I restarted my clinic again after coming from the USA, the patients started to come regularly. The addition of the operating theater was beneficial to my patients. When the patient had his operation in a private hospital, they usually charge the patient four times what I charge them in my operating theater. The hospital is charging for the use of its operating theater only because I do the surgery. For me, I trust my operating theater much better. I am always sure of the sterilization of the instruments and the gowns and towels. In addition, it is much convenient for me not to travel to another place just to do the operation. The patients and their relatives felt more comfortable when they had their operation in my place.

I used to examine patients in my clinic from about 8:30 AM till 2:00 PM. Then I do one or two operations. I go home to get my lunch. This is usually the main meal of the day. I usually sleep till about 4:30 PM, take a shower, and go back to my clinic. I usually start at 5:30 PM and see patients till about 9:30 or 10:00 PM. I used to work every day except Sunday. On Fridays, I do the morning session only. A good number of my patients used to come to me, especially from New Halfa, where I was working from 1975 till 1983. Some others were Halfaweyeen but living in Khartoum or other cities. They usually come to me after hearing from their relatives in New Halfa. Many of the Copts living in Khartoum used to come to my clinic.

This was the first time for me to work full time in a private clinic. I used to work before my visit to the USA in the government hospital between 8:00 AM–2:00 PM and work in my private clinic between 5:30 PM–9:30 PM. There were more responsibilities. I had a full-time nurse, an operating assistant, and two shift secretaries. Most of the time, one secretary was able to do the two shifts, but sometimes we had two separate secretaries.

Leila was taking care of most things. She used to observe the nurse and the secretary. Leila sometimes helped me in the operations if, at any point, the operating assistant was unable to come. In all the cataract operations with the lens implantation, Leila was my first assistant. She knew exactly what I was doing and what I wanted to do.

My operating assistant was Khalil. He was about forty years old. He worked in Khartoum Eye Hospital. He used to come on his bike. He was very quiet and very adaptable to what I need.

As secretaries, I had many. Some of them were girls, and some were boys. One of the good secretaries was Mary. She was working with me and at the same time, was a full-time student in one of the universities.

She was studying accounts. She was a very calm person. Her father was a good carpenter. I asked him a few times to do some work for me. Mary graduated from her university. She gave us a picture of her with the graduation robe. I still have this picture. She got married and left her job with us. She moved with her husband to their new house. Next to their house was a new two-story building under construction. In this new building there was a temporary wall built on the second floor. This wall fell after a moderate sand storm. Mary, by chance, was passing in her house, and the floor fell on her. She immediately became paralyzed in her two legs. She was unable to regain her strength. I heard that she was living in a house for handicapped people in Egypt.

The nurse, most of the time, was a nurse at Khartoum Eye Hospital. She worked there from 8:00 AM to 2:00 PM and came to work and slept in my clinic from 2:30 PM till 8:00 AM. She usually helped the patient to go to the bathroom or give him water. Leila used to bring some juice and even bring food for some patients if she felt that they have no relatives.

There was a kitchen in the clinic equipped with all the basic utensils, a fridge, and a cooker. Most of the time, the relative of the patient helps himself by preparing tea or even a light meal. I usually keep the patient one night only, so there was no time to prepare food. Most of the patients bring their already made food with them.

I usually stay in the clinic to see regular patients till about 9:30 PM. The next morning I come in at about 8:00 AM to check the patient's eye and discharge him. So the patient was alone only during the night hours when the nurse was not available.

I was very satisfied with what I was doing. There were a lot of frustrations. The electricity cuts were very bad. The shortage of gas was another problem. We had two cars, a Land Rover and a Subaru. The ration for the gas was almost all the years when we were in Khartoum in 1983–1990. We had to go every three months to get coupons for purchasing gas. Each car was allowed to get gas once a week. I remember the Land Rover was Thursday and the Subaru was on Monday. On that day I had to go early in the morning because there were always long lines. Most of the time I went about 5:00 AM and stayed in line till I got the gas. If I was lucky, I would get it before the time of my children's school. Sometimes Leila was obliged to take them to school with the other car. We tried to avoid that because we always tried to use the Subaru. The Land Rover consumed a lot of gas. When we use the Subaru only, I used the gas in the Land Rover car for the generator. I forgot to mention that each car was allowed to have only four gallons of gas each week. Sometimes I had to withdraw the gas from the Land Rover to use it in the clinic generator.

Chapter 49

Living in Al-Gereif, Khartoum, in Our First-Owned House

In 1974 we bought the land to build a house on it. This was the habit in Sudan. Nobody bought an already built home. We started to build the house gradually starting in 1976. I asked one of my friends, who was a contractor, to build it for me. It took us from 1976–1987 till we had the house finished. In Sudan, there were no mortgages for homes. If you have money, you buy land, and when you get more money, you build the house gradually. This was the reason that in the USA we called it the American Dream. Even if you just got a job, you can buy a house and car and pay the money gradually. The bank usually took a lot of money in interest, but the family could get their dream house immediately. I like this American Dream system. You have to be careful not to borrow too much to the extent that you could not pay it back.

We moved to our new house in 1988. The house was in an area called Al-Gereif. It was to the southwest of downtown Khartoum, and to the west of our clinic. It was almost on the bank of the Blue Nile. It was about seven miles from our clinic. There was no paved road to Al-Gereif, so in the rainy season, it usually got very messy. This was the reason that we kept our Land Rover because it was a four-wheel drive and had extra-powered gears. I remember even with the Land Rover, once, I got stuck in the mud between our house and my clinic. Our new house was great. It was only one floor, a roof, and a large yard. In Sudan, most of the roofs are flat. Ours was flat and surrounded by a short wall. We used to spend all the nights on this roof and sleep on top as well. The weather was always hot, so being on the roof was a great blessing. Remember that the electricity cuts were constant at that time. So you cannot use an air conditioner or air cooler. In Sudan, there were no heaters for the rooms because the coldest temperature in the winter was always above 65 Fahrenheit.

We used to sleep on the roof every night. Some nights a wind storm may start in the middle of the night. Then we have to go in and tolerate the hot weather. In Al-Gereif there were some houses near our house under construction. This usually meant that there were more thieves in the area. For this reason and because Leila and I were in our clinics till late at night, we hired a guard to live in our house permanently. This guard's name was Khalil. He was about fifty years old. His job was just to stay at home all the time. In his first week on the job, a thief managed to enter our house. He was unable to get anything, but I think he tried to open one of the doors inside the house but was not successful. In Sudan, if you have a problem with thieves, the best solution was to get a dog.

Around Christmas time, the missionary pastor Welling announced that his wife found a newly born dog and asked if anyone wanted the dog. We took the dog; he was blind. This was the first time for me to see a newly born dog. The Wellings gave us the dog and a plastic ear pump to give him milk with the pump. Our children were very excited about the small dog. They gave him the name of Bambino. Amazingly Bambino grew very quickly. He became really big and strong. At this stage, we thought of keeping Bambino out in the yard to secure our house. Bambino did the job in more than a perfect way. Nobody could get near our house. When Bambino was on the street, he kept everyone away from there. This was a problem with the neighbors and the people passing by. Bambino would bark and attack anybody passing on the street. We had to keep Bambino inside the house yard for the safety of the people. One of our neighbors lived in the house just in front of our us called Mukhtar. We used to visit Mukhtar and his family. They were very good people. Mukhtar had a big problem with Bambino. Apparently, there was mutual hatred between the two. Mukhtar, on many occasions, tried to hit Bambino with stones. This of course would initiate a strong reaction from Bambino. Mukhtar's wife and children had no problems with Bambino.

Bambino was very intelligent. I remember once I took the children to school in the morning. Bambino managed to go out of the house and tried to follow our car. I tried to drive fast, but Bambino was still running faster to follow the car. After about ten minutes, I managed to turn quickly and left him behind. I was very worried about Bambino. I thought he might not be able to go back to the house. The way we passed was not straight, and the distance was long. Because there were no telephone services in our house, I could not know about Bambino until I returned home at about 3:00 PM. I found Bambino waiting at home safely.

Bambino had the habit of barking and hitting the outer door when he heard my car coming. It was amazing that he usually did that when the car was about one mile from the house. Leila and the children knew beforehand when I was coming. Apparently, dogs have some senses that we humans do not have.

Bambino did not like to have a bath. The children loved to give him his regular baths. When he was young, they managed to force him to do it. When he got bigger and stronger, it was a big challenge. They keep him tied on his leash and used the water hose from afar. Bambino's reaction was to shake his body and spread the water over everyone around. Most of the time, the children would have more water than Bambino. He was a big dog, and when one of the children came near him, he would be excited and jump over the child. Sometimes the child may fall from the weight of the Bambino. Even Leila and I tried to keep away from him.

Once Khalil, the guard, asked permission to go to his hometown to be with his wife for a few weeks. I asked him to bring another temporary guard. He got an old guard called Burma. This name was funny because it meant a pot to keep the water in. Burma had a problem with Bambino. Bambino started to bark at Burma. We tried to convince both parties to calm down and get used to each other. Burma's reaction was hitting Bambino with his stick. From that time, there was a big tension between the two. Burma, to protect himself, brought a big tree branch, about one and a half meters long (six feet). He was carrying this tree branch and hit Bambino if he dared to come near him.

Bambino lived a few years after we left Sudan and died at the age of seven. He was a lovely dog, and we missed him.

Burma used to work as a *fakki*. This was considered as a religious medical practitioner. The patient would come to him and explain his problem and ask for his advice. Most of the cases were ladies who wanted to be pregnant or her husband was dating another lady. Burma would write some of the Quran verses in a small paper and wrap it with cloth or leather (lucky charms). The Quran is the holy book of Islam. The patient had to wear this all day long. Sometimes he burned the paper and mixed the ashes with water. The patient had to drink it or spread it in her house. These were some examples, but fakki usually did more things. Burma usually spent most of his time in the mornings, writing those small papers. He used to have neat handwriting. Most of the people his age were illiterate, so he was a highly educated person. Sometimes when we were in the house, Burma would go out for some time. Most nights, he would come back fully drunk. By the way, in Islam, drinking is prohibited.

Our house in Gereif showing Leila, our children, and Bambino

Khalil came back from his journey. Thank God. After a few weeks, Khalil told us that Burma died.

The next-door neighbors were a man, his wife, and two young children. The man was working in Saudi Arabia. Usually, people who work in Saudi Arabia become rich. This was the case for our neighbor. Their house was very well built with many decorations. His wife used to wear fancy dresses. His children had high-technology toys. They moved to their house when we were in Al-Gereif. Leila, as the habit in Sudan, sent them food and drinks on their first day. We visited them a few times. We had one problem with those neighbors. As high-standard people, they had a nice garden. To keep it alive, he used to keep the hose of water all day long running on the grass. This grass area was next to our house. In a few weeks, we started to see cracks in our walls. Al-Gereif had very fertile soil. This soil was very dark in color and expanded when soaked in water to four times its size. This was the reason that with the expansion of the soil, the walls would move, creating cracks. I tried to tell him about the problem. He said he would build a wall under the ground between his grass area and our house.

There was a Coptic family four houses away from our house. This was the family of Sam. His mother was a second cousin to my father. We knew his sister. She was our priest's wife. Sam was working in one of the companies owned by a Syrian family in Khartoum. He worked hard and built a nice house. We visited them a few times. After we left Sudan in 1990, they immigrated to Canada as most of the Copts of Sudan. We saw them in Canada when we visited Toronto in 1997. They have two daughters. The older was married and moved to the USA through her work in the United Nations. The youngest was Nora. She was a friend of my daughter Sandra, and they used to be in the same class in school.

Life in Al-Gereif was quiet and pleasant.

We lived in our new house for only four months.

Chapter 50

The Khartoum Flood 1988

On Thursday evening, in July 1988, the rain started and did not stop. Usually, the rain in Khartoum lasted for a few minutes to one hour. This Thursday evening, the rain was heavy and continued far longer than usual. I was working in my clinic as usual. Leila was working in her clinic next to me. The rainwater started to accumulate on the clinic floor. Leila and the secretary began to sweep the water out of the clinic floor. Suddenly the electricity went off, and after a few minutes, the water supply was off as well. We started to be worried about our children. Tony, Sandra, Jennie, and Diana were in the American Missionary Sunday school. They usually went with their friends to the Coptic club, where we usually joined them. I went to the Coptic club in my Land Rover. I noticed that by now, all the streets were entirely covered by water. The height of the water was very high in all the streets. I saw only the walls of the houses on the sides of the streets. I tried to keep the car in the middle of the street. Most of the streets had deep gutters on one side. All the huge gutters were not covered, so any could dip in those gutters completely. I drove very slowly. I was afraid that the water might go into my car plugs in the engine, then the car would stop. I managed to reach the Coptic club. Inside the club I found Sandra, Jennie, and Diana in real terror. They told me that Tony was coming with other friends in another car. There were no telephones working to contact any place. I had to carry Diana to the car, and Sandra walked beside me. I went back to carry Jennie, who was nine at that time because the water level was high enough to cover her head if she walked. A family asked me to take them to their home with me. I agreed, and we started our journey from the club to our home. I drove the car slowly, and after about half a mile, a big truck passed from the opposite side. The waves created by that truck forced the water to my car's plugs, and the car stopped. At that point, it was a desperate situation. The time was about 10:00 PM. There were no street lights. All the streets surrounding our car were covered with water to about one meter high (three feet). If I decided to walk, I could not carry Jennie and Diana at the same time. Jennie said this was the same as Noah's flood. I asked my daughters to pray. I assured them that God would send help. After about five minutes, I found a big truck coming. I flashed my car lights to the driver to stop. I asked him if he could give us a ride to our house. His answer was NO. I explained to him that because of the children I could not walk. At last, the driver agreed to take us, and drop us on his way to the nearest place to our house. When he explained his way, I discovered that we had to walk about one mile. I agreed, and I moved the children to the truck. It was a truck to transport meat. So it was like a fridge, it was good that there was no meat, and it was not cold. All of us with the other family moved to the back of this meat truck. The driver dropped us as he promised on his way. Thank God, the street at that point was not covered with high water in the center. We started to walk carefully, and we reached our house safely. We found Tony there already. We were very happy to be safe and together again. I think at that point it was midnight. Now we were in the clinic. We were living in Al-Gereif. Nobody at that point thought about our home in Al-Gereif. We decided to stay in the clinic until the situation was better, then we could drive to Al-Greif. We had no food in the clinic. Our neighbors, Yvonne Faltaos and her family, brought some food for us. They brought as well some clothes for Diana from their son who was at the same age. They gave us some dates and peanuts as additional food. We used the clinic's operating theater gowns as pajamas. There were many gowns that everybody had one. For light, the generator was risky to use because of the level of water. I cannot remember if we had gas for the generator. I had an emergency light that worked with batteries. This emergency light could work for six hours, and then you have to recharge it with electricity. We tried to use this emergency light for a short period and saved the rest of it for the future.

The next morning the water receded a lot, and most of the streets were dry at the center. In Al-Imtidad where my car was, the streets still had high water levels. We left the Land Rover for another day. We took a tour to see the situation. Many houses had their walls crumbled to the floor. In one house, the kitchen fell down in addition to the house wall. We saw the lady cooking inside her open kitchen. Many houses fell down, especially in certain areas in Khartoum North. One of my cousins lost her kitchen. The houses in Sudan were unique. The weather was always hot or very hot. Most of the people use their yard to sleep on at night and to sit most of the evenings and nights. To keep privacy, every house had walls about eight feet high. The walls separate the house from the neighbors' houses and from the street. There were usually one or two doors opening to the street. Some houses had wide doors for the cars to get inside the yard. We call those doors garage doors. It was usually safer to keep the car inside the yard.

Most of the houses in Sudan were not well-founded. They just dug about one meter or sometimes even less and built the walls. The rain was usually moderate in most of the years, so most of the buildings survive the rain without problems. Most of the modern new houses were built with proper foundations like our house in Gereif. The clinic building was strong because all the walls were built with bricks and cement. In many of the houses in low-class areas, the walls were built with mud and mud bricks. Those were the houses that suffer most with heavy rain. In Om-Durman, which was part of the capital, most of the houses were built with *jaloose*. This was a combination of mud and animal stools. Strangely enough, this combination was very strong and nicely resisted the rain. The only problem with those houses was the special smell that came out after every rain.

The water supply continued to be off for five days. This was a big problem, no clean drinking water. In Sudan at that time there was no bottled water. The next morning, no stores were open in the nearest market Khartoum 2 Market, and only one store opened the next day. We were able to buy a few things, mainly food.

The electricity was off for fourteen days, yes for fourteen days continuously. We used to have electricity cuts for eight hours or twelve hours a day, but not for that long period. From the second day, the emergency light was not working. All my batteries of penlights were depleted, I bought them from Boston, rechargeable because there was always a shortage of regular batteries. We managed to cook because we had a butane gas cylinder at the clinic. This was a great blessing at that point. There were no gas pipelines in Khartoum.

We stayed in the clinic for a week, and then we went back to our house in Al-Gereif. It was a terrible experience to drink from the rainwater for five days. We survived. I think I opened my clinic on Monday when the water supply came back.

This was the worst rain and flood I ever experienced in my life. I think the drainage system was bad in Khartoum, but at the same time, the rain was very heavy in a short period. I had no idea what was the amount of rain that Thursday evening. I did not know if anyone of the officials measured it in millimeter or inches.

All of us would remember this flood forever. My daughter Jennie, seven years later, chose to write about this flood in her school assignment.

Chapter 51

Gas Shortage, Leaving Our House, and Moving to a Rented Apartment

After living in our new house, the petrol shortage became strict, and the electricity shortage was more frequent. The ration of gas given for each car was four gallons each week. So we had to decide to move to a flat near the clinic to save on petrol for the generator of the clinic. Some people used to get petrol from the black market. I refused to do that because it was against my principles, and it was risky. So we asked Khalil the guard to live in our house in Al-Gereif. We moved to a rented apartment in El-Zohour Fatahat. Now when I thought of that, this was a bad situation.

We put all our savings for thirteen years to build this house and to use it for four months only and spend a lot of money to rent a flat which was less convenient than our house. At the same time, we had to close our house and spend money to keep a guard for protection. Actually, we had to visit this guard every week to give him food, sugar, and food for our dog. This was the type of life in Sudan. We had to adapt to bad situations to live.

Chapter 52

The Political Changes in Sudan 1956–2019

I am not a historian or a politician. What I am writing may not be 100 percent historically correct. This is what I know and feel about the political changes in Sudan.

The name of Sudan till 1956 was the Anglo-Egyptian Sudan. It was governed by both the English and Egyptian governments. I was young when the last English troops left Sudan. I remember my dad took a picture of the troops leaving from Khartoum Railway Station. There was a referendum in 1955 asking the people in Sudan to choose Sudan's final political status. There were two choices. One was to let Sudan unite with Egypt. The other choice was to declare Sudan as an independent country. Most of the people at that time chose independence. The independence of Sudan was declared on January 1, 1956. On that day for the last time, they lowered the flags of Egypt and England. For the first time, a new flag of the Republic of Sudan was raised. The flag consisted of three equal stripes of green, yellow, and blue. Till now when I remember the first flag of Sudan, it initiates a very happy and proud feeling.

First Sudan Flag in 1956

There was a democratic election. There were three main parties and three smaller ones. The first of the main parties was Watani Democratti, which won the first election. Watani Democratti means national democratic. The leader of this party was a school teacher called Ismail Al-Azhari. He was the leader of most of the demonstrations against the Anglo-Egyptian government before independence. He was a clean politician; everybody respected him. He was elected as the first prime minister of the Republic of Sudan. The second party was the Omma Party. This was a party whose leader was Imam Al-Mahadi. Imam means the religious leader of Islam. The Mahadi family was the same family whose grandparent, Mohammed Al-Mahadi, led the war against the English invasion of Sudan in the 1880s. At that time he and his followers freed the capital from the English invaders. They ruled Sudan for a few years. The English government arranged another bigger attack, using some Egyptian troops and took over Sudan again. The English rulers in the 1950s bestowed the title of Sir to Mahadi's son. The Mahadi family had many followers. They called themselves Ansar. They were mainly living in a small town in the middle of Sudan called Jazeera Abba. The Ansar were very loyal to their leader. They worked for him in his vast agricultural lands. They had the impression that they would go to heaven if they served their leader. At that time most of the Ansar were illiterate. My father was working in a town called Kosti, which was very near Jazeera Abba. For many years after Sudan's independence, the Ansar used to come in big numbers to Khartoum the capital to show their power, especially around election time. Some of the Ansar used to carry swords. Al-Imam Al-Mahadi sent his sons to Egypt to have their secondary school studies. After they finished high school, he used to send them to England to complete their studies at

UK universities. The second generation was completely different from Al-Imam Al-Mahadi apparently because they were open to the outside world. Sadiq Al-Mahadi, who was the latest prime minister in 1988, was even opposing the implementation of the Islamic Sharia laws. Now I felt that to eradicate any fanatic Muslim groups, we had to provide them with education and contact with the outside world. This rule could be applied to any other fanatic religious group. When you see other cultures and people who believe differently from you, you will gradually leave your fanatic ideas.

The third-largest political party in Sudan after independence was the Itihadi Party. The leader of this party was Mohammed Al-Mirghani. He was a religious leader who, as far as I know, was created by the English-Egyptian authorities to oppose the Mahadi authority. The Mirghani had fewer followers. He used to go to Egypt very frequently and had many properties in Egypt. This party was advocating unity with Egypt. This was the reason for their name, which meant unity.

For us, when we were young, we used to differentiate between the Mahadi and Mirghani by the shape of their head cover. The Mahady used to wear the typical Sudanese emma, which was a long white cloth that was wrapped in layers around the head. The Mirghani leader used to wear a head cover, white with a blue top.

A few years after independence, Mirghani's Itihadi Party united with the Watani Democratti Party. The new united party was called the Watani Itihadi Party.

The other small parties were:

1. The Communist Party. This was usually a party that got about seven to eight percent of the votes. They usually promote communist ideas. Some of their leaders had their university studies in the Soviet Union. They usually had a lot of ads, and they were famous for their long speeches. Most of the moderate people do not like them because of their views against all religions. Some of my relatives joined the communist party. A few of the Copts in Sudan were leaders of the communist party. Apparently they felt that they were unable to join the

religious Islamic parties like the Omma and the union party, and later on the Watani Itihadi Party.

2. The Islamic Front Party. From its name, this was a pure Islamic party. They were advocating the implementation of Islamic Sharia laws. The leader most of the time was Professor Hassan Al-Turabi. He was a professor of law at the University of Khartoum. He finished his PhD at Sorbon University in France. At the independence election and after that, they usually got about three percent of the votes.
3. The Southern Sudan small parties. Those usually got some of the votes in Southern Sudan only. Most of the governments asked those small parties to join them in the formation of the government. Many of their leaders were ministers in almost every government.

The democracy in Sudan did not last that long. Three military coups took over the government of Sudan. And the three were removed by people's uprising.

I feel that the people of Sudan could remove any military ruler.

In 1958, two years after independence, a military coup took over the democratically elected government. The leader of this military coup was Ibrahim Abboud. He was the head of the military forces. He replaced all the civilian government and appointed a government; all of them were from the military leaders. Abboud and his government ruled Sudan until 1964. The military government was not that bad. They made a lot of good improvements in Sudan. They built new bridges along the Nile in the capital. They maintained most of the streets in the capital. They arranged the construction of the first highway in Sudan between the capital Khartoum and Wad Medani. This was considered the second city after the capital. The United States of America paid and built this highway for Sudan. Some demonstrations were started by the Khartoum University students against Abboud government. After many clashes between the police, armed forces, and the students, a student was killed. The student's name was Ahmad Al-Ghurashi. His death sparked massive demonstrations against the military government.

All the trade unions arranged a general strike. This was very effective in almost stopping all the life in the capital. Abboud and his colleagues were obliged to step down. This was the first uprising of the Sudanese people against a military government.

The chief justice appointed a civilian transition government to keep the government going till a general election was arranged. At that time, I was in Assiut, Egypt, studying for my university degree. We, the Sudanese students in Assiut, watched the events in Sudan carefully. I remember we celebrated the victory of the people's uprising by making a big ceremony at Assiut University. We invited many of the teaching staff and the Egyptian students. One of our colleagues was a good singer. He sang all the new songs that were written in Sudan during this uprising. One of the very nice songs was "Asbah al subho fala alsijno wala al sajan baghi." The meaning is the morning came, and there is no prison or prison guard there. The original singer of this song was Ahmad Wardi, a very popular singer at that time. Actually, in July 2000 I heard Ahmad Wardi singing in one of the Minneapolis, Minnesota TV stations.

A newly elected democratic government started to rule Sudan from 1964 till 1969.

Another military coup took over in 1969. This new military government was led by Jafaar Nimeiry. The same story was repeated again. They formed a military head of command to rule Sudan. At the same time, they appointed some civilian ministers. One of those civilian ministers was one of my relatives, He was the minister of Health. Before the military coup, he was the chief surgeon of Sudan. In 1972 another attempted military coup started. The leader was one of the current ruling head of command. His name was Hashim Al-Atta. They took over the power for four days. They imprisoned Nimerei in the presidential palace. The new military coup leaders were part of the Nimerei regimen, but they wanted to get the full power. Most of them were communists. On the fourth day, some military forces came from Al-Gadaref, another town in the east of Sudan. They started to attack the new military coup. I remember we were away from our house, and when we came back, we found a bullet inside one of our living halls. We were lucky because this was the place where we usually sat most of the day. Actually, the bullet made a hole in the glass of the window and went through the hall and settled inside the inner wall.

Nimeiri climbed the wall of the presidential palace and escaped from there. He found one of the tanks passing in front of the palace at that time. Apparently, it was one of his allies' tanks. He got in the tank and went to join the supporting forces. At the end of the day, Nimeiri's forces regained power again. They created a military court, and in two days they put to death about five of his colleagues who rebelled. An obstetrician had to kill for the first time some of the opponents in Sudan. Nimeiri ruled from 1969 till 1985. I remember an obstetrician told me that Nimeiri was one of his classmates. He said that he was at the top of the class, and Nimeiri got the worst grades in the same class. He said, "Look now, Nimeiri is the one who controls our lives."

Nimeiri was politically not stable. At the beginning of his ruling, he was a communist ruler. He took all the English companies and made them owned by the government. This was a big mistake. He put a military director for each one of those companies. Within a few years, all the companies lost all their assets and became a financial burden on the Sudan government. This was strange because all those companies had very high profits before the transition to government properties. The same thing happened in Egypt when President Jamal Abd Al-Naser did it in Egypt.

After the unsuccessful military coup in 1972, Nimeiri started to go away from the communist ideas. In 1983, Nimeiri became a fanatic Muslim. He decided to implement the Islamic Sharia laws. The extreme Islamic laws started to be applied. They declared that they would pour all the alcoholic drinks on the River Nile. In Islam, it was against Islam to drink alcohol. The national TV showed the celebration of life. I remember one of the jokes that people said at that time. They said that all the alcoholics would now eat fish all day long. The government declared that it was illegal to drink alcohol in Sudan. This was a very tough decision for many who drank marissa as food. In the only government TV, they started to show how the police implemented Islamic laws. Every night they announced, "The police found the following individuals drinking, and they would be whipped tomorrow in the public park at a certain time. The authorities invited all the people to come and watch this event." Most of those people were highly ranked people. The police used to raid some houses to discover those individuals. All the newspapers would announce the names on their front pages. One day they announced on the TV and all the newspapers that the police searched one of the Catholic priests' houses and found some wine. This priest was Italian. They announced that the priest would be whipped the next morning in a public place, and everybody was invited to come and attend this event. The Italian government and the Vatican tried to stop this unfair punishment. The Sudan government insisted to carry on with the whipping. The poor priest was whipped the next morning in a public place. The wine was the type the Catholic church used for communion.

The other side of the Islamic laws was cutting the hand of the thief. Unfortunately, one of the orthopedic surgeons volunteered to supervise the cutting of hands. He was one of the fanatic Muslims. I remember that I worked with him once. He was very rude to everyone. The authorities used to announce that the following person was found guilty and their right hands would be chopped out the next morning at ten o'clock. They invite all the public to come to Sijjn Kober prison to watch this live. Many people used to attend. For habitual thieves, they cut the right hand and the left foot. Once I remember that the government TV made an interview with one of the Coptic Christians. This Christian mentioned that Christianity agreed with the cutting of hands, and he quotes the verse in the Bible:

> *If your hand causes you to sin, cut it off. It is better for you to enter life maimed than with two hands to go into hell, where a fire will never go out. And if your foot causes you to sin, cut it off, it is better for you to enter life crippled than to have two feet and be thrown into hell. (Mark 9:43).*

The TV introduced this Christian as a leader in the Christian church. This was the way the Nimeiri government at that time was trying to convince everyone of the new Islamic rules. There was an accountant in one of the schools, I cannot remember his name. This accountant was put on trial because they thought that he stole some money. As usual, there was a quick trial, and the Islamic court found him guilty. They chopped his right hand. After a few months, they found evidence that he was not guilty. It was too late; nobody could put his hand back.

Another court rule that I read in the newspaper was they announced that in a fight a man hit another man in his mouth and broke one of his teeth. According to the Islamic rules, the judge asked a dentist to pull a similar tooth from the attacking person. When I read this, I was frightened. I am an eye doctor. Someday a judge may ask me to take out someone's good eye because he hit another person in his eye.

There was another regulation in the Islamic Sharia laws, which was not fair for the Christians. The Islamic law considered all the non-Muslims as not a legal witness. At that time a Christian doctor was asked by the court to give witness. He was by chance the doctor on duty in the emergency room. The lawyer of one of the parties told the judge that according to the Islamic Sharia law, "The court cannot take the witness of a non-Muslim." The judge agreed and ruled out that this witness was not a competent witness and discarded the case.

The statement of a woman as a witness was also considered as not legal. This incident happened when we were about to leave Sudan in 1990. At that time and till 2019 the Sharia Islamic laws were still in force. I went with my wife Leila and my brother Joseph to a lawyer to legally authorize my brother Joseph to sell my properties when I left. The lawyer did all the legal papers and at last, he needed a witness. I told him Leila could sign as a witness. He said, "Sorry, according to the current Islamic laws, she could not witness because she is a woman. I have my colleague, a lady lawyer; she as well could not be a witness. But my porter who was sitting outside the office, I will ask him to come and sign." I was amazed by those strange rules and thanked God that we were leaving the country soon.

Sudan's uprising against Nimeiri's government in 1985

Nimeiri's rule continued till 1985 when another people's uprising started.

After the 1985 uprising, a newly elected government was in place.

In 1989 another military coup by Omar El Bashir took over Sudan. This regime was very oppressive. They imprisoned many of the trade union leaders and all the opponents and tortured them.

In 2019 a big people uprising faced Omar El Bashir's military rule. Many were killed, but in the end, El Bashir was forced out.

Chapter 53

How God Helped Us to Go to the USA

The political situation in Sudan in 1998 started to be uncomfortable for many, especially Christians. The government was a military one with a clear fanatic Islamic direction. The Sudan government, for the first time, started to detain and torture anyone they think was against them.

At that time, my cousin was detained by the secret police for a few days. Many friends I know were detained and tortured for months by the new Sudan military government. The government was detaining the trade union leaders to oppress them even without any real evidence of involvement in anti-government activities. The military government ignored all the laws in detaining those people. No lawyers could defend the person. Actually, nobody knew where those detained were. Even the detained person's immediate family had no idea if he was still alive. I was the secretary of the Sudanese Ophthalmological Society. This was an academic society. I did not feel safe. The ophthalmological society was in the process of a big project. We were planning to raise some donations to build an up-to-date center for eye treatment. The center would contain an operating theater equipped with all the modern technologies that were not available in Sudan. Also, the center would have laser machines for the treatment of diabetic complications to the eye. All the diabetic patients who were in need of lasers used to travel to Egypt or England to have those procedures done.

The estimated cost of the new eye center was more than a million dollars. We managed to collect most of this amount from Sudanese individuals in Sudan and outside Sudan and their foreign friends. One of the donors was the brother of the ousted prime minister Al-Sadig Al-Mahadi. Our society used to have meetings with him and others to raise this money. Al-Sadig Al-Mahadi was detained at that time.

One night a secret police officer came to my private clinic. He mentioned to the secretary that he was a police officer and wanted to see Dr. Victor Zaki. The secretary asked him to wait until I finished examining the patient who was with me at that time. The police officer ignored the secretary and opened the door of my office and came in. He directly asked me if I knew the home of a certain doctor. I told him that I never heard about this doctor. He suddenly went out as when he came in. The patient who was with me was shocked. I was very scared. I knew that the authorities were detaining many medical doctors at that time. I did not feel safe for the first time in my own country Sudan.

By the way, after I left Sudan, the eye center was erected, and the laser and other equipment came. I heard they put my name with some other colleagues as founders of this center.

During Christmas time in 1989, I received a Christmas card from Dr. Simmons from Boston. I had my training in the USA with Dr. Simmons for four months in 1985. He mentioned in his card that he heard bad things were happening in Sudan and if he could help. He was referring to the implementation of the cruel Islamic laws in Sudan. When I read that, I asked myself, is this a special message for me? Why do I receive such a message now? Is God sending a good person like Dr. Simmons to help me go out of Sudan at that time?

Suddenly I thought, why not ask him to find a job for me in the USA. I mentioned it to Leila, what I thought. Her reaction was to laugh. She told me, "Are you dreaming? In the USA it is very difficult to hire a foreigner without a green card. If you want, we can go tomorrow to the US Embassy and ask them about our application for immigration."

In 1985 we applied for immigration to the USA through Leila's sister who held American citizenship. I went with Leila the next morning to the American Embassy in Khartoum. We asked about the situation of our application. Their answer was "We have no idea. According to what is happening now, we expect more than seven years for you to get the green card."

When we came back home, I told Leila I still had the feeling of writing to Dr. Simmons. Her answer was "Are you really serious? Who in the USA would bother himself to apply for you for a work permit?"

I took the Bible and told Leila, "I am going to ask God for advice, and I know He will give a clear answer." I opened the Bible. I found the verse that appeared to me was *Genesis 12:1, "The Lord had said to Abraham, 'Leave your country, your people and your father's household and go to the land I will show you.'"*

For me, it was a clear message from God. I noticed that Leila was not convinced. So I told her I would ask God again for another message. So I opened the Bible again and it was *Joshua 1:2, "Now then, you and all these people, get ready to cross the Jordan River into the land I am about to give to them—to the Israelites. I will give you every place where you set your foot."*

Many preachers do not agree by asking God and opening the Bible. They consider this as gambling. For me, I usually pray and ask God for His advice. I am always confident that if I ask God for advice, He will give it to me.

Leila was still hesitant. So I told her, "Let me send the letter and pray to God. If this is the best for us, God will facilitate all the paperwork. If it is not to our benefit, God will stop this channel."

At last, Leila agreed. I wrote a letter to Dr. Simmons shortly after Christmas 1989. I told him, "If you want to help, please find me a job in the USA, so I can come with my family in a legal way." I suggested he got me a J1 visa. This is a visa that gives the person permission to work and study at the same time. In a couple of weeks, I received the response. Dr. Simmons said he was willing to apply for a J-1 visa for me. He asked me to send some documents. I sent the documents, and I later received another letter from him. He said that the arrangement was going well, and I have to plan to come to the USA around April 15, 1990.

We felt that now we were facing reality. We were in the process of leaving for the USA. Leila said, "No way to leave in April. The children will finish their final exams in the last week of May 1990." I tried to convince Leila that the children will start a new system, and their grades here would not affect them there. I told her we had no idea about Dr. Simmons and his approval, no point in asking for postponing our arrival date. If God opened a gate, let us not close it. At last, I sent our approval of the date to Dr. Simmons. After a week, I received another letter from Dr. Simmons that the J-1 visa was not approved. They changed the application to H-1 visa. This was a working visa. He also mentioned that the arrival date has to be postponed to June instead of April. When I received this letter, I felt that God was a loving Father. God wanted everyone to be happy and relaxed. In June the children's exams would be over, and their final certificates would be ready.

After I came to the USA, I learned that H-1 visa was much better than J-1 visa. It is easy to get a green card with an H-1 visa. With a J-1 visa, if you got the green card, you have to go back to your country to apply for the green card. This would be very expensive for the six of us to go back to Sudan and at the same time, not safe at all. The Sudanese authorities may not let us go out again.

During this time, I noticed that all my mail was opened by the government. All the letters were opened and sealed with a sticker. So sending a letter to the USA to ask for a job was very risky. At that time, God prepared an American patient to come to me for an eye exam. This patient had a problem with her eyes that needed continuous follow-up. I explained to this patient my situation and showed her the opened and resealed letters. Then she told me that she was leaving for the USA on her annual vacation after a few days. She offered to take my documents to the USA with her and send them to Dr. Simmons from the USA. I managed to prepare the documents, and I gave them to this nice lady. When she arrived in the USA, she sent the documents to Dr. Simmons. She contacted them by phone and told them that she would be in the USA for two weeks. She asked them if the final approval was ready by that time, and they can send it to her. I think she was on the west coast of the USA. She spent her vacation and received nothing from Dr. Simmons. When she wanted to book for the return flight, there was a problem. The easiest way was to travel from the west coast to New

York then to Europe and Sudan. She tried all the airlines and found nothing on the day she planned to travel. The only flight she found was obliging her to go to Boston and to stay in Boston for four hours till she got the other flight to Europe. When she arrived in Boston, she thought of calling Dr. Simmons's office and ask about my papers. Dr. Simmons told her that they just received the final approval now. He sent his secretary with the final approval to Boston airport. She met the nice lady and gave her the final papers. The nice lady brought the papers with her to Sudan. She told me that this was God's plan to force her to go to Boston, especially to bring those papers to me. She was a good Christian.

When I think about this, I felt that God was in control, and God took care of us. Nothing happens by chance. God changes everything around us for our benefit.

We received the approval from the USA, but what about the approval from the Sudanese government? It was very difficult for a medical doctor to get approval to leave the country. In a normal situation, we usually go to the ministry of interior and apply for an exit visa. They used to give the visa within two hours. When I went there, they told me to go and get approval from Jihaz Al-Amn. This was the new department created by the new military government to control any rebellion among the people. Those were the same group that detained the people without any legal documents and tortured all the opponents of the government. Those were the same people who detained my cousin for four days in a secret place. When his brothers asked about him, they told them, "We do not have anyone with this name." Those were the same people who tortured my other friend for about four months.

I asked my colleagues about the usual time to get this approval if they would give it. One of the eye doctors who was sent by the Ministry of Health in Sudan to attend a course in Tunisia told me, "I have a relative working in Jihaz Al-Amn, and I was lucky. I got it in a month's time."

On that day I asked my wife and children to pray. I told them God would make it easy. Nobody could close the door God already opened. I went to Jihaz Al-Amn in the morning. I knew the place because it faced my daughter's school. On the front door, there were some guards wearing military uniforms and carrying their rifles. I asked them about the approval of medical doctors to leave the country. They asked me to step into the office where a person in a civilian dress was sitting on a desk. I gave him my passport, Sudanese passport, and asked for approval to leave Sudan. He looked at my passport for a few minutes and told me, "Come in the afternoon to take your passport."

On that afternoon, I went again and found the approval was ready. I was not amazed, but I felt that God was with my family and me. It was a nice feeling when we feel the presence of God in our life. When you read the Bible about how God was helping his people, you may doubt what you read. Now I saw God helping me. It was not a story but real life. God was in action! It was not just one incident that could happen by chance. Those were continuous, successive miracles every day.

Second Samuel 22:33 states, "God is my strength and power, And He makes my way perfect."

I always appreciate how Dr. Simmons cared about me and my family's safety.

He offered to help me to come with my family to America.

He contacted a lawyer and did all the paperwork. It shows the high-quality, loving person he is.

Chapter 54

Preparations to Leave Sudan 1990

When I received the approval from the USA and the exit visa from the Sudanese authorities, I felt that now we were really leaving. During the current military government, nothing was guaranteed. Jihaz Al-Amn could stop anyone from leaving the country at any point even if they gave him the approval to leave. They used to accuse the people of illegally taking money out of Sudan. I thought with those circumstances was to keep the decision of leaving Sudan very secret. I told my brothers. My brother Joseph tried to convince me that the political situation in Sudan was a temporary one, and this military government would be removed soon. I told him, "I am convinced that God prepared this for us." I know that God always does the best for us. This oppressive military regime continued to control Sudan until 2019. After a few years, my brother Joseph left Sudan. He and his family found it extremely difficult to survive with this suppressive regime.

For my clinic, I asked an ophthalmologist who was working at Juba University to work for me. Juba was the largest city in Southern Sudan. There was continuous war between the south and the military government of Sudan. The government decided to move the university of Juba to the capital Khartoum. I asked this doctor to work in my clinic while I was away. He kept my name in the clinic for ten years till we closed the clinic in about the year 2000. Keeping my name in the clinic brought to him many patients.

All our neighbors knew that we were leaving for a short period and coming back. For me, I was completely sure that this was our last time in Sudan, and we would never come back.

The military government had a very tight security system. They recruit high school students and college students to be their eyes in every block. They first gave them the impression that they were serving God. They gave them the idea that they were part of the authority, and they felt that when they reported to Jihaz Al-Amn about any person. Lastly, they gave them money, which changed their life completely. Most of them like most of the people in Sudan were very poor. In reality, some of them reported their own families. This was the reason that this Islamic military government without any popular support managed to track and detain anyone who just mentioned his opposition to them. The problem that young students could even report things that were not true in order to show their loyalty to the authorities. If you add this to the fact that there were no real trials, most of the people can be detained and tortured for months and then released without going through any court. When they release them, they usually warn them that nobody must know of what happened to them. If they even told the story to anyone, they could be detained and tortured again.

Those were the reasons that we decided to keep our departure from Sudan secret. We left our rented apartment as it was. We knew if we sold our furniture or even moved them to our owned house in Gereif, it might cause a problem for us. We were sure that some young kids were watching us and were ready to report to Jihaz Al-Amn.

We applied to get some money transferred from the Sudanese currency to dollars. This process had to go from our regular bank to the central bank of Sudan. This central bank was called Bank of Sudan. I was the ophthalmologist of Bank of Sudan employees, and Leila was the dermatologist. When I went there, the official of the bank, who was my patient at the same time, told me the story. For myself, I was allowed to transfer fifty dollars. Leila, because she was holding an Egyptian passport, was not allowed to transfer any money. He said,

"But because you are my doctor and she is my doctor as well, I will give her special permission to transfer fifty dollars. For the children, because they were under eighteen years of age, they were not allowed to transfer any money. So for the whole family, we were allowed to transfer from Sudan one hundred dollars." Some people gamble by buying some dollars illegally and hide them in their bags. We decided not to do that. We usually did what was legal and according to the law even if it was an unfair law. At that time it was completely forbidden to transfer any money from a Sudanese bank to another bank outside Sudan. Imagine a family of six was traveling to the USA with one hundred dollars to cover all their expenses. We knew that Leila's two brothers and sister would be waiting for us in New York.

Leila started the packing of our bags. Leila decided to carry all the children's personal belongings. I mean all their toys and Barbies and the games. She said, "They are going to another country with no friends. Let us give them some security by taking their beloved toys." I agreed but the result was we had to carry thirteen bags. Some of the bags were small, but some were big. Tony, Sandra, and Jennie were keen to take their bikes with them. I told them no way. Their immediate question was "Are you going to buy new bikes for us there?"

My answer was "God would provide you with all that you need."

Tony also asked about our cars, "Are we going to take them with us?" I told him no! Then he asked, "Are we going to buy a new car there?" I told him yes but definitely after some time. He asked, "What type of car are you going to buy there?" I told him, "I like to buy a station wagon car."

It was sad to leave our house, cars, and all our furniture and money. The only valuable thing was one hundred dollars. I knew that I might not be able to get anything from what we left. Our income in Sudan was ten times our expenses. Now we were leaving with only one hundred dollars. For anyone, this may look crazy, but for me, I was very confident in God's promises to me. I was quite sure that God would provide all our needs as usual. I was sure that everything would be perfect.

Each of my brothers invited us to their homes.

We took many pictures. We took them with us to the USA and still kept them with us. We left all our other pictures, including our wedding pictures in Sudan.

Every few days, my brother Joseph was asking me if I changed my mind and canceled our move to the USA. My answer was always, "I am sure that it would be much better for us to go since God arranged this journey."

Chapter 55

Our Journey from Sudan to the USA

Our last days in Khartoum were hectic. My cousin Amal Mingerios came to help Leila in packing the bags. She brought with her, as usual, the high-quality homemade cake. She brought lemon and made lemonade. The weather in Khartoum was always hot and cold drinks helped a lot. Each of my brothers invited us to his home for a nice homemade dinner. All my brothers and my mother joined those dinners. In a suitcase, Leila put some of our old clothes and hid among the clothes a ten-dollar bill. I brought this ten-dollar bill with me when I went to the USA in 1987 to attend a conference. It was a big crime to possess foreign currency. We could not take it with us to the USA because it was not approved by the Bank of Sudan. Leila told my nephew Nader to be careful because this suitcase had the ten-dollar bill among the clothes. Nader took the suitcase with him to be hidden in my brother Joseph's house. The problem was that we could not trash the ten-dollar bill because someone may find it.

Our flight was scheduled to leave Khartoum airport at 2:00 AM on June 20, 1990. My brother Baheeg invited us to stay in his home for that night. He got a special curfew passage permit to take us to the airport. The reason was the curfew in Khartoum started at 11:00 PM.

We had thirteen suitcases for the six of us. Some of the suitcases were small and others were big. We were very careful not to carry anything that could cause problems with the Sudanese customs and security authorities. At that time, it was illegal to go out of Sudan with any money, except with written approval from the Bank of Sudan. It was also forbidden to take jewelry or electric equipment out of Sudan. Leila left most of her jewelry. The customs department was known to be managed by the secret police (Jihaz Al-Amn). We knew that we did everything within their rules and regulations but still no guarantee that we could pass safely. They opened all our bags and searched them carefully. One of the children's suitcases was an old one with a bad lock. We were unable to open it quickly. We agreed that they break the lock and open the suitcase. We had to wrap the suitcase with a rope to keep it closed. This was one of the children's jumping ropes.

At last, we safely went through the customs department and the security department. We went to the waiting area inside the airport. Even in this area, we felt not safe. Many passengers were called to go back for more security checks. The time passed very slowly. We were unable to buy any food or drink from this waiting area. We had only $100 and no Sudanese currency. The last part was the security check before entering the airplane. We heard that Jihaz Al-Amn asked many passengers to undress to ensure they were not carrying money or jewelry. We were lucky; they did the check without this undressing part.

At last, we reached the plane. It was the German Lufthansa Airline. It was a great change for us, from the suspicious attitude of all the officials inside the airport to the friendly attitude of the flight attendants. My daughter Diana told me the other day that she still kept a pen the flight attendant of Lufthansa gave her on that flight.

At this point, we were extremely exhausted. This was the accumulation of many days of packing and in addition the psychological tension. All of us were, at the same time, very alert and excited. We were happy that God managed to deliver us safely. In certain instances, we were not sure that we really were outside Sudan. We felt that we were just dreaming. The plane's first stop was in Cairo, Egypt. From Khartoum to Cairo, the plane took about two and a half hours. They kept us inside the plane for the two-hour stop in Cairo. They apologized that those were the instructions of the security authorities at Cairo Airport. The plane left Cairo and reached Frankfurt, Germany, after about six hours of flight. In Frankfurt, we waited at the airport for about four hours. We felt life was different here. The airport was very clean with no leaking toilets. The strange thing for us was the absence of police.

We left Frankfurt on another plane to the USA. This flight took about nine hours. So we reached the USA at about 8:00 PM. It took us twenty-three hours from leaving Khartoum airport until we reached the USA. When we passed by the airport immigration office, they checked our entry visa and gave us permission to stay in the USA for three years. When we proceeded to the customs department, they asked us to open the bags to check. They found three lemon seeds. My daughter Sandra put those three seeds in her suitcase. Sandra took those lemons after my cousin Amal prepared lemonade for us in Sudan on our last day. She thought that she would plant them in the USA and have similar lemons in the USA. Sandra laughed at the customs officer and told him those were lemon seeds, took them from him, and tried to throw them in the trash. The officer asked many other officers to come and told them, "They have seeds."

It took a long time for us to clarify the matter. In the end, they let us go after searching all our bags very carefully.

My daughters told me later that they had other seeds as well. They had a game where they played it with dried fava beans. They put about eighteen dry beans in a small metal case. This metal case was used for the geometry set. The customs officer picked this case and shook it, then put it back without opening it.

It was very exhausting to travel for about twenty-three hours continuously to end by having all our luggage searched again.

At last, we went out to look for Leila's brothers and sister. Leila's brothers Nazeeh and Maged and her sister Suad were living in Queens, New York. We found nobody waiting for us. We thought they may be late because of the traffic. We waited for about an hour then we decided to call them. They knew that we were coming to New York at that time.

Nobody was answering the phone. At last, we decided to take a taxi and go to their place. The taxi could not take all of us and the luggage.

We decided that I go with the children and most of the suitcases and leave Leila with the rest of the luggage.

The taxi driver told us that this would cost about ninety dollars because we were at Newark Airport in New Jersey state. This was a surprise for us. All the time we thought that we were going to New York airport. The reason for the confusion was the spelling in Arabic of New York was similar to Newark. On the plane, the pilot mentioned Newark, but we thought that this was the German pronunciation of New York. We discovered that Leila's family went to JFK Airport in New York. They waited there for us all this time. I took the taxi with the children except for Diana the youngest to Leila's family apartments in Queens. When I reached there, I found nobody. We stayed outside the building until Nazeeh came.

Maged, Leila's youngest brother, went to bring Leila and Diana from Newark Airport. Leila's mother went with Maged to the airport. Leila was unable to recognize her brother Maged in Newark Airport until she saw her mother with him. I think they last met about ten years ago. Maged lost some of his hair during those years. Maged recognized Leila easily.

Nazeeh, Maged, and Suad decided to make room for all of us. Maged took Leila, Diana, and myself to his flat. Tony went with Nazeeh. Sandra and Jennie went to Suad's apartment where Leila's mother was staying.

We were very tired, but we were unable to stop talking with them. It took us more than four hours until we finally slept.

Now I am thinking of how Nazeeh, Maged, and Suad helped us in our first weeks in the USA. How could we manage with one hundred dollars to live in New York?

Chapter 56

Our First Weeks in the USA as a Family 1990

For Leila and me, New York was not new. We visited New York a few times. For the children, this was their first experience in the USA. We were busy talking and chatting with Leila's family. It had been a long time since we saw them. The children were sticking to their grandmother. She was the only one whom they saw last and remembered more.

In the morning, I called Dr. Simmons in Boston to see what I was going to do? His answer was "Come alone now to arrange a place for your family. You could stay at our house till you find a place for them."

I left the next day for Boston. I stayed in Dr. Simmons's house. I went to the office with him. First he asked one of the secretaries to help me to find an apartment for us as a family. The secretary asked me first, "How big is your family and how old are your children?" I told her that I have four children, and they range from seven to fifteen years old. Her next question was "How much can you pay for the apartment?" I told her, "I have no idea." She said most of the people pay one third to one half of their salary for the rent. I told her I have no idea what my salary would be. This was the truth. I never asked Dr. Simmons about the salary. I had complete confidence that God helped me in every step to come to the States. I was sure that God would arrange everything in the best way. I went to the office of the administrator and asked her about my salary. She was shocked that I had no idea about the salary. She told me, "It is written in the contract we sent to you in Sudan." I looked in the contract, and I found the salary was clearly written. Apparently, I did not read the contract at all.

The secretary started to look in the newspapers for apartments for rent. She helped give me an idea about each town, how far it was from the office, and how the schools were in this town.

I went to Park Street Church and met Joseph Sabounjie, the pastor of the international students. He was a good friend of my visit in 1985. I asked Joe for his advice about the apartments. He told me, "The best town for you is Newton." It had the best schools and was near to the office. When I told him about my salary, he immediately said, "Forget about Newton. It is a very expensive city to live in."

About one week passed, and I was still looking for apartments without any success. At the same time, I had full confidence that God would give me a perfect apartment. I was not worried at all. After the week, Dr. Simmons told me that he had an apartment over their garages. His son lived in it after his wedding then moved. This apartment was rented to a girl who was living in it for the last four years. Today suddenly, she told Dr. Simmons that she was leaving.

Dr. Simmons told me, "If this apartment is suitable for you and your family, you can have it. You do not need to pay rent, just pay the utility bill." Dr. Simmons's house was in Newton. He showed me the apartment. It had two bedrooms and a large hall, and in the attic, there was a small room. The kitchen was in the hall. When I saw the apartment, I thanked God for His love and care and for providing good, loving people to help me. Later, when I met Joe Sabounjie, I told him that I found an apartment, which I could afford in Newton. He was amazed by how God helped me.

Dr. Simmons told me that the girl who was living in the apartment had a roommate. He had to give her notice to leave in a month. Dr. Simmons mentioned that Leila and the children could come and stay in his house for that month then move to the apartment. I called Leila and asked her to come from New York. Dr. Simmons had a large house with many rooms and bathrooms. He told me that they usually live all week in his sailing boat and come to the house on the weekend only. Leila and the children came from New York. We settled in Dr. Simmons's house. Mrs. Simmons arranged a place for everyone. Dr. Simmons and his wife were a very loving and caring couple. We felt that they were happy to have us in their home. My daughter Sandra mentioned that living in a house with other people would not be a convenient thing. I told her we have no choice, and Dr. Simmons and his wife were very generous to accommodate all of us in their house, and they were practically not living in the house except one day in the week. The next day after Leila and the children arrived from New York, we discovered that the girls living in the apartment had left. They decided to leave and not use the month's notice. I felt that God heard Sandra's comment and wanted all of us to be happy.

We moved to our new apartment. It was a nice sensation to be in our own place.

The first apartment we lived in the USA

Immediately after the arrival of Leila and the children from New York, Dr. Simmons told me, "You have a large family, and you need a car. I have a car that I am not using. You can use it all the time except when one of my daughters comes to the Boston area, and then she will use it." He showed me the car. It was a station wagon. Immediately I remembered in Sudan when my son Tony asked about the car I wanted to have in the States, and I told him a station wagon. It was amazing how God gave us all the things that we dreamt of.

Our first month in Newton, Massachusetts

Leila started to arrange the schools for the children. Tony and Sandra went to Newton High School. Jennie and Diana were accepted in William's primary school. They accepted their certificates from Sudan, and they went to the equivalent grades as in Sudan. Newton High School was the school for Tony and Sandra. It was less than a mile from our house, so Tony and Sandra would not need transportation. They could walk. William's school was a bit far away from the house. The school headmaster told Leila that they would arrange the school bus to come, but not for the first two weeks. During the first two days of school, Dr. Simmons's daughter came from North Carolina and would use the car. Leila was worried. We had no idea about using public transportation or taxis. One day before the beginning of school, there was a phone call from the school authorities. They apologized because they had to change Jennie and Diana from William's school to another school, Burr School. They said as well that the school bus would pick them up from our house starting from the first day of school. We thanked God for all his care. Diana remained in this school for the next five years. Jennie moved after one year to junior high school.

The first week after the arrival of Leila and the children, Mrs. Simmons showed us three bikes. She told me that those were her children's bikes, and nobody was using them now. She said that our children could use them. Those bikes were in good condition, and all of them had changeable speeds. I remembered when we were in Sudan the children were asking if they could take their bikes with them to the States. Tony was asking for a bike with changeable speeds for many years. I was unable to buy it because it was available only if you paid in dollars and not in Sudanese currency from the Khartoum airport free market.

I thanked God and Mrs. Simmons for providing the three bikes.

We went with the children to Star Supermarket, which was near our house. We spent a long time in front of the bread section. In Sudan, there was a severe shortage of bread. During our last few years in Sudan, we were allowed to buy a few loaves every day. Some days the bread was not available. In Star Supermarket, we found different varieties of bread. The one we liked more was the toast because it was not available in Sudan. So we bought a toaster and we started to eat bread with butter and marmalade every day at breakfast. This was our favorite breakfast when we were in London in 1972–1974.

We searched for bacon because that was what we used to eat in London also. We found it after some difficulty. Apparently, bacon and eggs became less popular now because of the cholesterol issue.

We found all types of fruits in the Star Supermarket. In Sudan, grapes, pears, peaches, apricots, and cherries were not available. They started to import apples in Sudan during the last few years, but they were very expensive. We bought all the fruit in Star Supermarket.

The children started their schools. I think Tony and Sandra managed better than Jennie and Diana because they knew English. Definitely it was tough for all of them to come from a different country with limited English and no cultural knowledge. Diana was the one who was unable to speak or understand English when she started. I am not sure if the teachers asked Jennie to translate it for her. After three months, Diana came to me and asked, "What is the meaning of brown in Arabic?" I was amazed that she managed to know English that quickly and at the same time started to forget Arabic. This was strange because we never used English at home.

Chapter 57

Our First Winter in Boston 1990

In Sudan, the weather was always hot or very hot. The coldest weather in winter was 65 Fahrenheit, and this was always for a few hours in the early morning in one or two days a year. Boston, on the other hand, was very cold in winter. The temperature could drop to 10 Fahrenheit or even rarely can reach zero. For us, this was not comfortable. We were not familiar with winter clothes. Coats were not available in Sudan. Leila and I used them in London. For the children, this was a completely new experience.

The first time the children saw snow, they were very excited. They want to play all day outside in the snow. We discovered the burden of shoveling the snow later on. The heating system in our apartment was strange. The bedrooms had electric heaters, so they were warm. The heating of the large hall was by a fireplace. It was a big challenge for us to start the fire. One of our neighbors was Bob. He used to come and visit us. He showed us how to start the fire. The hall had a high colonial sealing, so it was always cold unless we sat near the fireplace. We discovered the great pleasure of looking at the fire and feeling the warmth of the heat in winter. God was kind to us, so the first two winters were mild ones.

Victor shovelling the snow, Boston 1990

First winter in the USA

Walking on the snow was not that easy. Many times we slid on the snow and more when it melted and froze again in the morning. Later on, we learned even the technical terms of black ice.

It was a very scary experience when my car slid into the snow. I was driving during the day. The weather was good with no snow or rain. There was about two inches of snow on the street the other night. The car in front of me stopped at the stop sign. I was driving very slowly. I pushed the break till the end, but the car continued to move without stopping or even reducing its speed. After a few seconds, I found my car hitting the car in front of me. There was no damage to my car or the other car. I learned the lesson, to hit the break at least 200 feet earlier in the snowy roads.

Leila took the driver's test first. Our neighbor Bob went with her. She passed the test. She had few mistakes, but apparently, the years of experience in driving in Sudan helped.

I did my test later. We used our international driver's license during the first few months. They asked me to bring someone with a license in Massachusetts. I told them I had an international license, so I was authorized now to drive. After a lot of hesitation, they agreed. The police officer asked me to do a three-point turn in a small street. I did but I went into a driveway. It was easier for me. The police officer was upset. He told me that it was illegal to go into any driveway. He was kind enough to pass me and gave me the license.

Driving was different in Sudan than in the USA. In Sudan, there were no lanes. Here we need to drive on the right side and stay on our lane. If there is no incoming car, we can drive on the other side of the street. It was difficult for me the first few weeks to change lanes. Signaling the trafficator when you change lanes was a completely new concept for me.

Chapter 58

We Bought a House in America

In 1992 after some changes in the rules of transferring money from Sudan, my brother Joseph was able to sell our house and send us the money. We thought of buying a house. We looked at different houses on sale. Leila was more active than me. One day Leila told me, "Come and see this house." It looked good. The house was in West Newton. This meant that our children would not change their schools. In front of the house was an old middle school called Warren Middle School. The school was closed for at least ten years.

The owner of the house was an old lady. She wanted to get rid of the house because she was moving from the area. The asking price was 175,000 dollars. I told Leila, "I like the house. Let us put an offer. I am going to offer 160." We put the offer, and they said, "No, this is too low." I remember it was the afternoon after work. I told them 161, and this was my final I was not going to pay more than this.

Leila told me, "This is a good house. Why not to make it 165?" We looked at different houses, and this was the best. I told her no. After a few hours, they accepted our offer.

The next step was to apply for a mortgage. The bank representative asked about our credit history. At this point, I had no idea what credit history was. I told him, "I am paying everything in cash. I don't owe any money to anybody," so in my thinking, this was perfect credit history.

He explained that to create a good credit history, I had to get a credit card, a car loan, or a house mortgage, and I pay them on time, then I would create a good credit history.

I asked my office to give me a letter showing that I would be able to pay the mortgage. The bank accepted that.

Our house in America
The middle school and now Warren House

We discovered that the house was cheap because of the deserted middle school in front of the house. After we bought the house in six months, the city started to renovate the school, and it was converted to a condo complex. They put eight tennis courts and playgrounds for kids.

One month after buying the house, a financial advisor from an investment company came and offered his services. He would evaluate our income and advise how we might invest our money. I thought if the service is free, why not try it.

He asked me about our expenses and our income. He commented about our monthly payment to our church. He said, "With your financial situation, you have to get from the church, not give it."

Malachi 3:10 states, *"'Bring all the* tithes *into the storehouse, That there may be food in My house, And try Me now in this,' Says the Lord of hosts, 'If I will not open for you the windows of heaven And pour it. out for you such blessing That there will not be_room enough to receive it.'"*

After the financial advisor evaluated our situation, he said, "In one year, you will sell this house. You will not be able to pay the mortgage." I smiled and I thanked him for his evaluation.

Psalm 119:165 says, "165 Great peace have those who love Your law."

I had full peace, and I was quite sure that God would provide us with all our needs. I told him I knew that I was not going to sell the house. We paid our monthly payments on time and after two years changed the heating system to a new one from oil to gas, and after a few more years, we added a sunroom, and we finished the basement. I am very confident that God was the one who takes care of me all the time.

Chapter 59

I Became a Full-Time Student at New England College of Optometry

I noticed some changes in the office. Four of the glaucoma specialists split.

One of the optometrists in the office advised me to study in the college of optometry and get my license as an optometrist.

Research jobs depended on funds, so they were usually not stable jobs.

New England College of Optometry had an accelerated course for medical doctors from other countries or people with PhD. The course was a full-time course continuous for twenty-five months without vacations. The regular course was four years after four years of undergraduate college.

Dr. Simmons encouraged me to do it and gave me a recommendation letter. Also, Dr. Kenyon who was working with us and was the head of the cornea department at Harvard medical school gave me a similar letter.

I passed the optometry entrance exam. I was ready to start.

The annual college fees were $32,000 a year. The year I started college, my son Tony started his studies as a freshman at Boston University college of computer science. In my second year, my daughter Sandra started her undergraduate college at Brandies University.

I was hesitant at the beginning, but Leila encouraged me. Especially so, after she dropped me to do the entrance exam while driving on the highway back, she saw a big rainbow. She told me that this was a sign from God that He approved of my study.

In the accelerated class, we were ten. Four were MDs, two were from China, one from Brazil, and me. All the others were holders of PhD degrees.

One of them was a close friend. He was a professor in ocean ecology. He told me that academic positions had poor income, about $27,000 a year. We visited their home. He had a large tank filled with ocean water, different types of fish and plants. He explained to us how each of the fish and plants help each other to survive.

He was living in Belmont, which was about nine miles from the college. He used his roller skates to come to college most of the year.

I have another friend. He came from England, but he lived for many years in Africa. His wife is Greek. They are very good friends. Another close friend was a Chinese ophthalmologist. I used to speak with her about God. She was always saying she did not believe in the presence of God. I used to tell her every time that I would pray for her. And I regularly did for years even after we graduated and she left for Georgia. After about five years, she contacted me and told me that now she believes in God and reads the Bible regularly. I believe in the power of prayer.

The course was very intense. We had to work for many hours and stay late in the evenings. We had to pass many exams. It was funny when they failed me in checking the pressure of the eye. All my specialization in glaucoma was not helpful. He failed me because after checking the pressure, I did not check if I scratched the cornea or not.

In general, all the professors were treating us as colleagues and not students.

I graduated from New College of Optometry in 1995

During my study, I tried to work a few hours in an optical chain EyeWorld to get some practical experience with glasses.

I worked in the lab, where I managed to cut glasses and watch all the processes of making glasses. At the same time, I learned how the system of the optical chain worked.

Chapter 60

Work as an Optometrist

As soon as I finished the studies, I worked with an ophthalmologist, Dr. Morris in Lawrence, Massachusetts.

The city population was about 80,000 and one of the poorest cities in Massachusetts with more than 39 percent of Hispanic origin.

Lawrence was in the northern part of the state next to New Hampshire.

The work was nice; we had long lunch hours. Dr. Macool was very good and trusted me in treating the patients.

During the long lunch hour, I used to walk around. I found a supermarket that was cheap, compared to Star Market and Stop and Shop. The store name was Market Basket.

The owners were of Greek origin. All my grocery shopping shifted to Market Basket.

There was a problem. The distance between my home and the clinic was more than forty-five minutes. In the first three months, I did fine, but then I started to feel sleepy while driving. I found myself going over the elevated separations between lanes. As soon as I heard the click sound, I woke up.

I told Dr. Morris that I could not continue. He tried to offer more money or even to find a house for me in Lawrence.

I applied for a job as an optometrist in a store EyeWorld.

It was a chain of optical shops with a fully equipped office for an optometrist. I used to pay monthly rent. I charged my patient and their insurance with the rate that I decided. I was very happy.

EyeWorld had twenty-four stores in Massachusetts and New Hampshire states. They used to do a patient satisfaction survey in all the stores. Every month, they announce who of the optometrists got the best report, and they give him a gift. I used to get number one almost every month. I remember one of the gifts was a big bucket filled with honey-covered popcorn.

My store was in Southshore Plaza, Braintree. In the beginning, the number of patients was small, but in a short period, the numbers increased. I started to have my own loyal patients and their relatives. The store was in the mall and had to match the mall hours. But I had my own working hours. I used to work Saturday and take Sunday and Wednesday off. Working hours were 10:00 AM–6:00 PM and one day from 11:00 AM to 7:00 PM.

Because I start late, some days I used to put meat, vegetables in the slow cooker and turn it on so Leila would find it ready for dinner. I am not a good cook, but I found this was easy and the taste was good.

The owner of EyeWorld was a Japanese businessman. He was very polite. His main business was the steel industry in Japan. He suddenly lost a lot of money and came one day and sold his EyeWorld stores to LensCrafters which was an Italian company.

LensCrafters had another store in the same mall. They decided to let me continue until the end of the contract with the mall, then they would close my store.

I worked in the optical chains for eleven years.

In 2006 while working with LensCrafters, Joslin Clinic, where my wife Leila was working, asked me if I could work with them on my day off, Wednesdays. The job was to work in Joslin Vision Network, JVN.

They had remote places like some Arab countries or places in New Mexico where there were no ophthalmologists to examine diabetic patients. They put a high-quality camera to take photos of the back of the eye. Trained technicians take photos and send them to JVN. My job was to look at the photos on a large computer screen with 3-D glasses. Evaluate if there are diabetic changes in the eye and what grade. Then send instructions on what the patient had to do.

Chapter 61

Leila's Work in the USA

When we came to Boston, my wife Leila had H-2 visa, which entitled her to legally stay in the USA but not to work.

Leila got her MD degree from Egypt and her diploma in dermatology from London University. She worked as MD in Sudan and the UK.

To work as MD in the USA, she had to pass a qualifying exam, USMLE.

Leila studied and sat for the first part of USMLE, United States Medical Licensing Exam. She got 73 percent and for the foreign doctors, the passing number was 75 percent.

I was working full time, and Leila was taking care of our four children and at the same time the house. She decided that she would not have enough time to study again for this exam, which was the first step of three more tests.

She went to Physicians for Human Rights and did some volunteer work.

She did some volunteer work for the New England Glaucoma Foundation. When her work permit came, the foundation asked her to work as an ophthalmic assistant. In a few months, she passed the exam and became a Certified Ophthalmic Assistant.

Leila in a few more months became an expert in eye photography, ultrasound of the eye, and visual fields. She went to Minneapolis, Minnesota, to do the ophthalmic technician test and got her degree.

She worked at Lexington Eye Associates as an ophthalmic technician from 1994 until 1996. Because she did not like to drive every day, she left LEA and worked in Brigham and Women's eye department then Joslin Diabetes Center.

In a couple of years, she became a Certified Medical Technologist. Also, she got two degrees in ultrasound:

1. Registered Ophthalmic Ultrasound Biometrist
2. Certified Diagnostic Ophthalmic Sonographer

Leila in front of her office in Joslin Diabetes Center

Leila participated in almost all the research in Joslin. Her name was written in many papers.

Chapter 62

Lexington Eye Associates

Lexington Eye Associates is an ophthalmology/optometry practice

My wife Leila worked in Lexington Eye Associates (LEA) for two years from 1994 to 1996.

In 2005 my daughter Sandra joined LEA as an optometrist till 2007.

I worked in LEA from 2006 until I retired in April 2020.

I found the managers and the staff were very friendly. I worked for most of my fourteen years in the Westford Office.

I felt that it had a family atmosphere; everyone cared about others. We used to celebrate every birthday with homemade food. The manager treated all the staff in an excellent, respectable way.

I started to fit scleral contact lenses in about 2007. I was one of the early doctors who fit this type of lens. I used scleral lenses in more than 200 patients to treat keratoconus, severe dry eye, exophthalmos, neurotropic keratopathy, band shape keratopathy, and facial palsy.

I fitted scleral lenses for three patients with facial palsy. Those patients were suffering a lot from pain, watery eyes, and poor vision for seventeen years. After using the scleral lenses, all their symptoms disappeared. The vision of the two of them improved from just seeing hand motion to 20/25. I followed them for two years. I put my findings in a paper published in 2017 in *Medicine*.

I still feel I am part and will be part of Lexington Eye Associates, Westford Office.

Chapter 63

What Is My Experience at Seventy-Five Years of Life?

I enjoyed every day of my life. I am happy, and I have peace because my God is with me all my life.

My Advice to You

1. *Trust in the Lord. He will fill your heart with His peace and joy.*

   Psalm 91:2 states, "I will say of the Lord, 'is my refuge and my fortress; My God, in Him I will trust.'"

2. *Thank God* every day for what God gave you.

   Psalm 136:1 says, "Oh, give thanks to the Lord, for He is good! For His mercy endures forever."

3. *Enjoy what God gave you.*

   Ecclesiastes 2:24 says, "Nothing is better for a man than that he should eat and drink, and that his soul should enjoy good in his labor. This also, I saw, was from the hand of God."

4. *Do not envy* what others have because the gifts of God is different for each person.
5. *Love the people* around you, and you will be happy.

   A new commandment I give to you, that you love one another; as I have loved you, that you also love one another. By this all will know that you are My disciples, if you have love for one another. (John 13:34–35)

6. *Forgive others.* When you forgive, you will relieve yourself from the grudges that you carry against others, then you will be happy.

   Matthew 6:15 states, *"But if you do not forgive men their trespasses, neither will your Father forgive your trespasses."*

7. *Do not hate people* who hurt you, but hate their actions. No one is without sin, including us.

   First John 1:8 says, "8 If we say that we have no sin, we deceive ourselves, and the truth is not in us.'

8. *Be humble.*

   Galatians 6:3 says, "3 For if anyone thinks himself to be something, when he is nothing, he deceives himself."

9. *Set high goals* for yourself and work hard to achieve them. Nothing is impossible, trust the Lord, and He will help you.
10. *Travel to different countries* to learn more about other cultures.

Life is good. Enjoy it and be happy.

Victor Zaki
2020

CPSIA information can be obtained
at www.ICGtesting.com
Printed in the USA
LVHW030942070121
675848LV00015B/394/J

9 781664 145610